# The European
# Communities

# INTERNATIONAL RELATIONS INFORMATION GUIDE SERIES

Series Editor: Garold W. Thumm, Professor of Government and Chairman of the Department, Bates College, Lewiston, Maine

*Also in this series:*

ARMS CONTROL AND MILITARY POLICY—*Edited by Donald F. Bletz**

ECONOMICS AND FOREIGN POLICY—*Edited by Mark R. Amstutz*

INTELLIGENCE, ESPIONAGE, COUNTERESPIONAGE, AND COVERT OPERATIONS—*Edited by Paul W. Blackstock and Frank Schaf, Jr.*

INTERNATIONAL AND REGIONAL POLITICS IN THE MIDDLE EAST AND NORTH AFRICA—*Edited by Ann Schulz*

INTERNATIONAL ORGANIZATIONS—*Edited by Alexine Atherton*

THE INTERNATIONAL RELATIONS OF EASTERN EUROPE—*Edited by Robin Alison Remington*

LATIN AMERICA—*Edited by John J. Finan**

THE MULTINATIONAL CORPORATION—*Edited by Helga Hernes*

POLITICAL DEVELOPMENT—*Edited by Arpad von Lazar and Bruce Magid**

SOUTH ASIA—*Edited by Richard J. Kozicki**

SOUTHEAST ASIA—*Edited by Richard Butwell**

THE STUDY OF INTERNATIONAL RELATIONS—*Edited by Robert L. Pfaltzgraff, Jr.*

SUB-SAHARAN AFRICA—*Edited by W.A.E. Skurnik*

U.S. INVOLVEMENT IN VIETNAM—*Edited by Allan W. Cameron**

*in preparation

---

The above series is part of the
# GALE INFORMATION GUIDE LIBRARY

The Library consists of a number of separate series of guides covering major areas in the social sciences, humanities, and current affairs.

General Editor: Paul Wasserman, Professor and former Dean, School of Library and Information Services, University of Maryland

Managing Editor: Denise Allard Adzigian, Gale Research Company

# The European Communities

## A GUIDE TO INFORMATION SOURCES

*Volume 9 in the International Relations
Information Guide Series*

**J. Bryan Collester**

*Associate Professor of Political Science*

*and*

*Department Head*

*Principia College
Elsah, Illinois*

*Gale Research Company*
Book Tower, Detroit, Michigan 48226

**Library of Congress Cataloging in Publication Data**

Collester, J     Bryan.
      The European Communities.

      (International relations information guide series ; v. 9)
      Bibliography:  p. 265
      Includes indexes.
      1.  European Economic Community—Bibliography.
2.  European cooperation—Bibliography.  3.  European
Economic Community countries—Foreign relations—
Bibliography.  I.  Title.
Z7165.E8C58   [JN94.A91]     016.382'9142     73-17506
ISBN 0-8103-1322-7

For My Fondest
Information Sources
Mary,
Esther,
Sue, and
Colette

# VITA

J. Bryan Collester is an associate professor of political science at Principia College, Elsah, Illinois. He holds a Ph.D. from Indiana University and specializes in the politics of the European Communities.

# CONTENTS

# Contents

# FOREWORD

The publication of Professor Collester's work fills a need that has long been felt by English-speaking scholars and others interested in the European Community. This bibliography, categorized and annotated, is a valuable tool for the study of a unique system of government, its development and its goals.

The idea of a unified Europe had been bruted about in earlier centuries, but it had always been combined with conquest. The Europe that emerged from World War II was a continent sick of war and seeking to repair wartime damages and find peace. Two Frenchmen--Jean Monnet, the author of France's National Economic Plan, and Robert Schuman, France's postwar foreign minister-- proposed a plan for European economic unity. Under this incentive, the coal and steel resources of six nations (Belgium, France, the Federal Republic of Germany, Italy, Luxembourg, and the Netherlands) were merged. This consolidation in 1952--called the European Coal and Steel Community--was so successful that it led in 1958 to two other joinings--the European Economic Community (commonly called the Common Market) and the European Atomic Energy Community (known as EURATOM). The EEC made possible the free movement of goods and workers throughout the six nations, and EURATOM provided for cooperation in the field of nuclear energy.

These Communities, which later combined their organizational machinery into one, now often called "the European Community," soon gained considerable economic power. With the accession of Britain, Denmark, and Ireland in 1973, the Community had a population of more than 260 million. In 1976 its gross domestic product reached about $1.4 trillion and, with roughly 40 percent of the world's trade, it could claim to be the largest trading bloc.

Yet the Community is unique less for its economic strength and importance than for its political achievement. Although political unity is still far from complete, the Community represents a rare instance of national governments ceding parts of their sovereignty to supranational institutions. Its goal, however, is not to decrease the role of the nation-state, but to combine those elements that can be integrated for the common good into a European unity--while still maintaining the cultural and historical diversity that has enriched Europe, and much of the world, for centuries. The Community has established separate "European" institutions: the Commission, which is its executive branch; the Council of Ministers and the Parliament, its legislative branch; and the Court of Justice, its judicial branch.

With the strengthening and growth of the European Community, its relations with the United States have developed toward partnership. The EC has been particularly active in foreign aid through trade to the Third World. Since 1975, the Lome Convention has linked the Community to fifty-two developing countries in Africa, the Caribbean, and the Pacific. The Community also has bilateral trade agreements with Asian and Latin American countries and offers preferential treatment to goods from 112 developing nations. The Community's need for imported goods, raw materials, and export outlets makes good relations with the rest of the world imperative. The EC imports 60 percent of its energy supplies and 44 percent of its agricultural goods. Hence, the elaboration of a common external trading policy touched upon vital economic and political interests of the Community's trading partners.

How the Community develops in years to come--its prospective structure and dynamics--will be of major importance to the world. Emphasis on the Community's regional and social policies is expected to lessen the still-disturbing disparities between rich and poor regions within its borders. Problems with inflation and unemployment continue, and the hoped-for monetary union by 1980 seems unlikely. But the Community will hold direct elections to the European Parliament in 1978, a step that is expected to give new impetus to movement toward unity. Decisions will be made within the coming years on the membership applications of Greece, Portugal, and Spain.

The Community, therefore, is expected to continue its growth--politically and in terms of world importance. This well-researched book by Professor Collester provides a clear view of its past and present.

M. Fernand Spaak
Head, Delegation of the
   Commission of the
   European Communities
Washington, D.C.

# PREFACE

Compiling a bibliography is akin to catching sand in a sieve. It is frustrat-
ingly unending, and before this work is usefully shelved, much new material
will be available. Alas, I know of no simple solution to such a problem.

This bibliography, nonetheless, will undertake to list and describe in brief the
literature concerning the political aspects of European integration generally and
the European Community* specifically. By "political," I mean roughly those
aspects dealing with public policy creation. By "integration," I mean the
process of building popular consensus or a community of shared attitudes and
beliefs.

Since such boundaries are amorphous and arbitrary, however, I have tried to
include as much perspective in the materials as seemed to be pertinent. But I
would hasten to add that, although I am unaware of a more comprehensive bibliography available on the subject, this is not a definitive assessment of all the
literature--not even all of the political literature on the European Community.
I have excluded documentation and official reports, except where a document
was a major information source, because bibliographies of all documentation
are already available from the information offices of the respective agencies.
In addition, few foreign-language publications have been included, though on
some subjects they are richer than the English-language publications. This was
a necessary, if regrettable, limitation. Likewise, it was necessary to exclude
most magazine and journal articles, though in a few cases professional journals
have been included when an entire issue has been devoted to the topic of European integration. In a few instances when a chapter of a book was deemed
to be of greater relevance than the whole work, I have cited only the individual chapter.

This bibliographer has labored under the usual limitations of time and space,
and as a result each citation is listed only once. The user, therefore, will
need to exercise some creativity and perseverance in locating the information
that he or she wants. The following suggestions should prove helpful. Check
the headings and subheadings of the table of contents for cues to your topic.

*See Glossary of Abbreviations.

# Preface

Wherever there seemed to be a dominant theme or focus, I have used that as a guide for categorizing the citation. If you do not find the information you are seeking in the table of contents, check the subject index. Where possible each citation has been given at least three entries in the subject index: (1) geographical location (e.g., Britain, France), (2) an institutional or structural location (e.g., Court of Justice of the European Communities), and (3) a functional or procedural category (e.g., agriculture, foreign policy).

I should like to note, also, that certain citations have been included, without an annotation, when neither the study nor any summation of its content could be found. Thus, if there was a reason to believe a work useful, based on another's judgment, it has been included. Likewise, in some cases, citations have been listed but are incomplete, without dates or pagination. Where such occurs, the information was unobtainable even when checked against the NATIONAL UNION CATALOG and LIBRARY OF CONGRESS CATALOG, the CUMULATIVE BOOK INDEX, the BRITISH NATIONAL BIBLIOGRAPHY, or BRITISH GENERAL CATALOGUE OF PRINTED BOOKS. I have included these partial listings in the hope that they may be located in libraries other than those I have used, or directly from the respective publishers. Practical scholarship seems better served by including incomplete, and in some instances unverifiable, entries than by insisting on what may well be impossible anyway, confirmed knowledge of accuracy.

At length I should like to express a note of deep appreciation to those who gave aid and comfort in this endeavor; Marilyn Shapiro, a superb student assistant; Gary Thumm, editor of this series and scholar-friend; Barbara Sloan, information specialist for the European Community Information Service in Washington, D.C., and my peerless partner, Colette Collester. Likewise I wish to thank Principia College and Miami University (Ohio) for their gracious institutional support.

J. Bryan Collester

# GLOSSARY OF ABBREVIATIONS

| | |
|---|---|
| ABM | Antiballistic Missile System |
| AID | Agency for International Development (U.S.) |
| BENELUX | Belgium/Netherlands/Luxembourg Customs Union |
| BLEU | Belgo-Luxembourg Economic Union |
| BTO | Brussels Treaty Organization |
| CAP | Common Agricultural Policy (EC) |
| CDU/CSU | Christian Democratic Union/Christian Social Union (German Federal Republic) |
| CERN | European Center for Nuclear Research |
| CET | Common External Tariff (EC) |
| COMECON | Council for Mutual Economic Assistance |
| COMMISSION | EC Executive Commission |
| COUNCIL | EC Council of Ministers |
| CSCE | Conference on Security and Cooperation in Europe |
| EC | European Community or Communities (Member countries include Britain, France, Germany, Italy, Ireland, Denmark, Belgium, Netherlands, Luxembourg) |
| ECA | Economic Cooperation Administration (U.S.) |
| ECE | Economic Commission for Europe (UN) |
| ECMT | European Conference of Ministers of Transport |

# Abbreviations

| | |
|---|---|
| ECSC | European Coal and Steel Community |
| EDC | European Defense Community |
| EDF | European Development Fund |
| EEC | European Economic Community |
| EFTA | European Free Trade Association |
| EIB | European Investment Bank |
| ELDO | European Launching Development Organization |
| EMA | European Monetary Agreement |
| ENA | European Nuclear Energy Agency |
| EPC | European Political Community |
| EPU | European Payments Union |
| ERP | European Recovery Program (U.S.) |
| ESRO | European Space Research Organization |
| EURATOM | European Atomic Energy Community |
| EUROCOURT | Court of Justice of the European Communities |
| EUROPEAN COMMUNITIES | The three European organizations (EEC, ECSC, EURATOM) whose executives merged in 1967 |
| EUROPEAN COMMUNITY | The term used generally to refer to the European Communities |
| FNSP | Fondation Nationale de Science Politique |
| GATT | General Agreement on Tariffs and Trade |
| HIGH AUTHORITY | Executive Body of the ECSC |
| IAEA | International Atomic Energy Agency |
| IBRD | International Bank for Reconstruction and Development (World Bank) |
| ICAO | International Civil Aviation Organization |
| ILO | International Labor Organization |
| IMF | International Monetary Fund |
| MBFR | Mutual and Balanced Force Reductions |
| MLF | Multilateral Nuclear Force |
| NATO | North Atlantic Treaty Organization |

| | |
|---|---|
| OAS | Organization of American States |
| OAU | Organization of African Unity |
| OECD/OEEC | Organization for Economic Cooperation and Development/Organization for European Economic Cooperation |
| PCI | Italian Communist Party |
| PEP | Political and Economic Planning (Britain) |
| SALT | Strategic Arms Limitation Talks |
| SFIO | Section Francaise de l'Internationale Ouvriere |
| the six | The six founding members of the European Communities |
| SPD | Social Democratic Party (German Federal Republic) |
| UAR | United Arab Republic |
| U.K. | United Kingdom of Great Britain and Northern Ireland |
| UNA | United Nations Association |
| UNCTAD | United Nations Conference on Trade and Development |
| UNDP | United Nations Development Program |
| UNESCO | United Nations Educational, Scientific, Cultural Organization |
| UNIDO | United Nations Industrial Development Organization |
| USIA | United States Information Agency |
| WEU | Western European Union |

# INTRODUCTION

Like a "blue chip stock," the literature on European integration has grown bullishly since the early 1940s, and with seldom a recession. Indeed there were even "go-go" years when expansion of the European Communities and British accession to them were in the fore. In the mid- to late 1940s, the volumes published annually in English relating to European integration numbered less than twenty, and usually closer to ten. A decade later when the Rome Treaty was signed, the annual output was about thirty volumes. That number doubled by 1962-63 during the first debate on British accession. During Britain's second attempted accession in 1966-67, the number of polemics and prognoses trebled with the annual outpouring reaching some ninety volumes. With Britain's successful entry in 1973, the number reached one hundred volumes.

It is worth noting that the character of the literature also has changed in the last thirty-five years. The earlier volumes largely, though not exclusively, were general histories and comprised the first generation of literature on the subject of European integration. Since the early 1960s, with a surfeit of institutional description, authors have turned their attention largely to the policies of the European Communities, both internal and external. Sectoral concerns like agriculture, administration, energy, parliament, transport, and foreign relations, among others, opened a wide vista for further investigation and produced a second generation of literature. In all likelihood, these areas will continue to provide yet more seed for scholarship, but I also expect that the future direction of writing on European integration will lead to a third generation of literature that will integrate the European sectoral analyses into the broader fields of comparative political studies. I expect, for example, that studies of bureaucracy and administration will become less tied to their European pinnings, and more integrated with the field of public administration. Thus, the geographic and particular will slowly, but certainly, yield to the universal and general, following the paradigm of scientific research. Of course, before this third generation will have exhausted itself, the revisionists will be upon us, reinterpreting the "real" reasons for the earliest institutions, and we shall probably start the cycle anew.

In the following chapters, commentary and suggestions on specific volumes correspond to the six substantive parts of the bibliography: theoretical and conceptual studies of integration, general, historical, and institutional studies of integration, background and policy studies on the European Communities (EC), EC and member-state relations, EC and external relations, and European security.

The theoretical literature on political integration is vast and crosscuts several conceptual focuses. Those seeking to understand the phenomenon better can benefit not only from surveying the national and regional West European materials, but also by assessing the vast literature on global and international relations, as well as subnational studies from ethnic and minority group research. This literature is covered in chapter 1.

To link the broader international and more specific, regional or West European approaches to integration, Karl Deutsch's several works on aspects of communication's theory (1953, 1954, 1957, 1969)* are well-known and important references. The works of Ronald Yalem (1965), Paul Taylor (1971), R.O. Keohane and Joseph S. Nye (1972), and Charles Pentland (1973) are useful also.

Regarding West European integration, specifically, there are two major groups of theoretical studies, functionalism and federalism. These are frequently considered the two most likely processes through which an integrated European Community will result. Investigations of functionalism usually begin with David Mitrany's classic study (1943, reissued 1966) and are supplemented by the seminal work on neofunctionalism in Western Europe by Ernst Haas (1958, 1964). Leon N. Lindberg and Stuart A. Scheingold's reformulation of neofunctionalism (1970) is an important theoretical extension of the Mitrany-Haas functional quiltwork.

The other conceptual approach to integration, federalism, is analyzed in Robert Bowie and Carl J. Friedrich's classic (1954), and William Riker's resummarization of the topic (1968). Neither of these works is concerned expressly with applying federalism to Western Europe, but Friedrich's later work (1968) is.

In addition to what might be described as the "political" theory of European integration, a rich and complementary body of literature has come from the field of economics. Thus the study of economic influences and their consequences on the policy process is a major part of the political literature on European integration. These studies fall roughly into three complementary groups. The first group contains those analyzing the post-World War II era, or particular aspects and institutions of the reconstruction like the Marshall Plan, the Pleven Plan, the OEEC and OECD, or the European Coal and Steel Community. A particularly useful work here is Bela Balassa's (1962). A second group of economic theorists typified by Murry Edelman and R.W. Fleming (1965) is concerned with the components of contemporary regional decision making, but not

---

* The titles of these and subsequent works mentioned in this essay, together with their publication dates, may be located through the author's name in the author index of this bibliography.

integration itself. And a third group, Tibor Scitovsky (1958) and Sidney Dell (1963), is concerned with European regional integration as a specific consequence of various economic arrangements.

Finally, for those seeking an overview of theory and the theoretical literature--rather than specific theoretical approaches--Leon N. Lindberg and Stuart A. Scheingold (1971), Gunnar Sjostedt (1974), and Reginald J. Harrison (1974) are helpful compendiums.

Chapter 2 deals with general, historical, and institutional studies of integration. The largest portion of the integration literature has focused on Western Europe because of the European Communities created in 1958 and their predecessors which abetted the regeneration of Europe after World War II. The EC is, however, not the exclusive concern of students of integration. In this section, I emphasize several important works of pre- or non-EC topics, including general studies on integration. Nonetheless, note that analyses of specific functional areas, like agriculture or energy, which precede the EC, but which led to the shaping of their policies, have been grouped primarily in chapter 3. In chapter 2 will be found, also, several selections on African and Nordic cooperation which provide a contrast to "Europe of the Nine." In the case of Africa, culture appears more divergent than among EC countries, while in the Nordic case, culture is probably less divergent. Still, the conceptual study of integration has evolved very largely from studies of Western Europe, and studies of other areas tend to be cross-cultural or cross-regional comparisons.

The first concern, however, of chapter 2 is human rights, including the studies done for the European Convention and Commission on Human Rights. One of the best books on the subject, concentrating on practical applications, is by J.E.S. Fawcett (1969). In addition, the classic studies on human rights are by A.H. Robertson (1963, 1965). And a more recent introduction to the subject, and of particular interest to students of law, is by Frede Castberg (1974).

The Council of Europe has been presented best by A.H. Robertson's study of the Council's activities (1961) and by the Council's own manual (1970) which profiles twenty years. Ernst Haas's monograph on concensus formation in the Council (1960) is a significant link between European integration and national integration. The idea of Europe as one cultural unit has been a theme interestingly treated by the head of the European Cultural Center, Denis de Rougemont (1965, 1966), who chronicled "Europe" from ancient Greece to the present. In a more skeptical vein, Richard Mayne (1972) sought to separate fact from faith, and a European journalist, Guido Piovene (1975), probed the values and traditions of twelve European countries to try to find what is common to all, and what is not.

Three important studies of the European Coal and Steel Community which treat the ECSC as an experiment in European cooperation are those by Henry L. Mason (1955), William Diebold (1959), and Louis Lister (1960). Mason's work is a political view of supranational cooperation; Diebold and Lister view the ECSC as an experiment in economic union. Norman J.G. Pounds and William N. Parker (1957) approach the ECSC from the geographer's point of view. A specialized, but important, part of the ECSC's activity is its Court of Justice, detailed by D.G. Valentine (1955).

Several volumes treat the "fathers of Europe" of famous Europeans. Don Cook (1965) provides anecdotal accounts of various "fathers," including Monnet, de Gaulle, Adenauer, and others. A more personal view of these men has been given in the memoirs of a former Secretary-General of NATO, Dirk Stikker (1966). And for younger readers, Ton Oosterhuis's stories of twenty Europeans from Socrates to Masaryk (1970) is well written. Of the "giants," Paul-Henri Spaak's memoirs (1971) and Jakob Herman Huizinga's biography (1961) of the political life of Spaak are signal contributions. Jean Monnet's life and role in building Europe have been favorably reviewed by the Brombergers (1969), and an earlier dissertation by John C. Satra (1961) viewed Monnet more critically. The writings on Winston Churchill, and those by him, are manifold and marvels of insight. One collection of his post-World War II speeches, edited by Randolph Churchill (1948), reveals Sir Winston at his ambiguous best, an English European.

Most economic studies of European integration include threads of the period prior to World War I, but two which emphasize the prewar era and are especially helpful economic histories of Europe for the period between 1900 and 1950 are by Paul Alpert (1951) and Shepard B. Clough (1968). In addition W.O. Henderson's study (1959) of the German Customs Union, the Zollverein, provides an excellent background for understanding both Germany's contemporary role in an integrated Europe and the role early economic organizations played in the process of integration. Three other important historical and descriptive studies of the economic history of integration have been written by Geoffrey Crowther (1948), editor of the ECONOMIST, M.A.G. van Meerhaeghe (1966), and Sidney Pollard (1974). These three link prewar European economic history, reconstruction, and the drive for unification. Four very important economic studies focus on trade and monetary questions and their relationship to European integration: William Diebold (1952), Robert Triffin (1957), Bela Balassa (1967), and Pierre Uri (1971). In addition Werner J. Feld's (1972) tract on multinational corporations and nongovernmental forces, and the studies by Geoffrey R. Denton (1972) and James E. Meade et al. (1962) supplement the functional perspective with case studies in European economic union (ECSC, BENELUX, EFTA, etc.). Finally, J. Frederick Dewhurst's (1961) massive compilation of Europe's needs and resources in eighteen countries is a trove of information. Though several years old now, Dewhurst's work reveals patterns that will outlive the usefulness of his technical data.

Political studies, like economic ones, may be divided into those which emphasize the pre-World War II era, and those more voluminous ones which address more contemporary aspects of political integration in Europe. Three authors focus uniquely on aspects of the pre-World War I era: C. Deslisle Burns (1947) likens medieval Christendom to a united Europe; a journalist, W.T. Stead (1899), reviews the possibilities of a "United States of Europe" which emerged from the Hague Conference of 1898; and F.S.L. Lyons (1963) studies the origins of the process of integration from the period between the Congress of Vienna and the onset of World War I. Three more works also focus on the interwar period: Paul Hutchinson (1929) and Edouard Herriot (1930) are concerned with the conditions of a "U.S. of Europe," while a dissertation by Peter Rowe (1960) emphasizes European federation projects between 1929 and 1933. Two additional comprehensive studies which link the pre- and post-World War II periods are by Rene Albrecht-Carrie (1965) and Frans A.M. Alting von Geusau (1969, 1975).

Studies on the political situation in post-World War II Europe, still excluding the EC itself, are manifold and almost defy abbreviated comment. Nonetheless I have grouped several selections I find useful under three headings: descriptive histories, comparative institutional surveys, and what might be called sectoral or functional analyses. The classic journalistic accounts of Europe are those of Raymond Aron (1954) and Theodore H. White (1954). More recent, and hence more inclusive, accounts are those of Arnold Zurcher (1958), Walter Laqueur (1970), Derek W. Urwin (1972), and Clyde H. Farnsworth (1974). Such a list varies in its degree of "scholarliness," but each of these suggestions provides eminently readable history.

There are four comparative, institutional surveys of particular merit. Martin O. Heisler's work (1974) and the much briefer sketches by Michael Curtis (1965) are both textbook-type surveys. Michael Palmer (1968) and A.H. Robertson (1973), on the other hand, give us more comprehensive research tools.

The abbreviated list for sectoral or functional analyses includes seven works: C. Grove Haines (1957), David P. Calleo (1965), Richard L. Merritt and Donald J. Puchala (1968), Frans A.M. Alting von Geusau (1969), Mattei Dogan and Richard Rose (1971), Richard Mayne (1972), and Norman Luxemburg (1973).

Concerning U.S. aid policy and the Marshall Plan, three scholarly works are of special import: William Adams Brown, Jr., and Opie Redevers's massive analysis published for Brookings Institution (1953), and H. Field Haviland, Jr.'s six lectures given at Haverford College (1957). The third work by Richard Allen Goldman (1971) is a dissertation, more readable than most, tracing the effect of U.S. aid on European integration. The brief, classic history of the Marshall Plan's creation is by Joseph M. Jones (1955); Harry Bayard Price (1955) renders a view for the layman. For a British view of U.S. aid to Europe, see R.B. Manderson-Jones (1972).

When considering regional organizations like the EC, in the broader, international context, there are two readers or compendiums of particular interest. One is by Joseph S. Nye, Jr. (1968); the other is by Louis Cantori and Steven Spiegel (1970). Both are college-level texts. Paul A. Tharp, Jr. (1971), reviews the structures and functions of numerous regional organizations with a view towards similarities in approach, and Lincoln P. Bloomfield (1959) appraises European attitudes toward the United Nations.

# Introduction

In chapter 3 there is an overview of the European Communities--background, policies, and institutions--from which is a host of descriptions, analyses, and opinions by journalists, scholars, and participants. Some of the earlier accounts of
the formative years are still among the best, though no longer inclusive, like
those of J.F. Deniau (1961) and Uwe W. Kitzinger (1963). Miriam Camps
(1965, 1966) also has crafted numerous, evenhanded accounts, especially of the
middling, Gaullist years. There was a spate of excellent assessments of the
Communities resulting from the last and successful British bid for entry. Those
include Richard Mayne (1973), Roy Pryce (1973), Walter Hallstein (1973), and
Walter Farr (1973). An excellent collection of readings on the EC was edited
by Michael Hodges (1972), and Leon N. Lindberg and Stuart A. Scheingold
(1970) produced an unusually good conceptual analysis of institutional change
based on case studies of the EC. For emphasis on the economist's view of the
Communities see Finn B. Jensen and Ingo Walter (1965). In addition, two very
readable explications of the Rome Treaty and other documents can be found in
the works of Howard Bliss (1970) and P. Minet (1962). One critical, but very
interesting, view of the EC is that of Johan Galtung (1973).

The Common Agricultural Policy (CAP) has brought forth numerous short, but
excellent, studies by Britain's research organization, Political and Economic
Planning (PEP). In this regard, see the Library of Congress card listing PEP-
Occasional Paper (nos. 1, 3, 5, 13, 14). Nina Heathcote (1971) has, likewise,
a short but perceptive review of the CAP and Mansholt Plan. John Newhouse's
1967 account of the 30 June 1965 crisis is a view of the politics of the CAP,
and John S. Marsh (1973) analyzes the effects of the CAP on associate countries. Two other areas which have received considerable attention, besides the
CAP itself, are the effects of the CAP on the United States and on Britain.
Two well-acclaimed studies of the US-EC agricultural nexus are by John O.
Coppock (1963) and Stanley Andrews (1973). Concerning the problems created
for Britain by the CAP, see Graham Hallett (1968), Michael Butterwick and
Edmund Neville Rolfe (1968, 1971), and John S. Marsh and Christopher Ritson
(1971).

Research into the nature of the bureaucracy and administration has produced
fewer works than some more general areas. Nonetheless, David Coombes (1976)
and Isaac E. Druker (1975) offer comprehensive and scholarly treatments of the
system for financing the Communities and the locus of authority in the budgetary process. In addition, three studies are especially helpful in reviewing the
executive bureaucracy. A member of the EC Executive Commission, Altiero
Spinelli (1966) offers a classic study of the interaction between the European
bureaucrats and particular interest groups. Another study by David Coombes
(1970) of the EC Executive Commission is comprehensive and an important contribution. Glenda Goldstone Rosenthal's 1975 study is especially interesting
both for the substance of her findings about how decisions are made, and for
the method she uses to present those findings: five case studies, each analyzed
through three conceptual lenses and each through the personal perspectives of
three Eurocrats.

Monetary and commercial policy of the communities is yet more technical, but there are six analyses which are of special interest for the political assessment of the EC: Dennis Swann (1975) develops an economic theory of political decision making; Werner J. Feld (1970) analyzes the role of business executives in political integration; Ingo Walter (1967) uses trade patterns to assess functional integration; Etienne-Sadi Kirschen and others (1969) study the conflict in economic and political objectives; Lawrence B. Krause and Walter S. Salant (1973) detail the consequences to the United States of European monetary integration; and, finally, a general assessment by five economists of the policy consequences of integration by Alec Cairncross and others (1974).

In education and socialization, three works are of particular import: the work of Robert H. Beck (1971), whose interest is in the harmonization of educational practices; that of Carl J. Friedrich (1969), who focuses upon the more informal processes of "European" socialization in business, agriculture, and other areas; and John Patrick Corbett's study (1959) which is older but still useful, as he assesses the normative considerations underlying European unity.

Energy also is becoming a burgeoning field and is changing rapidly since the oil crisis of 1973. Three more recent analyses are interesting for their investigation of the relationship between technology and politics: Steven Jarrold Baker's dissertation (1973) is a case study of the Italian nuclear program and political integration; Henry R. Nau's study (1974) is broader, providing a look at national politics and nuclear reactor developments; and the work of Frans A.M. Alting von Geusau (1975) focuses directly upon the Communities' common energy policy.

Perhaps the easiest-to-read, nontechnical introduction to community law is by Stuart A. Scheingold (1965). It is, nonetheless, a sophisticated view of the law and the political role of the Court of Justice. Three more recent and more technical explications for students of law are by P.J.G. Kapteyn and P. Verloren van Themaat (1973), D. Lasok and J.W. Bridge (1973), and Anthony Parry and Stephen Hardy (1973). In addition, there are three comprehensive legal references containing the evolved case and treaty law: K.R. Simmonds (1972); H.J. Everson and others (1974); and EUROPEAN LEGISLATION 1952-1972, a massive compilation of community law from Butterworth Publishers (1975). Finally, for those interested specifically in the European Court of Justice, see Gerhard Bebr (1962), Werner J. Feld (1964), and Andrew Wilson Green (1969). These are very readable analyses of the structure and political function of the Court of Justice.

With direct elections to the European Parliament scheduled to be held in 1978, the Strasbourg legislature is a topic of increasing concern. The most complete analysis of direct elections, though now somewhat dated, was published by the European Parliament's Directorate-General in 1969. The European Movement (1974) sponsored a much abbreviated, though more recent, study of alternative methods of electing representatives.

# Introduction

A broader overview of the Parliament's structure and influence may be found in the work of Sir Barnett Cocks (1973) or in insightful dissertation by John Erwin Schwarz (1967). A current and worthwhile study of party groups in Parliament is by John Fitzmaurice (1975).

An excellent study of regional development in the communities has been written by Sergio Barzanti (1965), though it is now somewhat dated and is limited in that it focuses only upon Italy and France. A much broader and more recent analysis of regional planning in Europe is by Morgan Sant (1974). A brief but pithy study has been made by Harold Lind and Christopher Flockton for PEP (1970).

One of the early and comprehensive analyses of labor policy and trade union activity in the EC is by R. Colin Beever (1960). Following that, he wrote a short monograph for PEP (1969) on the EC's social policy, focusing specifically on the free movement of labor. Labor movements in the EC were also the subject of Marguerite Bouvard (1972) whose dissertation was rewritten for Praeger Publishers. It is a thorough look at unionism in the European Communities. Midway between labor and social policy is a study of industrial relations in the Common Market by Campbell Balfour (1972), and the work of Doreen Collins (1975) who addresses the Communities' common social policy specifically.

For a wide-ranging introduction to transport policy, see Bryant T. Bayliss (1965) who relates the development of a transport policy to the development of a custom's union. A more recent discussion of the EC's common transport policy is contained in a dissertation by Kurt Beran (1974).

In chapter 4 the reader may be amazed that an overweening half of the entries are on Britain and its relations with the European Communities. Rather than a prejudice, however, this situation results first from the fact, noted in the preface, that the size of this project regrettably precluded most foreign-language studies. And since most studies of EC member-state relations are in the indigenous language, they were, thereby, excluded. Britain and Ireland are, of course, the beneficiaries of this parsimony.

Second, because Britain is one of the "Big Four" countries, and because she was admitted into the EC in 1973 only after the third application, many "additional" analyses were generated over the chronic political imbroglio.

Finally, there is a third point to make about the quantity of British literature on the EC. All materials relating generally to Britain, even though most of them were written prior to the 1973 accession, have been included in this chapter. Treating the works written prior to 1973 as part of the EC's external relations and those written afterward as part of its internal affairs seemed confusing and arbitrary. I believe, thus, that treating all materials on Britain in one place and category will be more helpful for most users. It does, however, distend this chapter a bit.

For an introduction to the subject of the EC member-state relations, see Helen Wallace's study for PEP (1973) or the dissertation by Don Bentley Rhoades (1972). A slightly different perspective focusing on the extension of collective decision making and its effects on member governments has been written by Suzanne J. Bodenheimer (1967). And, a comprehensive view of the main features of the 1973 accessions is given by Jean-Pierre Puissochet (1975).

Though the BENELUX states have been grouped together because there are so few analyses, no single work treats the three as a unit vis-a-vis the EC, excepting that of Gordon L. Weil (1970), and he does so only as part of a larger study.

Despite the voluminous literature available on Britain, I have discovered on trips to London and Brussels that much of the written debate has not even reached American shores, partly because of copyrights. Nonetheless, several of the most noteworthy and available analyses of the early phases of the EC, and Britain's conjunction with it, are by John Pinder (1961), Michael Shanks and John Lambert (1962), and Miriam Camps (1964). A more recent and very general explanation of Britain's relation to the EC is by Derek H. Hene (1970). For analyses of the three entry petitions by Britain, see Nora Beloff (1963) for the first bid, and Uwe W. Kitzinger (1968, 1973) for the subsequent two bids, respectively.

Most of the literature on Britain is pervaded by a pro-Market or anti-Market flavor. The pro-Marketeers can be divided, prescriptively, into three additional categories: those who favor Britain's regional and European commitment over an Atlantic one, such as W. Horsfall Carter (1966); those who see no conflict between a "European" and an "Atlantic" approach, like Edward Heath (1970); and those who argue that Britain's new world role should be to lead Europe back into an Atlantic conjunction with the United States, like Drew Middleton (1963). A more analytic study of Britain's orientation to the EC has been made by Robert L. Pfaltzgraff, Jr. (1969).

Those taking the opposite viewpoint, the anti-Marketeers, are well characterized by the "Atlanticists": Lionel Morris Gelber (1966) and George E.G. Catlin (1969), or by the "patriots" like J. Enoch Powell (1971, 1973) and William Pickles (1962, 1967).

Studies in English of Denmark and the EC are very limited. One broad and early overview is a dissertation by Gunnar Preben Nielsson (1966). Ireland fares a bit better; an early study by Joseph Johnson (1962) focuses on agriculture. However, the most complete study is the Irish government's White Paper (1972).

Like Britain, France has been a controversial and pivotal part of the development of the European Communities--especially because of President de Gaulle whose leadership coincided with the first decade of the EC. Growing out of that controversial and formative period is a large body of literature on France

# Introduction

and on de Gaulle's leadership. Interestingly, most of the studies in English have been done by Americans and Britons, and are not simply translations of French studies. Conceivably, as translations are made, interpretations of de Gaulle and the French role will evince a more personal and national flavor, and may also reveal more subtle interpretations than those usually given by British and American scholars for de Gaulle's attitudes. For now, however, there is a well-stocked library on the Franco-British dispute over the EC. This dispute, analyzed by Britons, may be found in John Pinder (1963), Dorthy Pickles (1966), and Gladwyn Jebb (Lord Gladwyn) (1969). A history and analysis of France's interests in the other direction, with Germany, have been ably set forth by F. Roy Willis (1968). For a broader perspective on France and the Communities, see the compendium edited by Sydney Nettleton Fisher (1964). Finally, two excellent empirical studies of French elite attitudes toward integration are by Karl Deutsch (1967) and Jeremy G. Haritos (1974). The latter is an interesting, cross-temporal comparison to the earlier Deutsch study.

There are a large number of studies on Germany, too, but surprisingly few on the bilateral relations with the EC. Rather, most of the more general studies on Germany and integration put the EC into an East-West equation. Characteristic of this approach are two clear introductions to the topic by Gerald Freund (1961) and Ernst Majonica (1969). The news and statements of the federal government on the EC, specifically, have been collected in an official publication which includes the protocols on the accession of Britain, Ireland, and Denmark (1972).

Finally, Italy has not been as exhaustively treated as the other "Big Three," but three very good, general studies of Italy and the EC are by F. Roy Willis (1971), James J. Divita (1972), and Primo Vannicelli (1974). The Divita work is a dissertation; Vannicelli's analysis is an abbreviated monograph from a dissertation. One scholarly, specialized, and excellent study of the Italian Communist Party and the European Communities has been written by Donald L.M. Blackmer (1968).

In chapter 5 on external relations there are a number of current and estimable overviews of the EC's external relations like those of Frans A.M. Alting von Geusau (1974), Werner J. Feld (1976), Stanley Henig (1971), Max Kohnstamm and Wolfgang Hager (1973), and Kenneth J. Twitchett (1976). All of these are background studies for considering the idea of a Communities "foreign policy," and all interrelate the patterns of EC external interest to the "First, Second, and Third Worlds."

For a view of the EC's external relations with developing areas, generally, see a brief report by Michael Lipton and others (1973). For an analysis of EC aid programs and especially the Yaounde Convention, see David Jones (1973). This is a bibliography with an introductory section discussing developing areas. It also contains studies of several individual, developing countries, like Spain and Israel, which were too few to categorize independently.

Some of the earlier surveys of African-EC relations are among the best and most comprehensive. For example, see the work of Arnold Rivkin (1962, 1966), P.N.C. Okigbo (1967), and, also, I. William Zartman (1971).

There are many analyses of EFTA-EC relations, too, again because of Britain. Joining the EC meant, of course, leaving EFTA. Several early studies of "The Outer Seven" are still very good period histories like those of Frederick Victor Meyer (1960) and Emile Benoit (1961). Equally good are the later studies: that of Pierre Uri (1968), the Geneva Graduate Institute of International Studies (1968), and Paul Streeten and Hugh Corbet (1971).

In addition to the general and British-focused studies of EFTA, three works on Norway are of particular interest and chronicle the unsuccessful accession bid: Klaus Tornudd (1969), which includes Nordic and EC relations, generally; Nils Orvik (1972); and T.K. Derry (1973). Derry's work is the broadest history covering the period from 1814 to 1972; Orvik is the narrowest, focusing upon the prospect of EC entry.

A case study of Austria by William T. Bluhm (1973) is particularly interesting among the EFTA analyses, because it is a comparative, theoretical study challenging the earlier integration work by Deutsch.

The influence of the EC on the relations between West European states and East Bloc states varies considerably, depending on the state and the functional area concerned. For example, EC influence tends to be less in security matters than in economic and political ones. Johan Galtung (1971) has tried to detail that interface in various fields, including security, whereas John P. DeGara (1964) emphasized the economic relations and sought to assess the EC as a functional integrator. In addition, a very recent collection of analyses of the EC's policies toward the East Bloc by European and American scholars has been edited by Ieuan John (1975). One particularly impressive piece of speculation has been written by Charles Ransom (1973) to consider the possible effects of EC enlargement on its relations with COMECON and a wider European system of integration.

As might be expected, concern for the EC's relations with the United States and Atlantic Community has been of considerable interest to U.S. scholars and writers, judging from the outpouring on the subject. Excluding security relations, which are covered in the next chapter (6), there are two major focuses into which studies of the Atlantic area have been divided: those primarily political, and those primarily economic.

I will address the political studies first and divide them yet again between those essentially favorable to Atlantic and European cooperation and who do not find fundamental conflict between the two approaches, and those who oppose such positions.

# Introduction

Representative of the early Atlanticist studies are those of H.C. Allen (1960), a prescription; George Lichtheim (1963), for the nonspecialist; Francis O. Wilcox and H. Field Haviland, Jr. (1963), a compendium; Zbigniew Brzezinski (1965); and George M. Taber (1969), a journalistic account of President Kennedy's European policy. A current argument for closer Atlantic union is by Eliot R. Goodman (1975).

Opponents of the Atlanticist position, or those who have found it unworkable, are equally prolific. William C. Cromwell (1969) found what might have been a good idea souring as conditions changed. Equally certain of the disintegration of Atlantic relations due to "imbalances" is Robert L. Pfaltzgraff, Jr. (1969). David P. Calleo (1970, 1973) believes, quite simply, that the United States is wrong to try to govern the Atlantic alliance from Washington. And in two separate and current studies, Gerhard Mally (1974, 1976) assesses the inherent conflict between intra-European and trans-Atlantic integration. Finally, Phillip H. Trezise (1975) and J. Robert Schaetzel (1975) critique past policy failures and urge new policy prescriptions, if the United States is to regain its respect and its position of responsibility.

Two compendiums worthy of professional consideration are those by Wolfram F. Hanrieder (1974) and Richard Mayne (1975). Contributions to both collections are by eminent European and American scholars and practitioners.

The political consequences of the EC's economic policies on the United States, and vice versa, can be readily followed in five general studies of the subject: a brief monograph published by the CED (Committee for Economic Development) (1971); two analyses of trade relations by Randall Hinshaw (1964) and Don D. Humphrey (1964); an appraisal of the differences and consequences of the formation of the EEC and EFTA by Lawrence B. Krause (1968); and a series of papers given under the auspices of the International Economic Association, edited by Charles P. Kindleberger and Andrew Shonfield (1971).

Finally there are three works of especial bearing tracing the potentially negative effects of American business on Europe: the works of Edward McCreary (1964) and Raymond Vernon (1971), both of whom are concerned about the consequences for multinational corporations; and Jean-Jacques Servan-Schreiber (1968) whose LE DEFI AMERICAIN [The American Challenge] raised a tempest of protest in France.

European security is the subject of chapter 6. The Rome Treaty of 1957 establishing the European Communities did not provide for European security or defense arrangements since those concerns were largely relegated to existing organizations, NATO and WEU. Nonetheless, the concept of an integrated European defense community, formally proposed as the Pleven Plan, but defeated in 1954, attested to the "logic" or "reasonableness" of the idea. Later, with the uneven success, indeed growth, of economic and political integration in the EC, concomitant proposals for inclusion of the defense sector were expectable. But, as painful lessons are long remembered, so proposals for a new

EDC, or for the specific inclusion of security in the Rome concept, have been few.

Accordingly, the largest section of security studies in this bibliography concerns NATO. Unhappily however, many, in fact probably most, of the NATO studies concern European integration only in a small or peripheral way, and it has been necessary, thus, to winnow out a great portion of those studies, oftentimes all too arbitrarily. For those interested in a more comprehensive view of NATO and the elements of European integration, I would suggest sifting through NATO's own bibliographies. A massive one was produced in 1964, but smaller and more recent ones are available.

There are several studies, however, which do make the existing EC organizational arrangements the centerpiece of analysis. Among them are those of Alastair Buchan (1969), Sir Bernard Burrows and Christopher Irwin (1972), and Ghita Ionescu (1974). Geoffrey Lee Williams and Alan Lee Williams (1974) rely upon the "dumbbell theory" or "Europeanist vs. Atlanticist" perspectives to frame their analyses of the EC and NATO, and George W. Ball (1968) and Stephen Denis Kertesz (1967) use a yet broader backdrop of regional and global organizations like the United Nations and OECD to try to assess the EC's possible and expanded role in promoting peace.

Finally, two older, but important, studies focusing on popular and elite attitudes of Europeans toward their own role in European security are by Daniel Lerner and Morton Gorden (1960), and Richard L. Merritt and Donald J. Puchala (1966).

Two studies of British strategic potential are tied to the question of her request for EC accession: the first is by Ivor Richard and others (1971), and the second by Sherwood S. Cordier (1973).

The trade-offs between CSCE and MBFR, early seen as European and U.S. positions, respectively, have been well framed in Michael Palmer's 1971 study for PEP, in the study by Wolfgang Klaiber and others (1973), and in an edited compendium by Z. Michael Szaz (1974).

A summary study of the EDC and the evolution to WEU was written for the RAND Corporation by Nathan Leites and Christian de la Malene (1954). A more recent dissertation linking the ECD and MLF has been written by Ralph John Thompson (1968).

The role of France in European security has been analyzed well in an older study by Edgar S. Furniss, Jr. (1954). For a study of the relationship between France and the EDC, see Daniel Lerner and Raymond Aron (1957), and for a study of France in the nuclear context, Wilfrid Kohl (1972) is commendable.

# Introduction

Germany's role in European security is always tied to the so-called "German Question," to some aspect of the reunification issue, or its pivotal role between East and West. There are numerous, well-written studies on these aspects, but two scholarly ones especially noteworthy are by James L. Richardson (1966) and Robert McGeehan (1971).

As mentioned, the available material on NATO is seemingly endless and multi-faceted. A few suggestions may be helpful. From the perspective of the EC or Europe and NATO, see the works of: Mary Margaret Ball (1959), Carl H. Amme (1967), or a brief monograph from the Atlantic Institute by Lothar Ruehl (1974).

European security and NATO's role viewed from the perspective of the United States may be found in the study of Theodore Geiger and Harold van B. Cleveland (1951), and that of Robert E. Osgood (1962). Arnold Wolfers (1964) has an edited volume focused on similar concerns. John Newhouse and others (1971) analyze the question of U.S. troops in Europe, while Warner R. Schilling and others (1973) have produced an arms control report. In addition, Louis J. Mensonides and James A. Kuhlman (1975, vol. 2) have edited a series of contemporary studies on the United States and NATO.

Finally, two studies representing, essentially, the "get-out/stay-in" NATO arguments are by Richard J. Barnet and Marcus G. Raskin (1965), and Morton A. Kaplan (1971). Barnet and Raskin hold the "get-out-of-NATO" position; Kaplan defends the opposite view.

For an overview of European and East Bloc relations see Robert R. King and Robert W. Dean (1974), or Louis J. Mensonides and James A. Kuhlman (1975, vol.1). Both are edited volumes, or compendiums.

The last section on European security contains studies of WEU. For an early view of the significance of the organization see J.G. Foster (1956). A view of a decade of activities was published in 1964 by WEU itself, and a review of WEU's role in European integration is the theme of a dissertation by Diane Arlene Kressler (1967).

# Chapter 1

# THEORETICAL AND CONCEPTUAL STUDIES
# OF INTEGRATION AND COOPERATION

## A. GENERAL

1   Ake, Claude. A THEORY OF POLITICAL INTEGRATION. Home-
    wood, Ill.: Dorsey Press, 1967. 164 p.

    A conceptual study of integration which is drawn partly
    from the West European experience.

2   DeVree, Johan K. POLITICAL INTEGRATION: THE FORMATION
    OF THEORY AND ITS PROBLEMS. The Hague: Mouton, 1972.
    389 p.

    The development of a theory of integration and a criti-
    cism of the major American theorists, Haas, Deutsch,
    Etzioni, and Lindberg. An admirable, descriptive his-
    tory of the theory of integration.

3   Etzioni, Amitai. POLITICAL UNIFICATION: A COMPARATIVE
    STUDY OF LEADERS AND FORCES. New York: Holt, Rinehart
    and Winston, 1965. 346 p.

    A paradigm derived from Parsons's structural-functional
    systems theory for the analysis of the international in-
    tegration process. On the basis of the paradigm, Etzioni
    posits twenty-two testable propositions and then tests
    them in four comparative case studies of political inte-
    gration: the UAR, the Federation of the West Indies,
    the Nordic Association, and the EEC.

4   GOVERNMENT AND OPPOSITION 9, no. 1 (1974). Special issue:
    "Between Sovereignty and Integration." 119 p.

    Eight articles by Ionescu, Beloff, Deutsch, and others
    address sovereignty and integration.

5    Lijphart, Arend. WORLD POLITICS: THE WRITINGS OF THEO-
     RISTS AND PRACTITIONERS, CLASSICAL AND MODERN. Boston:
     Allyn and Bacon, 1966. 448 p.

     A book of readings on international relations which con-
     tains two sections directly useful to European integra-
     tion: chapter 12 on "International Relations," and chap-
     ter 13 on "Functionalism and Regionalism."

6    Plischke, Elmer, ed. SYSTEMS OF INTEGRATING THE INTERNA-
     TIONAL COMMUNITY. Princeton, N.J.: D. Van Nostrand, 1964.
     198 p.

     A collection of five essays giving a broad overview of
     certain aspects of the coalescing process in the func-
     tional perspective. A consideration of Europe included
     in a world perspective of confederalism and federal in-
     tegration.

## B. ALLIANCES

7    Beer, Francis A. ALLIANCES: LATENT WAR COMMUNITIES IN
     THE CONTEMPORARY WORLD. New York: Holt, Rinehart and
     Winston, 1970. 384 p.

     Eleven essays, primarily conceptual, analyzing the ex-
     ternal conflict and the internal cohesion of alliances.
     Several deal specifically with NATO and the Atlantic
     Alliance.

8    Liska, George. NATIONS IN ALLIANCE: THE LIMITS OF IN-
     TERDEPENDENCE. Baltimore: Johns Hopkins Press, 1962. 301 p.

     A theoretical analysis of the dynamics and structure of
     alliances drawn from a vast historical background. Should
     be read as a companion to Liska's EUROPE ASCENDANT:
     THE INTERNATIONAL POLITICS OF UNIFICATION
     (see no. 242).

9    Osgood, Robert E. ALLIANCES AND AMERICAN FOREIGN POL-
     ICY. Baltimore: Johns Hopkins Press, 1968. 171 p.

     A comprehensive, conceptual analysis of the nature of
     alliances, especially U.S. alliances, which includes a
     section on U.S. alliances in Europe, especially NATO.

10   Rood, Robert Magruder. "Agreement in the International System:
     A Comparison of Some Theoretical Aspects of Alliance Structures
     in a Balance of Power International System with the European State
     System of 1814-1914." Ph.D. dissertation, Syracuse University, 1973.

11    Rosenau, James N., ed. LINKAGE POLITICS. New York: Free
      Press, 1969. 352 p.

      See especially the chapter by O.R. Holsti and J.D.
      Sullivan, "National-International Linkages: France and
      China as Non-Conforming Alliance Members" which com-
      pares the nonconformity of the two in their respective
      alliances and seeks to identify aspects of the interna-
      tional political process that relate to alliance and inte-
      gration.

## C. ECONOMICS

12    Balassa, Bela. THE THEORY OF ECONOMIC INTEGRATION.
      London: George Allen and Unwin, 1962. 304 p.

      A clearly written, theoretical exposition of economic
      integration drawn from European organizations like the
      ECSC.

13    Dell, Sidney. TRADE BLOCS AND COMMON MARKETS. London:
      Alfred A. Knopf, 1963. 384 p.

      A study of the origins of trade groupings and the rationale
      for economic integration in Europe including the post-
      war efforts and problems in Western Europe, in the de-
      veloping countries, and in the Socialist countries.

14    Edelman, Murry, and Fleming, R.W. THE POLITICS OF WAGE-
      PRICE DECISIONS: A FOUR COUNTRY ANALYSIS. Urbana:
      University of Illinois Press, 1965. 331 p.

      Not a study about the EC directly but a four-country
      comparative study about the organizations and politics
      that influence wage and price decisions. Results in an
      attempt at developing theory which is derived from, and
      is clearly applicable to, integration generally and to
      Europe specifically.

15    Krauss, Melvyn, ed. THE ECONOMICS OF INTEGRATION: A
      BOOK OF READINGS. London: George Allen and Unwin, 1973.
      300 p.

16    Meade, James E. PROBLEMS OF ECONOMIC UNION. Chicago:
      University of Chicago Press, 1953. 102 p.

      A discussion of the problems connected with forming a
      customs union between sovereign states, and the impli-
      cations for the individual state economies which draw
      upon the European experience.

17 _____. THE THEORY OF CUSTOMS UNIONS. Amsterdam: North Holland Publishing Co., 1955. 121 p.

> Three lectures on the theoretical aspects of customs unions, their advantages, problems, and influences upon integration. BENELUX used as a case study.

18 Robson, Peter, ed. INTERNATIONAL ECONOMIC INTEGRATION: SELECTED READINGS. Baltimore: Penguin Books, 1972. 458 p.

> A collection of essays concerning the theory, formation, and results of various forms of economic integration: customs unions; common markets; free trade areas; and full economic unity, including the European Economic Community.

19 Sannwald, Rolf F., and Stohler, Jacques. ECONOMIC INTEGRATION: THEORETICAL ASSUMPTIONS AND CONSEQUENCES OF EUROPEAN UNIFICATION. Princeton, N.J.: Princeton University Press, 1959. 260 p.

> A theoretical treatise on economic integration, specifically European economic integration, including world free trade, regional free trade, methods of integration, and currency questions. Also a functional and institutional discussion on the ECSC as "partial integration."

20 Scitovsky, Tibor. ECONOMIC THEORY AND WESTERN EUROPEAN INTEGRATION. Stanford, Calif.: Stanford University Press, 1958. 154 p.

> Four essays applying general principles of economic theory to the particular problems of economic union in Western Europe: economic integration; common currency; competition; and comparative advantage.

21 Streeten, Paul. ECONOMIC INTEGRATION: ASPECTS AND PROBLEMS. Leiden, Netherlands: A.W. Sijthoff, 1961. 151 p.

> A study of the meaning of "balanced" integration and the problems and advantages of "unbalanced" growth. Maintains that unbalanced growth is the core of the argument for integrating a community like Europe.

22 Tinbergen, Jan. INTERNATIONAL ECONOMIC INTEGRATION. 2d rev. ed. Amsterdam: Elsevier Publishing Co., 1965. 142 p.

> A simplified but not simple analysis of the theory of economic integration including minimum conditions for integration. Intended for those untrained in economics and is a useful prologue to an understanding of the economics of political integration.

23    Viner, Jacob. THE CUSTOMS UNION ISSUE. New York: Car-
      negie Endowment for Peace, 1950. 221 p.

      A review of the nature, purposes, and mode of operation
      of the customs union as one form of integration.

## D. FEDERALISM

24    Bingham, Alfred M. THE UNITED STATES OF EUROPE. New
      York: Duell, Sloan and Pearce, 1940. 336 p.

      A study of European federation and the possible organi-
      zational structure in light of the events preceding World
      War II.

25    Bowie, Robert R., and Friedrich, Carl J., eds. STUDIES IN FED-
      ERALISM. Boston: Little, Brown and Co., 1954. 887 p.

      A series of sixteen edited studies submitted to the Euro-
      pean Movement on the principles and practice of feder-
      alism.

26    Davies, Lord David. FEDERATED EUROPE. London: Victor Gollancz,
      1940. 141 p.

      A design from 1940 that analyzes the doctrines of fed-
      eralism and at the same time offers a plan of establish-
      ing a federated Europe.

27    Friedrich, Carl J. TRENDS OF FEDERALISM IN THEORY AND
      PRACTICE. New York: Frederick A. Praeger, 1968. xii, 193 p.

      A study of "federal behavior," what actually occurs in
      communities that federate. Besides a general and theo-
      retical discussion, one chapter devoted specifically to
      a united Europe.

28    Goodwin, Geoffrey L. EUROPEAN UNITY: A RETURN TO RE-
      ALITIES. Leeds, Engl.: Leeds University Press, 1972. 23 p.

      A monograph criticizing the federalist approach to Euro-
      pean integration.

29    Macmahon, Arthur Whittier, ed. FEDERALISM: MATURE AND
      EMERGENT. Garden City, N.Y.: Doubleday and Co., 1955.
      557 p.

      Twenty-six articles on federalism. Parts 1 and 2, the-
      oretical considerations of federalism and its application

to party systems, courts, and states. Part 3, functional
federalism and its applications, and part 4, supranational
union in Western Europe.

30    McWhinney, Edward. FEDERAL CONSTITUTION-MAKING FOR
A MULTINATIONAL WORLD. Leiden, Netherlands: A.W. Sijthoff,
1966. xii, 150 p.

A review of a broad range of experiments in federalism,
some enduring, some not. Also analyzes the opposing
forces of integration and fragmentation in various historical contexts--when and on what basis a federal form
should be entered into, and when national communities
should go their own ways.

31    Mitchell, J.B.D. EUROPE: THE POLITICS OF PIG IN THE MID-
DLE. Leeds, Engl.: Leeds University Press, n.d. 30 p.

A short clarification of the problems of federalism and
supranationalism. Seeks to offer an alternative perspective.

32    Mouskheli, Michel. CONFEDERATION OR FEDERATION? Paris:
European Youth Campaign, 1952. 43 p.

33    Parmelee, Maurice Farr. GEO-ECONOMIC REGIONAL AND
WORLD FEDERATION. New York: Exposition Press, 1949. 137 p.

An analysis of integration or federation based on geographic and economic principles, including the nature,
bases, and functions of such federations.

34    Riker, William H. FEDERALISM: ORIGIN, OPERATION, SIGNIF-
ICANCE. Boston: Little, Brown and Co., 1964. 169 p.

A study of the theory of federalism, its origins and conditions for application under varying political situations.

35    Watson, Alan. EUROPE AT RISK. London: George G. Harrap
and Co., 1972. 224 p.

An essay on sovereignty and the long-term problems
facing an integrated Europe within a federal framework.

## E. FUNCTIONALISM

36    Brenner, Michael Joseph. "The Functionalist Theory of Integra-

tion and the Process of Adherence to a Supranational Organization: A Case Study of Britain and the European Economic Community." Ph.D. dissertation, University of California, Berkeley, 1968.

37 _____. TECHNOCRATIC POLITICS AND THE FUNCTIONALIST THEORY OF EUROPEAN INTEGRATION. Ithaca, N.Y.: Cornell University Press, 1969. 164 p.

> Concerned with domestic determinants of policy choice in Britain and in Europe. Explanation of policy formation in Britain (application for membership) and in France (the veto) framed in terms of the political and technocratic elites of each country. A critique of functionalist explanation.

38 Groom, A.J.R., and Taylor, Paul, eds. FUNCTIONALISM AND INTERNATIONAL RELATIONS THEORY AND PRACTICE. London: University of London Press, 1975. 354 p.

39 Haas, Ernst B. BEYOND THE NATION-STATE: FUNCTIONALISM AND INTERNATIONAL ORGANIZATION. Stanford, Calif.: Stanford University Press, 1964. x, 595 p.

> A classic study of functionalism and the development of neofunctionalism as a theory of integration. Uses the ILO as a case study.

40 _____. THE UNITING OF EUROPE: POLITICAL, SOCIAL, AND ECONOMIC FORCES, 1950-57. Stanford, Calif.: Stanford University Press, 1958. 552 p.

> A conceptual study of neofunctionalism and the integration process using the ECSC as a case to substantiate the pluralist thesis that political community can be developed if the behavior of the key groups can be refocused on integrated institutions.

41 Jordan, Robert S., ed. MULTINATIONAL COOPERATION: ECONOMIC, SOCIAL AND SCIENTIFIC DEVELOPMENT. New York: Oxford University Press, 1972. 392 p.

> A collection of studies on multinational cooperation in economics, social affairs, and science. Includes studies of specific organizations like OAS and UNESCO in relation to economic cooperation and trading. A study of functional integration.

42 Mitrany, David A. A WORKING PEACE SYSTEM. 1943. Reprint. Chicago: Quadrangle Books, 1966. 221 p.

An explication of the theory of the functional approach to integration and its application both to European and world conditions.

## F. INTERNATIONAL COOPERATION

43    Brickman, Howard Joseph. "Towards an Integrated Earth System: The European Model of the Integrative Process." Ph.D. dissertation, Northwestern University, 1973.

44    Cosgrove, Carol Ann, and Twitchett, Kenneth J., eds. THE NEW INTERNATIONAL ACTORS: THE UN AND THE EEC. London: St. Martin's Press, 1970. 272 p.

A compendium of fifteen articles by scholars on the theory of international cooperation and aspects of that cooperation in the UN and EEC.

45    Deutsch, Karl W. THE ANALYSIS OF INTERNATIONAL RELATIONS. Englewood Cliffs, N.J.: Prentice-Hall, 1968. 214 p.

Analyzes basic concepts of international relations including power, elites, conflicts and coalitions as well as international and supranational integration.

46    Keohane, R.O., and Nye, J[oseph]. S., Jr., eds. TRANSNATIONAL RELATIONS AND WORLD POLITICS. Cambridge, Mass.: Harvard University Press, 1972. 398 p.

A collection of essays which seeks to identify and categorize transnational actors like airlines and multinational businesses to show whether or not structural transformation of interstate relations is taking place, and to conceptualize a new "world view" of politics based on transnational actors.

47    Pentland, Charles. INTERNATIONAL THEORY AND EUROPEAN INTEGRATION. New York: Free Press, 1973. 283 p.

A conceptual study of European political integration as a process. A reformulation of European integration which places it in the broader context of international relations theory.

48    Taylor, Paul. INTERNATIONAL COOPERATION TODAY: THE EUROPEAN AND UNIVERSAL PATTERN. London: Elek Books, 1971. 165 p.

A study of international cooperation from a theoretical

perspective including a critique of the functionalist, neofunctionalist, and federalist positions.

## G. NATIONALISM

49    Deutsch, Karl W. NATIONALISM AND SOCIAL COMMUNICA-
      TION: AN INQUIRY INTO THE FOUNDATIONS OF NATIONAL-
      ITY. Cambridge, Mass.: M.I.T. Press, 1953. 292 p.

      Develops a theory of social communication to study na-
      tionalist ideas and why they are strong at some times,
      weak at others. Includes empirical indicators and quan-
      titative tests for nationalism.

50    Kohn, Hans. NATIONALISM IN THE NORTH ATLANTIC COM-
      MUNITY. Research Monograph no. 3. Philadelphia: University
      of Pennsylvania for the Foreign Policy Research Institute, 1965.
      41 p.

      An assessment nationalism in the post-World War II At-
      lantic Community including its origins and effects on the
      development of an integrated Europe.

51    Nussle-Kramer, Marguerite. "The Passing of Nationalism in West-
      ern Europe: A Study of Internationalism, Based on French, British,
      and German Elite Panel Surveys 1955-61." Ph.D. dissertation,
      Massachusetts Institute of Technology, 1963.

## H. REGIONALISM

52    Cobb, Roger W., and Elder, Charles. INTERNATIONAL COM-
      MUNITY: A REGIONAL AND GLOBAL STUDY. New York:
      Hold, Rinehart and Winston, 1970. 160 p.

      A digest of the existing literature on integration theory
      and an attempt to test empirically eighteen of these ex-
      trapolated propositions. Examines trends in community
      formation at the regional and global level by transac-
      tion analysis.

53    Deutsch, Karl W. POLITICAL COMMUNITY AT THE INTERNA-
      TIONAL LEVEL. New York: Doubleday and Co., 1954. 70 p.

      A transaction analysis of the evolution of political com-
      munity, historically, conceptually, and methodologically.

54    Deutsch, Karl W., et al. POLITICAL COMMUNITY AND THE

NORTH ATLANTIC AREA. Princeton, N.J.: Princeton University Press, 1957. 227 p.

One of the classic studies on integration which seeks to develop the topic theoretically: the background conditions for integration, its process, and current state.

55  Haas, Ernst B. REGIONAL INTEGRATION AND NATIONAL POLICY. International Conciliation, no. 513. New York: Carnegie Endowment for International Peace, 1957. 61 p.

A survey of the problems which have grown out of various regional groupings as well as the advantages of regionalism, like stability.

56  Harrison, Reginald J. EUROPE IN QUESTION: THEORIES OF REGIONAL INTERNATIONAL INTEGRATION. London: George Allen and Unwin, 1974. 256 p.

57  Jacob, Phillip E., and Toscano, James V., eds. THE INTEGRATION OF POLITICAL COMMUNITIES. By Karl W. Deutsch et al. Philadelphia: J.B. Lippincott Co., 1964. 314 p.

Ten studies on integrated political behavior developed around theoretical perspectives of a research seminar on integration. Includes a discussion of communication theory, transaction flow analysis, and the learning of integrative habits.

58  Lindberg, Leon N[ord]., and Scheingold, Stuart A[llen]., eds. REGIONAL INTEGRATION: THEORY AND RESEARCH. Cambridge, Mass.: Harvard University Press, 1971. 398 p.

A collection of essays viewing the theoretical literature, its contributions and future directions, by eminent contributors like Haas, Alker, Nye, and Schmitter.

59  Nye, Joseph S., Jr. PEACE IN PARTS: INTEGRATION AND CONFLICT IN REGIONAL ORGANIZATION. Boston: Little, Brown and Co., 1971. 210 p.

A study of regional organizations, their organizational structure, and their functions and goals as international actors shaping peace and security. Evaluates several regional organizations, including the EEC.

60  Russett, Bruce M. INTERNATIONAL REGIONS AND THE INTERNATIONAL SYSTEM: A STUDY IN POLITICAL ECOLOGY. Chicago: Rand McNally and Co., 1967. xvi, 252 p.

A theoretical and methodological study of regions and

regionalism. Part of chapter 2 devoted to a comparison of the theory of regionalism and Western Europe.

61    Sjostedt, Gunnar. INTEGRATION AND ACTOR CAPABILITY: A SURVEY OF THE THEORIES OF REGIONAL, POLITICAL INTEGRATION. Research report, Swedish Institute of International Affairs, UL-74-1. Stockholm: Swedish Institute of International Affairs, 1974. 101 p.

62    Slaughter, Richard Arthur. "Toward Modification of European Integration Theory: Policy Spillover in the European Community, 1958-71." Ph.D. dissertation, University of Denver, 1974.

63    Yalem, Ronald J. REGIONALISM AND WORLD ORDER. Washington, D.C.: Public Affairs Press, 1965. 160 p.

An analysis and assessment of the interplay between regional organizations and international organizations in creating world order.

# Chapter 2

## GENERAL, HISTORICAL, AND INSTITUTIONAL
## STUDIES OF INTEGRATION

(Excluding the European Economic and Atomic Energy Communities)

## A. AFRICA

64    Nye, Joseph S., Jr. PAN-AFRICANISM AND EAST AFRICAN IN-
      TEGRATION. Cambridge, Mass.: Harvard University Press, 1965.
      307 p.

> An excellent study of the initial East African rejection
> of Common Market Associate status, in chapter 7. How-
> ever, the main thrust of the book in a study of regional
> integration using Africa to test the hypotheses found in
> a European setting.

65    Wallerstein, Immanuel. AFRICA, THE POLITICS OF UNITY. AN
      ANALYSIS OF A CONTEMPORARY SOCIAL MOVEMENT. New
      York: Random House, 1967. xi, 274 p.

> Primarily a study of African integration of the late 1950s.
> Has many obvious parallels to the process of integration
> in Western Europe.

## B. EUROPE

### 1. Convention and Commission on Human Rights

66    Castberg, Frede. THE EUROPEAN CONVENTION ON HUMAN
      RIGHTS. Leiden, Netherlands: A.W. Sijthoff, 1974. 198 p.

> An introduction to the European Convention on Human
> Rights. Of particular interest to students of law.

67    Council of Europe. Directorate of Information. THE RIGHTS OF
      THE EUROPEAN CITIZEN. Strasbourg, France: 1961. 87 p.

> Useful for both novice and jurist. A study of the es-

sence, effects, and machinery of the European law on human rights. The text of the European Convention on Human Rights also included.

68    Eide, Asbjorn, and Schou, August, eds. INTERNATIONAL PRO-TECTION OF HUMAN RIGHTS. New York: Interscience Publications, 1968. 300 p.

See the chapter by A.B. McNulty, "Practical Application of the European Convention," a review of the value of the protection and effectiveness of the EC Executive Commission and its procedures. See also other articles on the convention.

69    Fawcett, J.E.S. THE APPLICATION OF THE EUROPEAN CON-VENTION ON HUMAN RIGHTS. Oxford: Clarendon Press, 1969. 368 p.

One of the best books on the subject concentrating on the practical application of the Convention on Human Rights, and how the convention has been interpreted. Treaty explained article by article, thoroughly, but very readably.

70    Kadijk, Jozef H. "The European Convention for the Protection of Human Rights and Fundamental Freedoms, 1953-63: Its Political Aspects and Integrative Effect in Europe." Ph.D. dissertation, New York University, 1967.

71    Morrisson, Clovis C[lyde, Jr.]. THE DEVELOPING EUROPEAN LAW OF HUMAN RIGHTS. Leiden, Netherlands: A.W. Sijthoff, 1967. 247 p.

An evaluation of the first twelve years and the practical results of the European Law of Human Rights. More attention given to the activities of the Commission on Human Rights than to the court.

72    _____. "The Developing European Law of Human Rights." Ph.D. dissertation, University of Colorado, 1965.

73    Robertson, A.H. HUMAN RIGHTS IN EUROPE. Manchester, Engl.: Manchester University Press, 1963. 280 p.

An analysis of the Human Rights Convention ten years after its conception focusing on the application of the ideals set forth in the charter, the bodies created to carry out the doctrines, and drawing conclusions about its effectiveness by using case studies.

74 _____, ed. HUMAN RIGHTS IN NATIONAL AND INTERNA-
TIONAL LAW: THE PROCEEDINGS OF THE SECOND INTERNA-
TIONAL CONFERENCE ON THE EUROPEAN CONVENTION ON
HUMAN RIGHTS, HELD IN VIENNA UNDER THE AUSPICES OF
THE COUNCIL OF EUROPE AND THE UNIVERSITY OF VIENNA,
18-20 OCTOBER 1965. Manchester, Engl.: Manchester University
Press, Oceana Publications, 1968. 396 p.

> A series of studies on human rights and how the Human
> Rights Convention is applied both in national law and
> in European community law.

75 Weil, Gordon L[ee]. THE EUROPEAN CONVENTION ON HUMAN
RIGHTS: BACKGROUND, DEVELOPMENT AND PROSPECTS. European Aspects, series C. Leiden, Netherlands: A.W. Sijthoff, 1963.
260 p.

> A history, commentary, and evaluation of the Conven-
> tion and Protocol of the European Convention on Human
> Rights through the summer of 1961.

76 _____. "The European Convention on Human Rights: Background,
Development and Prospects." Ph.D. dissertation, Columbia University, 1961.

## 2. Council of Europe

77 Council of Europe. Directorate of Information. THE COUNCIL
OF EUROPE AND THE SCHUMAN PLAN. Strasbourg, France:
1952. 40 p.

78 Council of Europe. Secretariat. MANUAL OF THE COUNCIL OF
EUROPE: STRUCTURE, FUNCTIONS AND ACHIEVEMENTS. London: Stevens and Sons, 1970. ix, 322 p.

> An explanation of the structure, functions, and activi-
> ties of the Council of Europe during the past twenty
> years in various fields: political, social, economic,
> human rights, and others.

79 European Movement [Britain]. THE EUROPEAN MOVEMENT AND
THE COUNCIL OF EUROPE. London: published for the European
Movement by Hutchinson and Co., 1950. 203 p.

> A history of the European Movement, its role at the
> Hague Congress of 1948, and Europe and the integra-
> tion process, culturally, politically, and economically.

80 Gellner, C.R. THE COUNCIL OF EUROPE: A BRIEF SURVEY OF

ITS ORIGIN AND DEVELOPMENT. Washington, D.C.: Library of Congress, Legislative Reference Service, 1951. 24 p.

81    Haas, Ernst B. CONSENSUS FORMATION IN THE COUNCIL OF EUROPE. Berkeley and Los Angeles: University of California Press, 1960. 70 p.

A monographic study on the Council of Europe's role in European unification, including the areas in which it has been most integrative, and those in which it has been least integrative (based upon roll-call voting), data of national affiliation, and political affiliation.

82    Hurd, Volney D. THE COUNCIL OF EUROPE: DESIGN FOR A UNITED STATES OF EUROPE. New York: Manhattan Publishing Co., 1958. 58 p.

A very brief description of the history and activities of the Council of Europe.

83    Pluhar, Ivan. "The Inconspicuous Integration: The Council of Europe in West European Unification." Ph.D. dissertation, Harvard University, 1959.

84    Robertson, A.H. CONSTITUTIONAL DEVELOPMENTS IN THE COUNCIL OF EUROPE. Brussels: Universitaire Libre de Bruxelles, 1964. 47 p.

85    _____. THE COUNCIL OF EUROPE: ITS STRUCTURE, FUNCTIONS AND ACHIEVEMENTS. 2d ed. London: published for the London Institute of World Affairs by Stevens and Sons, 1961. 288 p.

A thorough recounting of the origins, aims, and institutions of the Council of Europe by an official of that organization.

86    Rohn, Peter H. "Relations Between the Council of Europe and International Non-Governmental Organizations." Master's thesis, Union of International Associations, Brussels, 1957.

A consideration of the problem of relations between international organizations (composed of states) and non-statal international organizations.

87    Shockley, Barbara Jean Larson. "Conventions of the Council of Europe with Special Reference to the Concepts of Nationality and Status: A Documentary History." Ph.D. dissertation, University of Pennsylvania, 1958.

## 3. Cultural Unity

88    Hay, Denys.  EUROPE:  THE EMERGENCE OF AN IDEA.  Rev. ed.
      Edinburgh:  Edinburgh University Press, 1968.  151 p.

> Traces the development of the concept of "Europe," be-
> ginning with antiquity's "Europa."  Also discusses med-
> ieval and Renaissance competition between Christendom
> and Europe as well as more recent developments in the
> concept of Europe like the EEC.

89    Hazard, Paul.  THE EUROPEAN MIND.  Translated by J.L. May.
      New Haven, Conn.:  Yale University Press, 1953.  454 p.

90    Lukacs, John A.  DECLINE AND RISE OF EUROPE:  A STUDY IN
      RECENT HISTORY WITH PARTICULAR EMPHASIS ON THE DEVELOP-
      MENT OF A EUROPEAN CONSCIOUSNESS.  Garden City, N.Y.:
      Doubleday and Co., 1965.  295 p.

> A history of the development and unification of Europe
> during the last twenty years focusing upon European
> philosophy and attitudes.  Might well be considered a
> functional theorist's study of integration.

91    Madariaga, Salvador de.  EUROPE:  A UNIT OF HUMAN CUL-
      TURE.  Brussels:  European Movement, 1952.  32 p.

92    _____.  PORTRAIT OF EUROPE.  London:  Hollis and Carter, 1967.
      204 p.

> The author, a former representative to the League of
> Nations.  Views the "spiritual" side of Europe which
> both unites and divides Europeans.

93    Mayne, Richard.  THE EUROPEANS:  WHO ARE WE?  London:
      George Weidenfeld and Nicolson, 1972.  206 p.

> A look at the history and culture of "Europe" to see if
> there really is, or can be a "European" culture and tra-
> dition, or if nationalities are too prominent.  In short,
> is "Europe" founded in fact or faith?

94    Piovene, Guido.  IN SEARCH OF EUROPE:  PORTRAITS OF THE
      NON-COMMUNIST WEST.  Translated by John Shepley.  New
      York:  St. Martin's Press, 1975.  342 p.

> A journalist's probe into the values and traditions of
> Western Europe, country by country (twelve in all), seek-
> ing to determine if there is a tradition and culture com-
> mon enough to justify a "united Europe."

95    Rougemont, Denis de. THE IDEA OF EUROPE. Translated by N.
Guterman. New York: Macmillan Co., 1966. 434 p.

A chronicle of the way in which men from Grecian times
have come to think of Europe as a cultural entity. Also
includes the origins of the idea of European federation.

96    _____. THE MEANING OF EUROPE. Translated by Alan Braley.
London: Sidgwick and Jackson, 1965. 126 p.

Argues for a federated Europe through cultural activities
and suggests the way in which Europe is uniting culturally.
By the head of the European Culture Center.

## 4. ECSC (European Coal and Steel Community)

97    Bok, Derek Curtis. THE FIRST THREE YEARS OF THE SCHUMAN
PLAN. Princeton Studies in International Finance, no. 5. Princeton, N.J.: Princeton University Press, 1955. 79 p.

A short but scholarly analysis of the early years of the
Schuman Plan and an attempt to assess its economic and
political objectives, institutions, operations, and effects.

98    Diebold, William. THE SCHUMAN PLAN: A STUDY IN ECO-
NOMIC COOPERATION, 1950-59. New York: published for the
Council on Foreign Relations by Frederick A. Praeger, 1959. 750 p.

A description of the ECSC between 1950 and 1959, and
analysis of the Schuman Plan as a form of international
cooperation.

99    Giunta, Agatino John. "The European Coal and Steel Community:
An Evaluation of Achievements and Future Prospects." Ph.D. dissertation, Syracuse University, 1956.

100   Goormaghtigh, John. EUROPEAN COAL AND STEEL COMMU-
NITY. International Conciliation, no. 503. New York: Carnegie
Endowment for International Peace, 1955. 65 p.

101   Kohnstamm, Max. THE EUROPEAN COAL AND STEEL COMMU-
NITY. Recueil des Cours, vol. 90. Leiden, Netherlands: Academy
of International Law, 1957.

A discussion of the ECSC and its role in European federation, its success, and the lessons for unity and integration.

102   Lister, Louis. EUROPE'S COAL AND STEEL COMMUNITY: AN

EXPERIMENT IN ECONOMIC UNION. New York: Twentieth
Century Fund, 1960. 495 p.

An economic survey of the ECSC background, its methods and results. The ECSC viewed in the context of
the movement for European integration and used as an
illustration of the success of federal-type integration.

103 _____. "Europe's Coal and Steel Community: An Experiment in
Economic Union." Ph.D. dissertation, Columbia University, 1960.

104 Mason, Henry L. THE EUROPEAN COAL AND STEEL COMMUNI-
TY: EXPERIMENT IN SUPRANATIONALISM. The Hague: Martinus Nijhoff, 1955. 153 p.

A study of the political and constitutional problems of
the ECSC as a supranational organization and testing
ground for the development of international community.

105 Maxwell, Josette Lou. "The European Coal and Steel Community:
An International Government?" Ph.D. dissertation, Claremont
Graduate School, 1966.

106 Nichols, R.T. THE EUROPEAN COAL AND STEEL COMMUNITY.
Santa Monica, Calif.: RAND Corp., 1962. 38 p.

A focus on those aspects of the ECSC experience that
are relevant to an analysis of the institutions and limitations of the EEC, and therefore to an understanding
of the prospects for European political and military unity.

107 Padover, Saul K. EUROPE'S QUEST FOR UNITY. New York:
Foreign Policy Association, 1953. 63 p.

A short description of European integration and answers
to some of the main questions Americans ask about the
European Coal and Steel Community.

108 Philip, Andre. THE SCHUMAN PLAN: NUCLEUS OF A EURO-
PEAN COMMUNITY. Brussels: 1951. 46 p.

109 Pounds, Norman J.G., and Parker, William N. COAL AND
STEEL IN WESTERN EUROPE. London: Faber and Faber, 1957.
381 p.

"A history of the growth of the coal and steel sector and
the regional industrial groups affiliated with it. The
authors develop the technical, political, and economic

> problems of the coal and steel sector which is the basis
> for contemporary integration."
>
> BIBLIOGRAPHIE ZUR EURO-
> PAISCHEN INTEGRATION

110   Renfield, Richard Lee. "The Common Assembly of the European
Coal and Steel Community and the Community's Foreign Relations."
Ph.D. dissertation, American University, 1965.

111   Sherer, Walter. "The Coal and Steel Community: Stepping Stone
to European Integration." Ph.D. dissertation, New York University,
1961.

112   Speerenberg, D.P. THE EUROPEAN COAL AND STEEL COMMU-
NITY. Luxembourg: 1956.

113   Valentine, David Graham. THE COURT OF JUSTICE OF THE
EUROPEAN COAL AND STEEL COMMUNITY. The Hague: Martinus Nijhoff, 1955. xi, 273 p.

114   _____. "The Court of Justice of the European Coal and Steel
Community." Ph.D. dissertation, University of Utrecht, Netherlands, 1955. 271 p.

An examination of the Schuman Court, its organization,
procedures, and competence as well as the treaty covering these.

115   Weir, Sir Cecil. THE FIRST STEP IN EUROPEAN INTEGRATION:
THE EUROPEAN COAL AND STEEL COMMUNITY, THE SCHUMAN
PLAN. London: Federal Educational and Research Trust, 1957. 29 p.

116   Wentholt, Wyger. CONFEDERATE EUROPE OR WORLD REVOLU-
TION. Amsterdam: Buyten en Schipperheyn, 1962. 136 p.

Reflections on cooperation at the international level focusing specifically on the ECSC. Twelve appendixes
included.

## 5. Famous Europeans

117   Birch, Lionel, ed. INTO EUROPE: THE STORY OF THE CRU-
SADE FOR EUROPEAN UNITY, AND SOME OF THE PERSONALI-
TIES WHO HAVE PERSISTENTLY CAMPAIGNED FOR IT AND WHO
WILL CONTINUE TO DO SO IN THE FUTURE. London: Hulton
Publications, 1967. 152 p.

118 Bromberger, Merry, and Bromberger, Serge. JEAN MONNET AND THE UNITED STATES OF EUROPE. Translated by E.P. Halperin. New York: Coward-McCann, 1969. 349 p.

A biography of the "father" of Europe leading to a favorable assessment of his role.

119 Churchill, Winston S. THE SINEWS OF PEACE: POST-WAR SPEECHES. 2 vols. Edited by Randolph Churchill. London: Cassell and Co., 1948. 256 p.

The speeches by Winston Churchill, chairman of the United Europe Movement in Britain, spurring the drive for European cooperation.

120 Cook, Don. FLOODTIDE IN EUROPE. New York: G.P. Putnam's Sons, 1965. 384 p.

An interesting and anecdotal account of the persons and events surrounding the creation and activities of the European Community: Monnet, de Gaulle, Adenauer and others; also includes a look at the U.S. role.

121 Dziewanowski, M.K. JOSEPH PILSUDSKI: EUROPEAN FEDERALIST 1918-22. Stanford, Calif.: Hoover Institution Press, 1969. xiv, 379 p.

A study of Pilsudski's concept of a buffer zone of nations between Poland and Central Europe, their effects, and why they failed.

122 Huizinga, Jakob Herman. MR. EUROPE: A POLITICAL BIOGRAPHY OF PAUL-HENRI SPAAK. London: George Weidenfeld and Nicolson, 1961. 248 p.

A biography detailing the political life of Paul-Henri Spaak focused upon his Belgian career which shaped his "European" outlook, and upon Spaak as a European political force.

123 Oosterhuis, Ton. THESE WERE EUROPEANS. Translated by Adrienne Dixon. Amersham, Engl.: Hulton Educational Publications, 1970. 192 p.

For younger readers, twenty stories of famous Europeans from Socrates to Masaryk.

124 Satra, John C. "The Fate of Jean Monnet's Concept of European Integration in the Light of Cross Pressures on the European Coal and Steel Community." Ph.D. dissertation, University of Florida, 1961.

125 Spaak, Paul-Henri. THE CONTINUING BATTLE: MEMOIRS OF A EUROPEAN 1933-66. Translated by Henry Fox. London: George Weidenfeld and Nicolson, 1971. 512 p.

> An inside view from one of Europe's eminent spokesmen. Details his own role and perspective as a participant in the creation of an integrated Europe.

126 Stikker, Dirk U. MEN OF RESPONSIBILITY: A MEMOIR. New York: Harper and Row, 1966. 418 p.

> An autobiography of a former secretary-general of NATO describing his view of Europe, its problems, and its leaders like de Gaulle, Spaak, Adenauer, Schuman, and Bevan.

127 Zinn, Carolyn June. "Paul-Henri Spaak and the Political-Economic Integration of Europe: An American Perspective." Ph.D. dissertation, West Virginia University, 1967.

## 6. OECD and OEEC (Organization for Cooperation and Development and Organization for European Economic Cooperation)

128 Aubrey, Henry G. ATLANTIC ECONOMIC COOPERATION: THE CASE OF THE OECD. New York: Frederick A. Praeger, 1967. 214 p.

> An assessment of the OECD's effect on Europe and international cooperation, and a discussion of the institution's history and organization.

129 Organization for European Economic Cooperation. AT WORK FOR EUROPE: AN ACCOUNT OF THE ACTIVITIES OF THE ORGANIZATION. 4th ed. Paris: 1957. 139 p.

> A collection of essays on European cooperation through the OEEC: trade, manpower problems, energy, agriculture, maritime transport, and tourism.

130 _____. HISTORY AND STRUCTURE. 4th ed. Paris: 1954. 37 p.

131 Ouin, Marc. THE OEEC AND THE COMMON MARKET: WHY EUROPE NEEDS AN ECONOMIC UNION OF SEVENTEEN COUNTRIES. Paris: Organization for European Economic Cooperation, 1958. 32 p.

## 7. Other Economic Studies

### a. INCLUDING PRE-WORLD WAR II SUBJECTS

132 Alpert, Paul. TWENTIETH CENTURY ECONOMIC HISTORY OF EUROPE. New York: Schuman, 1951. xiv, 466 p.

> An economic history of Europe in the twentieth century. Reconstruction and attempts at unification since the end of World War II detailed in chapter 5.

133 Clough, Shepard B., et al. ECONOMIC HISTORY OF EUROPE: TWENTIETH CENTURY. New York: Harper Torchbooks, 1968. 384 p.

> Discusses the period from 1914 to the late 1950s in Britain, France, Germany, Italy, and the Soviet Union, including approaches to postwar recovery, the radical reconstruction of East Europe, and the development of regional cooperation.

134 Henderson, W.O. THE ZOLLVEREIN. 2d ed. Chicago: Quadrangle Books, 1959. 375 p.

> A history of the German Customs Union and German economy between 1815 and 1871. An excellent background study for an understanding both of Germany's particular economic history, which influences her present policy towards Europe, and the Customs Union as an integrating organization.

135 Palyi, Melchior. MANAGED MONEY AT THE CROSSROADS: THE EUROPEAN EXPERIENCE. Notre Dame, Ind.: University of Notre Dame Press, 1958. 196 p.

> A survey of the financial centers of Europe and an analysis of the methods of managing and converting money since the 1900s. Also covers postwar recovery methods, inflation controls, and devaluation tactics.

136 Roussakis, Emmanuel N. FRIEDRICH LIST: THE ZOLLVEREIN AND THE UNITING OF EUROPE. Studies in Contemporary European Issues, no. 1. Bruges, Belgium: College of Europe, 1968. 149 p.

137 Watson, William Braasch. "A Common Market in Fifteenth Century Europe: The Structure of Genoese, Venetian, Florentine, and Catalan Trade with Flanders and England." Ph.D. dissertation, Harvard University, 1963.

## b. POST-WORLD WAR II

138    Balassa, Bela, et al.  STUDIES IN TRADE LIBERALIZATION.  Bal-
       timore:  Johns Hopkins Press, 1967.  338 p.

    Implications for major industrial nations of possible al-
    ternative approaches to trade liberalization, including
    an Atlantic Free Trade Area, periodic tariff reductions
    under the most-favored-nation clause, and European in-
    tegration, among others.  Political and economic objec-
    tives and alternatives assessed for each country or group
    of countries.

139    Barach, Arnold B.  THE NEW EUROPE AND ITS ECONOMIC FU-
       TURE.  New York:  Macmillan Co., 1964.  148 p.

    An updating of J. Frederick Dewhurst's 1961 study:
    EUROPE'S NEEDS AND RESOURCES:  TRENDS AND
    PROSPECTS IN EIGHTEEN COUNTRIES.  Provides an
    overview of European economic, social, labor, educa-
    tional, agricultural, and technological problems and re-
    sources.  Additional subjects also covered.

140    Brinton, Crane.  THE TEMPER OF WESTERN EUROPE.  Cambridge,
       Mass.:  Harvard University Press, 1953.  118 p.

    A look at the consequences of post-World War II re-
    covery:  the working conditions and the mentality which
    have arisen.  A useful background study for the prob-
    lems of labor integration.

141    Cohen, Stephen D.  INTERNATIONAL MONETARY REFORM, 1964-
       69: THE POLITICAL DIMENSION.  New York:  Frederick A. Praeger,
       1970.  222 p.

    An analysis of monetary reform which finds the subject
    more rooted in politics than in economics.

142    Council of Europe.  THE PRESENT STATE OF ECONOMIC INTE-
       GRATION IN WESTERN EUROPE.  Strasbourg, France:  1955.
       103 p.

    A summary of the progress towards economic integration
    in each of the economic organizations to 1955.

143    Crowther, Geoffrey.  THE ECONOMIC RECONSTRUCTION OF
       EUROPE.  Claremont, Calif.:  Claremont College, 1948.  79 p.

    Lectures by the editor of the ECONOMIST concerning
    the future economic development of Europe and the im-
    portance of the U.S. policy decisions toward Europe in
    order to integrate Germany and to avoid extremes of na-
    tionalism.

144 Denton, Geoffrey R., ed. ECONOMIC INTEGRATION IN EU-
ROPE. 2d ed. Reading University Studies on Contemporary Europe,
no. 3. London: George Weidenfeld and Nicolson, 1972. 365 p

Twelve essays on the theory and practice of the impact
of customs unions and free trade areas on members and
third countries. Also includes economic problems faced
by the EEC and EFTA.

145 Dewhurst, J. Frederick, et al. EUROPE'S NEEDS AND RESOURCES:
TRENDS AND PROSPECTS IN EIGHTEEN COUNTRIES. New York:
Twentieth Century Fund, 1961. 1,198 p.

A major resource book on Europe, technical but readable, covering topics of economic development and problems since World War II. Topics include population,
manpower, education, housing, and capital.

146 Diebold, William. TRADE AND PAYMENTS IN WESTERN EUROPE:
A STUDY IN ECONOMIC COOPERATION 1947-51. New York:
Harper and Row, 1952. 488 p.

A survey and analysis of the European Payments Union
and various programs for the removal of restrictions on
trade in Europe from their earliest beginnings to the present.

147 Feld, Werner J. NONGOVERNMENTAL FORCES AND WORLD
POLITICS: A STUDY OF BUSINESS, LABOR AND POLITICAL
GROUPS. New York: Frederick A. Praeger, 1972. 284 p.

A study of multinational enterprises and nongovernmental forces, and their vast influence on regional and global integration.

148 Franck, Thomas M., and Weisband, Edward, eds. A FREE TRADE
AREA ASSOCIATION. New York: New York University Press,
1968. xv, 239 p.

A collection of essays which grew out of Britain's second exclusion from the EEC. Purports to examine the
economic and political possibilities and the theory of
another free trade area including Britain, the United
States, and Canada.

149 Geary, Robert Charles, ed. EUROPE'S FUTURE IN FIGURES. Amsterdam: North Holland Publishing Co., 1962. 334 p.

Forecasts the GNP for 1970-75 in numerous small European nations with comparative figures for 1959-60. Emphasizes, analyzes, and criticizes various techniques of
forecasting. Provides a useful measure of integration
and comparative integrated growth.

150   Geoffrey, Denton, ed. ECONOMIC INTEGRATION IN EUROPE.
       (See Denton, Geoffrey R., no. 144.)


151   Gustavson, Carl G. EUROPE IN THE WORLD COMMUNITY SINCE
       1939. Boston: Allyn and Bacon, 1971. xii, 548 p.

       A comprehensive history of post-World War II Europe.
       Divided into three parts with the latter two parts deal-
       ing with the beginning of European integration and com-
       pletion of the EEC and EFTA.


152   Imrik, Andrew. "Development of the Idea of European Economic
       Integration." Ph.D. dissertation, St. Louis University, 1958.


153   Kravis, Irving B. DOMESTIC INTERESTS AND INTERNATIONAL
       OBLIGATIONS: SAFEGUARDS IN INTERNATIONAL TRADE OR-
       GANIZATIONS. Philadelphia: University of Pennsylvania Press,
       1963. 448 p.

       An examination of the nature of international commit-
       ments and the manner in which domestic interests have
       been safeguarded in three European arrangements, OECD,
       ECSC, and EEC.


154   Meade, James E., et al. CASE STUDIES IN EUROPEAN ECO-
       NOMIC UNION. Oxford: Oxford University Press, 1962. 424 p.

       Three case studies, the Belgo-Luxembourg Economic Un-
       ion, BENELUX, and the ECSC, which give specific fo-
       cus to the economic problems facing the builders of these
       three unions. Not an assessment so much as a guide to
       the problems encountered.


155   Meerhaeghe, M.A.G. van. INTERNATIONAL ECONOMIC INSTI-
       TUTIONS. New York: John Wiley and Sons, 1966. 404 p.

       A useful introduction to the theory of international eco-
       nomic relations and the European institutions, and their
       structures and functions: BENULUX, OEEC and OECD,
       ECSC, EEC, and EFTA.


156   Paelinck, Jean H.P., ed. PROGRAMMING FOR EUROPE'S COL-
       LECTIVE NEEDS. London and Amsterdam: North Holland Publish-
       ing Co., 1970. v, 358 p.

       A highly technical compendium of essays assessing Eu-
       rope's collective needs in health resource allocation,
       public funding, transport, and other areas. Also at-
       tempts to analyze needs on a regional and an integrated
       basis, rather than on a national basis.

157   Pollard, Sidney.   EUROPEAN ECONOMIC INTEGRATION: 1815–
      1970.  London:  Thames and Hudson, 1974.   180 p.

      An economic history of Europe stressing industrialization
      as the drive which led to unification.


158   Postan, M.M.   AN ECONOMIC HISTORY OF WESTERN EUROPE
      1945–64.  London:  Methuen and Co., 1967.   382 p.

      A study of the major developments in the post–World
      War II economy of Europe dealing specifically with the
      causes of economic expansion and assessing the benefits
      and penalties of the new economic and social policies.


159   Triffin, Robert.   EUROPE AND THE MONEY MUDDLE:  FROM BI-
      LATERALISM TO NEAR-CONVERTIBILITY, 1947–56.   New Haven,
      Conn.:  Yale University Press, 1957.   351 p.

      A comprehensive, if eliptical, study of national and
      European policies which begat Europe's monetary re-
      covery after World War II.  Should prove useful for
      experts and lay readers alike.


160   Uri, Pierre, ed.   TRADE AND INVESTMENT POLICIES FOR THE
      SEVENTIES:  NEW CHALLENGE FOR THE ATLANTIC AREA AND
      JAPAN.  New York:  Frederick A. Praeger, 1971.   286 p.

      The proceedings and an analysis of a Trade and Invest-
      ment Conference in Tokyo in 1971.  ˙ Focus upon the
      role of the new multinational enterprise, as well as
      trade policies of Europe, the United States, and East
      Europe.


161   Ward, Barbara.   POLICY FOR THE WEST.  Harmondsworth, Engl.:
      Penguin Books, 1951.   253 p.

      An analysis of European institutions, the OEEC, EPU,
      and the Schuman Plan, and an argument for an Atlan-
      tic Community as the most viable form of European com-
      mitment.


162   Wentholt, Wyger.   SOME COMMENTS ON THE LIQUIDATION
      OF THE EUROPEAN PAYMENTS UNION AND RELATED PROB-
      LEMS. Amsterdam: Amsterdam Stock Exchange Report, 1959.  23 p.

      A brief monograph assessing the European Monetary
      Agreement and the liquidation of the EPU, a result,
      the author seeks to show, of the conflict between France
      and England when the United States refused to make
      the dollar convertible to gold.

163 Wightman, David. ECONOMIC COOPERATION IN EUROPE: A STUDY OF THE UNITED NATIONS ECONOMIC COMMISSION FOR EUROPE. London: Stevens and Sons, 1956. 288 p.

> A detailed appraisal of the problems of intra-European trade and general economic cooperation within the framework of the UN's Economic Commission for Europe. Includes a discussion of the Marshall Plan, ECE machinery, agricultural, and other sectoral cooperation.

## 8. Other Political Studies

### a. INCLUDING PRE-WORLD WAR II SUBJECTS

164 Albrecht-Carrie, Rene. ONE EUROPE: THE HISTORICAL BACKGROUND OF EUROPEAN UNITY. New York: Doubleday and Co., 1965. 346 p.

> A broad survey of European unity from ancient times to the present including Napoleon's attempts at unifying Europe, the Concert of Europe, Briand Plan, Hitler, Council of Europe, Schuman Plan, and the European Community.

165 _____. THE UNITY OF EUROPE: AN HISTORICAL SURVEY. London: Martin Secker and Warburg, 1966. 346 p.

> See no. 164.

166 Alting von Geusau, Frans A.M. EUROPEAN PERSPECTIVES ON WORLD ORDER. John F. Kennedy Institute Series, no. 10. Leiden, Netherlands: A.W. Sijthoff, 1975. 275 p.

> An examination of Europe's role and view of world order: (1) from the historical perspective prior to World War II, (2) following World War II including a discussion of the effect of European unification on Europe's perspective on world order, and (3), a review of the national perspectives on world order.

167 Beloff, Max, ed. EUROPE AND THE EUROPEANS: AN INTERNATIONAL DISCUSSION. London: Chatto and Windus, 1957. 288 p.

> An edited round table discussion at the instance of the Council of Europe looking at "Europe" in its broadest perspectives: historical, economic, cultural, political, scientific, and philosophic, and showing the relationships among these perspectives.

168 Boyd, Andrew [K.H.], and Boyd, Frances. WESTERN UNION: A STUDY OF THE TREND TOWARD EUROPEAN UNITY. Washington, D.C.: Public Affairs Press, 1949. 183 p.

> A history of European integration, trends, ideas, organizations, personalities (like Rousseau, Kant, Churchill, Fulbright), pertinent speeches and treaties, as well as movements like the United Europe Movement, European Union of Federalists, BENELUX, and others.

169 _____. WESTERN UNION: UNA'S GUIDE TO EUROPEAN RECOVERY. London: Hutchinson and Co. for the United Nations Association, 1949. 183 p.

> See no. 168.

170 Brinton, Crane. FROM MANY ONE: THE PROCESS OF POLITICAL INTEGRATION: THE PROBLEM OF WORLD GOVERNMENT. Cambridge, Mass.: Harvard University Press, 1948. 126 p.

> An essay concerning the process and ideas of political integration drawn from ancient, medieval, and contemporary illustrations. Seeks to analyze the historical "realities" of the process rather than to encourage the mere hopes of proponents of world government.

171 Burns, C. Deslisle. THE FIRST EUROPE: A STUDY OF THE ESTABLISHMENT OF MEDIEVAL CHRISTENDOM, A.D. 400-800. London: George Allen and Unwin, 1947. 684 p.

> A study of the design of medieval Christendom, the "First Europe," and an attempt to draw an analogy for the study of the "Third Europe," or the European Community following World War II.

172 Chambers, J.D., and Madgwick, P.J. CONFLICT AND COMMUNITY: EUROPE SINCE 1750. London: George Philip and Son, 1968. 492 p.

> A history of the conflicts and steps toward European union since 1750. Europe up to World War I in parts 1-5; World War II in parts 6-8. Part 9 on post-World War II development of institutions and patterns of cooperation.

173 Dawson, Christopher. THE MAKING OF EUROPE: AN INTRODUCTION TO THE HISTORY OF EUROPEAN UNITY. New York: World Publishing Co., 1958. 274 p.

> By a Catholic historian. Writes of religious factors in the making of political Europe beginning with the period between the fall of the Roman Empire and medieval unity.

174   Fasel, George W.  MODERN EUROPE IN THE MAKING:  FROM THE FRENCH REVOLUTION TO THE COMMON MARKET.  New York:  Dodd, Mead and Co., 1974.  xii, 300 p.

175   Fogarty, Michael P.  CHRISTIAN DEMOCRACY IN WESTERN EUROPE, 1820-1953.  London:  Routledge and Kegan Paul, 1957.  xviii, 461 p.

> One of the few studies indicating the Christian Democratic party's policies and actions toward Europe.  Also covers CDU interests and actions in the Assembly of the ECSC, their reactions to the "Green Pool" and to supranational approaches.

176   Funk, A.L., ed.  EUROPE IN THE TWENTIETH CENTURY:  SOURCE STUDIES ON CONTEMPORARY ISSUES AND PROBLEMS.  Homewood, Ill.:  Dorsey Press, 1968.  469 p.

> A series of case studies on significant historical events from 1916 to the present including the shaping of European integration.  Also includes excerpts from official documents, correspondence, and memoirs.

177   Gilbert, Felix.  THE END OF THE EUROPEAN ERA:  1890 TO THE PRESENT.  New York:  W.W. Norton and Co., 1970.  426 p.

> A study of the clash of national interests which ended in World War I and the subsequent instability that led to totalitarian regimes in Germany, Italy, and Russia. Europe as a former world power, and now as an uncertain power analyzed by author.

178   Grosshans, H.  THE SEARCH FOR MODERN EUROPE.  Boston:  Houghton Mifflin Co., 1970.  440 p.

> A look at the major problems of Europe over the last 250 years, including revolution, secularism, industrialization, nationalism, war, and relations between Europe and the United States.  A useful guide to background problems of integration.

179   Herriot, Edouard.  THE UNITED STATES OF EUROPE.  Translated by R.J. Dingle.  London:  George G. Harrap and Co., 1930.  294 p.

> A history of the integration attempts and movements prior to 1930.

180   Hotchkiss, Alice.  "The Concert of Europe, 1813-23; Its Evolution and Development as an Experiment in Collective Action."  Ph.D. dissertation, University of California, Berkeley, 1940.

181 Hutchinson, Paul. THE UNITED STATES OF EUROPE. Chicago: Willett, Clark and Colby, 1929. 225 p.

> The historical circumstances of the "United States of Europe" and the factors in its growth: prewar problems, postwar politics, economics, and U.S., British, and Soviet influences.

182 Larkin, Maurice. GATHERING PACE: CONTINENTAL EUROPE 1870-1945. New York: Humanities Press, 1970. 483 p.

> A history of Europe from 1870 to 1945 emphasizing those developments most influential to most people. Each subject examined for its social, economic, and political outcome. Larkin's material improvement of the masses and the subsequent implications proves to be of central concern.

183 Lichtheim, George. EUROPE IN THE TWENTIETH CENTURY. New York: Praeger Publishers, 1972. 448 p.

> A history of Europe since 1900 which tries to show why the Europeans could not cope with integration after World War I, and how they have since World War II.

184 Lyons, F.S.L. INTERNATIONALISM IN EUROPE 1815-1914. Leiden, Netherlands: A.W. Sijthoff, 1963. 412 p.

> A history of the origins of the process of European integration and the organizations and activities of cooperation in the economic, intellectual, religious, humanitarian, scientific, and legal fields.

185 Martin, Laurence W., ed. DIPLOMACY IN MODERN EUROPEAN HISTORY. New York: Macmillan Co., 1966. vi, 138 p.

> Essays discussing the central importance of diplomacy in Western European political relations from the time of its origins in fifteenth-century Italy to its modification and refinement in the cold war era. The topics broad in scope and the orientation scholarly and technical. Emphasis is on social, historical, and political factors of diplomacy.

186 Mulvey, John J. "The United States of Europe: The Plans of Henry IV and Briand." Ph.D. dissertation, Georgetown University, 1931.

187 Rothman, Stanley. EUROPEAN SOCIETY AND POLITICS. Indianapolis: Bobbs-Merrill Co., 1970. 931 p.

A history describing the importance of Europe's Christian heritage, the emergence of nation-states, industrialization, ideologies, and the conflicts of the nineteenth century. Also examines the social and cultural bases of European politics as well as parties and institutions implementing public policy.

188 Rowe, Peter Niles. "European Federation Projects and National Policies, 1929-33." Ph.D. dissertation, Yale University, 1960.

189 Salter, Sir James Arthur. THE UNITED STATES OF EUROPE AND OTHER PAPERS. Edited with notes by W. Arnold-Foster. London: George Allen and Unwin, 1933. 303 p.

190 Stead, W.T. THE UNITED STATES OF EUROPE ON THE EVE OF THE PARLIAMENT OF PEACE. 1899. Reprint. New York: Garland, 1971. xv, 468 p.

A journalist's look at the possibilities of a United States of Europe as he talked with representatives at The Hague International Peace Conference of 1898.

## b. POST-WORLD WAR II

191 Alting von Geusau, Frans A.M. BEYOND THE EUROPEAN COMMUNITY. Leiden, Netherlands: published for the John F. Kennedy Institute, Center for International Studies, Tilburg, Netherlands, by A.W. Sijthoff, 1969. 247 p.

A systems analysis of European integration and its failure to achieve its objectives. Focuses upon Europe as a federal state and as a nucleus for political union and common defense.

192 American Academy of Arts and Sciences. "A New Europe?" DAEDALUS 93 (1964): entire issue.

Twenty-three essays on Europe by European and American experts.

193 Andrews, William G. EUROPEAN POLITICAL INSTITUTIONS: A GOVERNMENT READER. New York: D. Van Nostrand, 1962. 387 p.

A comparative reader organized functionally for Britain, France, Germany, and the USSR, but not concerning the European Community exclusively. This collection of speeches, documents, and essays a valuable resource of national policies toward political integration and the various European institutions.

194  Aron, Raymond. THE CENTURY OF TOTAL WAR. Garden City,
N.Y.: Doubleday and Co., 1954. 379 p.

A broad study of the nature and history of Europe and
European integration including the political and economic issues. Written by a well-known French political
scientist and journalist.

195  Barraclough, Geoffrey. EUROPEAN UNITY IN THOUGHT AND
ACTION. Oxford: Basil Blackwell, 1963. 60 p.

An inquiry into the doctrines held by various politicians
and philosophers on European unity, and an attempt to
assess their relevance to this era. The views of de Gaulle
among those assessed and found to be ungrounded in
historical context.

196  Birley, Robert. THE CONCEPT OF EUROPE: AN HISTORI-
CAL SURVEY. Exeter, Engl.: European-Atlantic Movement,
1974.  47 p.

197  Bolles, Blair. THE BIG CHANGE IN EUROPE. New York: W.W.
Norton, 1958. 527 p.

A history of post-World War II Europe, and especially
its leaders, and the impact of the United States and the
Soviet Union on Europe. Interesting for its anecdotal
and personal details.

198  Bonn, Moritz Julius. WHITHER EUROPE: UNION OR PARTNER-
SHIP? London: Cohen and West, 1952. 207 p.

Examines the possibilities of closer cooperation in Europe, predominantly from the American point of view,
and urges further integration through the functional approach of the OEEC, EPU, and the Council of Europe.

199  Brugmans, Hendrik. TOWARDS A EUROPEAN GOVERNMENT.
Paris: European Movement, International Youth Secretariat, 1953.
29 p.

200  Bruley, Edouard, and Dance, E.H. A HISTORY OF EUROPE.
European Aspects, Series A, no. 3. Leiden, Netherlands: A.S.
Sijthoff, 1960. 100 p.

201  Byrne, Gary C., and Pederson, Kenneth S. POLITICS IN WEST-
ERN EUROPEAN DEMOCRACIES: PATTERNS AND PROBLEMS.
New York: John Wiley and Sons, 1971. 435 p.

A collection of essays on a variety of integration subjects: European transition, alienation, political parties, national response to integration, technology, NATO, and a bit of conceptualizing.

202 Calleo, David P. EUROPE'S FUTURE: THE GRAND ALTERNA-
TIVES. New York: W.W. Norton and Co., 1965. 192 p.

Describes the grand alternatives: an Atlantic Europe of NATO, a supranational Europe and the Common Market, and de Gaulle's Europe of States. Also discusses the proponents presenting advantages and disadvantages of each view.

203 Campion, Lord, and Lidderdale, D.W.S. EUROPEAN PARLIAMEN-
TARY PROCEDURE. London: George Allen and Unwin, 1953. 270 p.

Focus upon the common bases of European parliamentary procedure as well as individual, national studies of countries in the Interparliamentary Union.

204 Carter, Gwendolyn M., and Westin, Alan F., eds. POLITICS IN
EUROPE. New York: Harcourt, Brace and Co., 1965. 205 p.

Case studies on Britain, France, Germany, the EEC, and the Soviet Union. Each case concentrates on a different aspect of political society, the press, the law, constitutionalism, pressure groups, and integration.

205 Chatham House/Political and Economic Planning. STATEMENTS
AND DECLARATIONS OF THE ACTION COMMITTEE FOR THE
UNITED STATES OF EUROPE 1955-67. European Series, no. 9.
London: 1969. 112 p.

The first English publication of the complete papers of the Action Committee regarding the concrete achievements towards a United States of Europe.

206 College of Europe. SYMPOSIUM EUROPA 1950-70. Studies in
Contemporary European Issues, no. 8. Bruges, Belgium: 1971.
517 p.

207 Commonwealth of World Citizens. THE BIRTH OF A WORLD PEOPLE.
London: Dennis Dobson, 1956. 59 p.

An organizational publication describing the origin, ideology, and functions of the Commonwealth of World Citi-
zens, an agency for world peace and security. Goals and constitution of the organization included.

208 Congress of Europe. EUROPE UNITES: THE STORY OF THE CAM-
PAIGN FOR EUROPEAN UNITY, INCLUDING A FULL REPORT OF
THE CONGRESS OF EUROPE HELD AT THE HAGUE, MAY 1948.
London: Hollis and Carter, 1949. viii, 120 p.

> A history of the ideas and institutions like the Marshall
> Plan, WEU, and others, which have carried the momen-
> tum of integration. The 1948 Congress of Europe also
> surveyed.

209 Coudenhove-Kalergi, Richard N. TOWARD A CONSTITUENT AS-
SEMBLY FOR EUROPE. Gstaad, Switzerland: European Parliamentary Union, 1947.

210 Council of Europe. Documentation Centre. NON-GOVERNMENTAL
ORGANIZATIONS FOR EUROPEAN COOPERATION. Strasbourg,
France: 1954. 15 p.

> A small but useful pamphlet discussing nongovernmental
> organizations in Europe.

211 Council of Europe. Secretariat. THE UNION OF EUROPE: ITS
PROGRESS, PROBLEMS, PROSPECTS AND PLACE IN THE WESTERN
WORLD. Strasbourg, France: 1951. 43 p.

212 Curtis, Michael. WESTERN EUROPEAN INTEGRATION. New
York: Harper and Row, 1965. 262 p.

> A description and an assessment of eight major European
> international organizations: Council of Europe, OECD,
> NATO, WEU, ECSC, EEC, EURATOM, and EFTA in
> their respective roles as contributors to European unity.

213 Dawson, Christopher. UNDERSTANDING EUROPE. London and
New York: Sheed and Ward, 1952. ix, 261 p.

214 Deutsch, Harold C., et al. THE CHANGING STRUCTURE OF EU-
ROPE. Minneapolis: University of Minnesota, 1970.

215 Dogan, Mattei, and Rose, Richard, eds. EUROPEAN POLITICS.
Boston: Little, Brown and Co., 1971. xviii, 590 p.

> A reader in the comparative politics of Britain, France,
> Germany, and Italy examining likenesses and differences
> in historical roots, political cultures, socialization, par-
> ties, voting alignments, and pressure groups.

216 European Institute of International Relations. EUROPE 1980: L'AVENIR

DES RELATIONS INTRA-EUROPEENNES/THE FUTURE OF INTRA-EUROPEAN RELATIONS. Leiden, Netherlands: A.W. Sijthoff, 1972. 301 p.

Reports, some French, some English, on the October 1972 Conference of Directors and Representatives of the European Institute of International Relations held at Vana, Bulgaria. Analyzes economic, political, and security aspects, as well as social, cultural, and technological facets of integration. Also comments on the relations between East and West.

217 Farnsworth, Clyde H. OUT OF THIS NETTLE: A HISTORY OF POST-WAR EUROPE. New York: John Day, 1974. 209 p.

218 Farr, Thomas S. "Some Considerations on Western European Federation." Ph.D. dissertation, University of Chicago, 1954.

219 Florinsky, Michael T. INTEGRATED EUROPE? New York: Macmillan Co., 1955. 182 p.

A historical description of European integration including economic, military, and political aspects as well as description of the institutions and issues from the period after World War II through 1954.

220 Foreign Policy Association, New York. CAN EUROPE UNITE? New York: 1950. 62 p.

Included are two articles, one by V.M. Dean detailing Europe's efforts to unite, and one by J.K. Galbraith reviewing the relationship between Western Europe and the United States.

221 Freymond, Jacques. THE SAAR CONFLICT, 1945-55. London: Stevens and Sons; New York: Frederick A. Praeger, 1960. xxviii, 395 p.

A case study exploring the post-World War II Saar conflict as well as a theoretical study of conflict and its resolution in a European setting. The study itself is about an important piece of European integration but also includes the activities of the EDC and the Council of Europe.

222 _____. WESTERN EUROPE SINCE THE WAR: A SHORT POLITICAL HISTORY. New York: Frederick A. Praeger, 1964. 236 p.

A historical essay on Europe following World War II including an appraisal of the postwar outlook and strategy,

economic redevelopment, the crises of 1950, and a debate on the "grand design," usually from the French
viewpoint.

223  Goerner, E.A., ed. DEMOCRACY IN CRISIS: NEW CHALLENGES
TO CONSTITUTIONAL DEMOCRACY IN THE ATLANTIC AREA.
Notre Dame, Ind.: University of Notre Dame Press, 1971. 199 p.

A collection of ten essays dealing with a variety of European political topics. See especially van der Esch's
article on the European Economic Community.

224  Goodwin, M., ed. ASPECTS AND PROBLEMS OF EUROPEAN
UNION. London: Nineteenth Century and After, 1952. 94 p.

A symposium of articles on European unification by Barbara Ward, Robert Boothby, Denis Healey, and others
on a variety of topics including a history of integration,
Britain's role, Germany's role and rearmament, and
economic problems.

225  Goormaghtigh, John. EUROPEAN INTEGRATION. International
Conciliation, no. 488. New York: Carnegie Endowment for International Peace, 1953. 60 p.

226  Gross, Feliks, ed. EUROPEAN IDEOLOGIES. New York: Philosophical Library, 1948. 1,075 p.

A broad range of articles dealing with European ideologies, including communism, trade unionism, regionalism,
and federalism providing a background to a "European"
integrated polity.

227  Guerard, Albert. EUROPE FREE AND UNITED. Stanford, Calif.:
Stanford University Press, 1945. 206 p.

228  Gunther, John. INSIDE EUROPE TODAY. Rev. ed. London: Hamish
Hamilton, 1962. 390 p.

229  Haines, C. Grove. WHAT FUTURE FOR EUROPE? Headline Series,
no. 124. New York: Foreign Policy Association, 1957. 62 p.

A basis for public discussion from the Foreign Policy Association. A short history of European unification prior
to 1957 with special emphasis on the Common Market and
the "relance European" [revival of Europe] included.

230 _____, ed. EUROPEAN INTEGRATION. Baltimore: Johns Hopkins Press, 1957. 310 p.

> A variety of papers given at a conference on the status of European integration held in Bologna, Italy, included here covering the historical setting of European integration and some of the main economic and political issues.

231 Hajda; Joseph. "Central European Federation." Ph.D. dissertation, Indiana University, 1955.

232 Hallberg, H. Peter, ed. SEVEN VOICES ON EUROPE: SYMPOSIUM 1972, LINKOPING UNIVERSITY. Lund, Sweden: Studenlitt, 1972. 106 p.

233 Heisler, Martin O., ed. POLITICS IN EUROPE: STRUCTURES AND PROCESSES IN SOME POSTINDUSTRIAL DEMOCRACIES. New York: David McKay Co., 1974. 415 p.

> A comparative reader on European politics. The first part devoted to conceptual and theoretical facets of European integration. Part 2: study of the European Community's political system. Part 3: institutions and processes of policy making in Europe.

234 Huang, R. Chu-Kua. "Toward European Union." Ph.D. dissertation, University of Kentucky, 1953.

235 Isenberg, Irwin, ed. THE OUTLOOK FOR WEST EUROPE. New York: H.W. Wilson Co., 1970. 213 p.

> A compendium of twenty-four journal and newspaper articles on the history of European unification, economic mechanisms, NATO and security, and various political questions.

236 Knapp, Wilfrid. UNITY AND NATIONALISM IN EUROPE SINCE 1945. New York: Pergamon Press, 1969. 146 p.

> A historical narrative of the forces for European unity in Western Europe in the twenty-year period after World War II.

237 Kramer, Marguerite Marie-Louise. "Passing of Nationalism in Western Europe." Ph.D. dissertation, Massachusetts Institute of Technology, 1963.

238 Laqueur, Walter. EUROPE SINCE HITLER. London: George

Weidenfeld and Nicolson, 1970. ix, 434 p.

> "In four general divisions--the period from the end of
> World War II to Stalin's death; the main economic and
> social trends; cultural developments in Europe since the
> middle fifties; and European politics since 1955--Professor
> Laqueur considers the particular problems and progress of
> each country as well as the common features and patterns
> which have affected the rebirth of Europe. He concludes
> with the prediction that Europe's astonishing resurrection
> may well signal the burgeoning of a new 'European Age.'"

BOOK REVIEW DIGEST

239 _____. THE REBIRTH OF EUROPE. New York: Holt, Rinehart
and Winston, 1970. 434 p.

The American title for no. 238.

240 Larkin, Patrick John. EUROPE AND WORLD AFFAIRS. London:
Hulton Educational Publications, 1969. 233 p.

241 LIMITS AND PROBLEMS OF EUROPEAN INTEGRATION: THE
CONFERENCE OF 30 MAY-2 JUNE 1961. Papers by Ernst B.
Haas et al., with an introduction by B. Landheer. The Hague:
published for the Stichting Grotius Seminarium by Martinus Nijhoff,
1963. 144 p.

> Nine essays dealing with the global versus European
> values and institutions. Also includes studies on a the-
> ory of integration, regional unity, law and politics,
> elections to the European Parliament, and consumerism.

242 Liska, George. EUROPE ASCENDANT: THE INTERNATIONAL
POLITICS OF UNIFICATION. Baltimore: Johns Hopkins Press,
1964. 182 p.

> Sets forth the political conditions, both historical and
> contemporary, for European integration. Suggests a
> strategy of regional economic cooperation that will even-
> tually include Communist Central Europe.

243 Luxemburg, Norman. EUROPE SINCE WORLD WAR II: THE BIG
CHANGE. Carbondale: Southern Illinois University Press, 1973.
260 p.

> An overview of the political, industrial, and psychologi-
> cal changes in Europe since 1939 that have shaped the
> conditions leading to interdependence and integration.

244 Mackay, R.W.G. EUROPEAN UNITY: THE STRASBOURG PLAN FOR A EUROPEAN POLITICAL AUTHORITY WITH LIMITED FUNCTIONS BUT REAL POWER. Foreword by Paul-Henri Spaak. Oxford: Basil Blackwell, 1951. 34 p.

245 _____. WESTERN UNION IN CRISIS: ECONOMIC ANARCHY OR POLITICAL UNION: FIVE PAPERS SUPPORTING THE PROPOSITION THAT POLITICAL SOLUTION PROVIDES THE ONLY KEY TO OUR ECONOMIC PROBLEMS. Oxford: Basil Blackwell, 1949. 138 p.

246 Manshel, Warren D. "Western European Integration." Ph.D. dissertation, Harvard University, 1952.

247 Mayne, Richard, ed. EUROPE TOMORROW: SIXTEEN EUROPEANS LOOK AHEAD. London: published for Chatham House, Political and Economic Planning by Fontana, 1972. 352 p.

   A collection of essays in which authors from five countries deal with various aspects of Europe's future policies, education, population, technology, and environment, among other topics.

248 Merritt, Richard L., and Puchala, Donald James, eds. WESTERN EUROPEAN PERSPECTIVES ON INTERNATIONAL AFFAIRS: PUBLIC OPINION STUDIES AND EVALUATIONS. New York: Frederick A. Praeger, 1968. xx, 552 p.

   A study of survey research and its methods on USIA data. Part 1 of general background interest, what the man in the European street is thinking about a variety of issues. Part 2, popular attitudes on European integration, NATO, and disarmament.

249 Meynaud, Jean, and Sidjanski, Dusan. EUROPEAN INTEGRATION AND POLITICAL SCIENCE. Geneva: 1965.

250 Newman, Bernard. THE NEW EUROPE. New York: Macmillan Co., 1943. viii, 568 p.

   A study of the European nations and a discussion of the expectations for European federation in the peace following World War II. The structure and function of federation included.

251 Owen, Richard Ewan. "United States of Europe: A Twentieth Century Challenge To Nationalism." Ph.D. dissertation, University of Southern California, 1964.

252 Palmer, Michael, et al. EUROPEAN UNITY: A SURVEY OF EU-
ROPEAN ORGANIZATIONS. London: published for Political and
Economic Planning by George Allen and Unwin, 1968. 519 p.

> An institutional overview and synthesis of the form and
> focus of ten European organizations, political, defensive,
> and economic in nature, and how these organizations
> have transformed relations among the countries of West-
> ern Europe.

253 _____. A HANDBOOK OF EUROPEAN ORGANIZATIONS. New York:
Frederick A. Praeger, 1968. 519 p.

> The American title of no. 252.

254 Patijn, S., ed. LANDMARKS IN EUROPEAN UNITY: TWENTY-
TWO TEXTS ON EUROPEAN INTEGRATION. Leiden, Netherlands:
A.W. Sijthoff, 1970. 223 p.

> A collection of studies (twenty-two texts) concerning the
> political process of European integration by luminaries
> like Churchill, Schuman, de Gaulle, and others.

255 Political and Economic Planning. EUROPEAN ORGANIZATIONS.
London: published for PEP by George Allen and Unwin, 1959.
372 p.

> A PEP report analyzing and assessing the work and con-
> tribution to European unity of eight principal European
> organizations: ECE, OEEC, Council of Europe, NATO,
> WEU, ECSC, EURATOM, and the EEC.

256 Price, Brian P. THE NEW EUROPE. London: Macdonald and Co.,
1974. 24 p.

257 Puchala, Donald J[ames]. EUROPEAN POLITICAL INTEGRATION:
PROGRESS AND PROSPECTS. New Haven, Conn.: Yale University Political Science Research Library, 1966. v, 135 p.

258 _____. "International Political Community Formation in Western
Europe: Progress and Prospects." Ph.D. dissertation, Yale University, 1966.

259 Robertson, A.H. EUROPEAN INSTITUTIONS: CO-OPERATION,
INTEGRATION, UNIFICATION. 3d ed. London: published for
the London Institute of World Affairs by Stevens and Sons, 1973.
427 p.

> A comprehensive description of the structure, functions,
> and activities of seventeen of the most important Euro-

pean organizations, excluding only the regional organizations of the United Nations and its specialized agencies.

260 _____. THE LAW OF INTERNATIONAL INSTITUTIONS IN EUROPE: BEING AN ACCOUNT OF SOME RECENT DEVELOPMENTS IN THE FIELD OF INTERNATIONAL LAW. New York: Oceana Publications, 1961. 140 p.

A discussion of the "European idea," its political significance and ideological connotation, which traces the historical development of the concept through major treaties, conferences, and cooperative organizations. Special attention on human rights in the Council of Europe philosophy.

261 Rohn, Peter H. "European Integration: A Comparison of Institutions." Ph.D. dissertation, University of Washington, Seattle, 1958.

262 Rubenstein, Alvin Zachary. "An Analysis of Soviet Policy in the Economic and Social Council and the Economic Commission for Europe 1946-51." Ph.D. dissertation, University of Pennsylvania, 1954.

263 Rundle, Stanley. LANGUAGE AS A SOCIAL AND POLITICAL FACTOR IN EUROPE. London: Faber and Faber, 1946. 207 p.

264 Schmitt, Hans A. EUROPEAN UNION: FROM HITLER TO DE GAULLE. New York: Van Nostrand Reinhold Co., 1969. 159 p.

A brief history of various attempts to form a European union as an alternative to the concept of the national state. Traces Hitler's attempt to form a united Europe under the Nazis, the Marshall Plan, the OEEC, BENELUX, and the Pleven Plan, and focuses on de Gaulle's objections to European integration.

265 Scott, J.H.M. EXPERIMENT IN INTERNATIONALISM. New York: Allyn and Bacon, 1967. 223 p.

An accounting of the international political activity of the European liberal parties from 1945 to 1965. Describes how the Liberal International came to be established and the difficulties faced cooperatively among liberals of different national backgrounds. Included also is the general problem of political parties and European integration.

266  Sennholz, Hans F.  HOW CAN EUROPE SURVIVE?  New York:
D. Van Nostrand Co., 1955.  336 p.

An analysis of the conflict between nationalism and the
forces and institutions working towards European integration, from the early European parliamentary movement
to the ECSC and NATO.

267  _____ .  "Inquiry into the Problems of International Cooperation
and European Unification."  Ph.D. dissertation, New York University, 1955.

268  Shackleton, M.R.  EUROPE: A REGIONAL GEOGRAPHY.  London:
Longmans, Green and Co., 1950.  525 p.

A regional geography of Europe primarily for university
students.  Relates geographic and political or physical
aspects and human activities, in order that the bases for
cooperation or integration are understandable.  Countries
considered both individually and by regions.

269  Smith, Gordon.  POLITICS IN WESTERN EUROPE: A COMPARA-
TIVE ANALYSIS.  London: William Heinemann, 1972.  403 p.

A general look at West European politics with the usual
fare of executive, legislative, and judicial structures.
Also includes chapters on political integration and the
significance of the European Community.

270  Smith, Howard K.  THE STATE OF EUROPE.  New York: Alfred
A. Knopf, 1949.  408 p.

A nation-by-nation look at postwar Europe along with
some generalizations about its unification.  Also useful
historical material on the origins of the Marshall Plan,
OEEC, and NATO.

271  Thumm, Garold W.  "The Western European Powers and International Control of the Ruhr."  Ph.D. dissertation, University of
Pennsylvania, 1954.

272  U.S. Army.  Office of the High Commissioner for Germany.  PUB-
LIC OPINION IN WESTERN EUROPE: ATTITUDES TOWARDS PO-
LITICAL, ECONOMIC, AND MILITARY INTEGRATION.  Reactions
Analysis Staff, Office of the High Commissioner for Germany, Jan-
uary 1953.

273  Urwin, Derek W.  WESTERN EUROPE SINCE 1945: A SHORT
POLITICAL HISTORY.  2d ed.  London: Longmans, Green and
Co., 1972.  349 p.

Three central themes addressed: national politics in Britain, France, West Germany, and Italy; the development of European integration; and Europe's role in international affairs.

274 Wales, Peter. EUROPE IS MY COUNTRY: THE STORY OF WEST EUROPEAN COOPERATION SINCE 1945. London: Methuen and Co., 1963. 117 p.

A survey of European integration, its political and social origins, and development since World War II.

275 White, Theodore H. FIRE IN THE ASHES: EUROPE IN MID-CENTURY. London: Cassell and Co., 1954. 383 p.

A journalist's account of the dramatic rejuvenation of Europe since the advent of the Marshall Plan in France, Germany, and Britain, and the portents for the future.

276 Wiskemann, Elizabeth. THE EUROPE I SAW. New York: St. Martin's Press, 1968. 255 p.

277 Woodward, James C. RECENT EFFORTS TOWARD EUROPEAN FEDERATION. Washington, D.C.: 1950. 173 p.

278 Zurcher, Arnold. THE STRUGGLE TO UNITE EUROPE, 1940-58: AN HISTORICAL ACCOUNT OF THE DEVELOPMENT OF THE CONTEMPORARY EUROPEAN MOVEMENT FROM ITS ORIGIN IN THE PAN-EUROPEAN UNION TO THE DRAFTING OF THE TREATIES FOR EURATOM AND THE EUROPEAN COMMON MARKET. New York: New York University Press, 1958. 254 p.

A good introduction to and a history of the European unity movement including the Council of Europe, the ECSC, and the EDC. Emphasizes the role of the United States in promoting an integrated Europe.

## 9. Polemics and Programs for European Integration

279 Cole, G.D.H. EUROPE, RUSSIA AND THE FUTURE. 3d ed. London: Victor Gollancz, 1943. 186 p.

A Socialist's appeal for all Socialists in Europe and in Russia to work for a Socialists' supranational state of Europe in which a non-Nazi Germany would be included, but controlled.

280 Coudenhove-Kalergi, Richard N. CRUSADE FOR PAN EUROPE:

AUTOBIOGRAPHY OF A MAN AND A MOVEMENT. New York: G.P. Putnam's Sons, 1943. 318 p.

> An autobiographical account of Coudenhove-Kalergi and the Pan-European Movement both before and after World War II, including his dreams and designs for a United States of Europe.

281 _____. EUROPE MUST UNITE. Glarus, Switzerland: Paneuropa Editions, 1940. 160 p.

> A history of the idea of European unification.

282 _____. EUROPE SEEKS UNITY. New York: Institute of Public Affairs and Regional Studies, 1948. 59 p.

> A monograph urging the necessity of European unification.

283 _____. AN IDEA CONQUERS THE WORLD. London: Hutchinson and Co., 1953. 310 p.

> The second autobiography of a European nobleman whose main interest is the advancement of a plan for a united Europe.

284 Crawford, Oliver. DONE THIS DAY: THE EUROPEAN IDEA IN ACTION. London: Rupert Hart-Davis, 1970. 399 p.

> Selective commentary by a partisan and federalist on various aspects of the "European idea": its conception in the Council of Europe; the early struggles of the ECSC; and human rights.

285 De Man, H. THE REMAKING OF A MIND. New York: Charles Scribner's Sons, 1919. 289 p.

> Traces the psychological effects that participation in World War I had on the author. Notes that before the war he had a feeling of identity as a European, so that for him the war was a civil one. Concludes that Europe must unite economically and also through socialism.

286 Firsoff, V.A. THE UNITY OF EUROPE: REALITIES AND ASPIRATIONS. London: Lindsay Drummond, 1946. 305 p.

> Develops a case for European federation based on a historical analysis of Europe.

287 Jennings, W. Ivor. A FEDERATION FOR WESTERN EUROPE. Cambridge: At the University Press, 1940. xi, 196 p.

A plan for federating Western Europe to be used as a proposal for and discussion by the organization called Federal Union.

288  Jordan, Peter. CENTRAL UNION OF EUROPE. New York: R.M. McBride and Co., 1944. 110 p.

A polemic arguing for regional groupings of states, specifically for a regional grouping of European states.

289  Miller, James Marshall. LAKE EUROPA: A NEW CAPITAL FOR A UNITED EUROPE. New York: Books International, 1963. 114 p.

A wide-ranging polemic for European unity which envisions a capital on Lake Europa bordering on France, Luxembourg, and Germany, complete with sketches and quotations to support the idea.

290  Mosley, Sir Orwald. EUROPE: FAITH AND PLAN; A WAY OUT FROM THE COMING CRISIS AND AN INTRODUCTION TO THINKING AS A EUROPEAN. London: Euphorion Books, 1958. iii, 147 p.

A program by the leader of the British Fascist Party for the "renovation" of Europe including the creation of a European government built upon a corporate basis and fascist wage-price theory.

291  Otto, Archduke of Austria. THE SOCIAL ORDER OF TOMORROW: STATE AND SOCIETY IN THE ATOMIC AGE. Translated by Ivo Jarosy. Westminster, Md.: Newman Press, 1959. 158 p.

A plea and an argument for European federation.

292  Pettee, George S. UNION FOR EUROPE. Human Events Pamphlets, no. 20. Chicago: Human Events Associates, 1947. 29 p.

A brief monograph in which the author argues the need and desirability for uniting Europe after the destruction caused by World War II.

293  Reynaud, Paul. UNITE OR PERISH: A DYNAMIC PROGRAM FOR A UNITED EUROPE. New York: Simon and Schuster, 1951. 214 p.

A former French premier argues for the necessity of uniting Europe based on the post-World War II experiences. He promotes the Council of Europe as the vehicle through which this should be done.

294    Schwarzenberger, Georg. ATLANTIC UNION: A PRACTICAL
       UTOPIA. London: Federal and Educational Trust, 1957. 14 p.

       An argument for Atlantic union, and against a more lim-
       ited European community.

295    Strauss, Franz-Josef. CHALLENGE AND RESPONSE: A PROGRAM
       FOR EUROPE. New York: Atheneum Publishers, 1970. 175 p.

       An analysis of the acute and urgent problems facing Eu-
       rope, with a program for their solution by a prominent
       German spokesman who is chairman of the German CSU
       party.

296    Streit, Clarence K. UNION NOW. New York: Harper and Brothers,
       1949.

       Advocates an Atlantic union between Europe and the
       United States along federalist lines. Not a sophistica-
       ted argument, but one which clearly exposes the prob-
       lems of the federalist position.

## 10.  U.S. Policy and Marshall Plan (Pre-Common Market)

297    Alexander, Sidney S. THE MARSHALL PLAN. Washington, D.C.:
       National Planning Association, 1948. 68 p.

       A description and discussion of the Marshall Plan as
       well as aspects of American foreign policy oriented to-
       wards Europe.

298    The American Assembly. Graduate School of Business. Columbia
       University. UNITED STATES--WESTERN EUROPE RELATIONS: AS
       VIEWED WITHIN THE PRESENT WORLD-WIDE INTERNATIONAL
       ENVIRONMENT. New York: 1951. 218 p.

       A compilation of research reports and documents on Eu-
       rope concerning business, labor, farm groups, professions,
       political parties, and government, so that citizens can
       be informed on the policies and problems the United
       States faces in its relations with Europe.

299    Balogh, Thomas. THE DOLLAR CRISIS: CAUSES AND CURE. New
       York: Macmillan Co., 1950. 269 p.

       A Fabian analysis of U.S. economic influence in Europe.
       Argues that the U.S. plans, especially the Marshall Plan,
       were based upon short-range objectives meant to counter
       postwar activities of the USSR rather than to promote
       long-range goals of an integrated Europe for its own sake.

300   Brown, William Adams, Jr., and Redevers, Opie. AMERICAN
      FOREIGN ASSISTANCE. Washington, D.C.: Brookings Institution,
      1953.  615 p.

> An admirable account of the American recovery program
> following World War II and its bearing on European in-
> tegration, including U.S. objectives and European re-
> sponses such as the ECSC.

301   Dean, Vera Micheles.  EUROPE AND THE UNITED STATES.  New
      York: Alfred A. Knopf, 1950.  349 p.

> An explanation for Europeans of American foreign poli-
> cy towards Europe as well as the historical background,
> ideologies, politics, and programs which begat European
> cooperation.

302   Ellis, Howard Sylvester.  THE ECONOMICS OF FREEDOM.  New
      York: published for the Council on Foreign Relations by Harper
      and Row Publishers, 1950.  549 p.

> An analysis of postwar Europe, France, West Germany,
> and Italy, and the economic and political effects of the
> Marshall Plan, both on the individual states and on re-
> gional progress and integration.

303   European Movement [Britain].  THE ECONOMIC FUTURE OF EU-
      ROPE: PRELIMINARY PAPERS OF THE SECOND CONFERENCE
      OF WESTMINSTER, 1954.  London:  Andre Deutsch for the Euro-
      pean Movement, 1954.  188 p.

> A discussion of the structure of the European economy
> and the necessity of unification vis-a-vis the American
> economy.

304   Goldman, Alan Richard.  "United States Foreign Policy Toward the
      Integration of Western Europe, 1947-54."  Ph.D. dissertation, Brown
      University, 1971.

305   Harris, Seymour.  THE EUROPEAN RECOVERY PROGRAM.  Cam-
      bridge, Mass.:  Harvard University Press, 1948.  309 p.

> An early analysis of the American aid program and its
> effects on European cooperation, though largely from
> an American perspective.

306   Haviland, H. Field, Jr., ed.  THE UNITED STATES AND THE WEST-
      ERN COMMUNITY.  Haverford, Pa.:  Haverford College Press, 1957.
      161 p.

> Six lectures given at Haverford on economic, political,

military interrelationships between the United States and
Western Europe including discussions on BENELUX, ECSC,
OEEC, GATT, and IMF.

307 Hickmann, Warren Leroy. GENESIS OF THE EUROPEAN RECOV-
ERY PROGRAM. Geneva: Universite de Geneve, Institut Universitaire des Hautes Etudes Internationales, 1949. 297 p.

308 Hitchens, Harold Lee. "Congress and the Adoption of the Marshall
Plan." Ph.D. dissertation, University of Chicago, 1959.

Examines the congressional debates over the Marshall
Plan and the personalities that shaped it. Also studies
the role of public opinion in the adoption of the plan
and finds that humanitarian concern was nearly as important as economic and political interests in extending
aid to Europe.

309 Hoffman, Paul. PEACE CAN BE WON. London: Michael Joseph,
1951. 158 p.

An account of the Economic Cooperation Administration
and its activities regarding post-World War II western
policy. Argues for a united Europe and discusses the
steps taken under the Schuman Plan including a description of U.S. assistance.

310 Jones, Joseph M. THE FIFTEEN WEEKS. New York: Viking Press,
1955. 296 p.

A detailed narrative of the events in Washington leading up to, and finally creating, the Marshall Plan.

311 Kirkpatrick, Ivone. THE INNER CIRCLE: MEMOIRS OF IVONE
KIRKPATRICK. London: St. Martin's Press; New York: Macmillan
Co., 1959. x, 275 p.

A history of the role of the U.S. policy makers in European reconstruction and integration after World War II.

312 Koefod, Paul Eric. NEW CONCEPT IN THE QUEST FOR PEACE:
MARSHALL PLAN; ASPECT OF POWER POLITICS. Geneva: Im-
primeries Populaires, 1950. 235 p.

A political consideration of the Marshall Plan and its
effect on the United States, on Europe, and on the
Soviet Union.

313 Manderson-Jones, R.B. THE SPECIAL RELATIONSHIP: ANGLO-

AMERICAN RELATIONS AND WESTERN EUROPEAN UNITY, 1947-56. London: London School of Economics and Political Science, 1972. 168 p.

A discussion of the interplay between American and British policy during most of the stages of progress towards European unity from the Marshall Plan to the creation of WEU.

314 Marjolin, Robert. EUROPE AND THE UNITED STATES IN THE WORLD ECONOMY. Durham, N.C.: Duke University Press, 1953. 105 p.

A description of the progress and developments in post-war Europe and the role of the United States in the world economy. Analyzes patterns of trade and financial relationships emerging from European and U.S. cooperation.

315 Northrop, F.S.C. EUROPEAN UNION AND UNITED STATES FOREIGN POLICY: A STUDY IN SOCIOLOGICAL JURISPRUDENCE. New York: Macmillan Co., 1954. 230 p.

Uses method of sociological jurisprudence for analysis. Focuses on the relations between the positive legal constitutions, institutions and procedures, and the underlying living habits, associations and beliefs of the United States and Western Europe. An attempt to show the effect of American foreign policy on European integration.

316 Price, Harry Bayard. THE MARSHALL PLAN AND ITS MEANING. Ithaca, N.Y.: Cornell University Press, 1955. 424 p.

For the informed layman, one of the most complete accounts of the history of the Marshall Plan and its meaning to both Europe and the United States.

317 Roberts, Henry L., and Wilson, Paul A., eds. BRITAIN AND THE UNITED STATES: PROBLEM IN COOPERATION. A Joint Report Prepared by Henry L. Roberts, rapporteur of the study group of the Council on Foreign Relations in New York, and Paul A. Wilson, rapporteur of the study group of the Royal Institute of International Affairs, London. New York: published for the Council on Foreign Relations by Harper and Row, 1953. xvi, 253 p.

A study of the intimate cooperation of two major democracies, the interplay of domestic and foreign policies, relations with the Soviet Union and East Europe, and other areas. Also, an in-depth look at the problem of the "special relationship" to both British and U.S. relations with Western Europe.

318　Summers, Robert E., ed. AID (ECONOMIC) TO EUROPE: THE
　　　MARSHALL PLAN. New York: H.W. Wilson, 1948. 271 p.

　　　　　Pronouncements and articles by President Truman, mem-
　　　　　bers of Congress, economists, and others, on aspects of
　　　　　the Marshall Plan, including America's capacity to aid
　　　　　Europe, and the effect of that aid on Europe.

## C. INTERNATIONAL AND REGIONAL

319　American Council on Public Affairs, Washington, D.C. REGION-
　　　ALISM AND WORLD ORGANIZATION: POST-WAR ASPECTS OF
　　　EUROPE'S GLOBAL RELATIONSHIPS. Washington, D.C.: 1944.
　　　162 p.

　　　　　A symposium report of the Institute on World Organiza-
　　　　　tion.

320　Bloomfield, Lincoln P. WESTERN EUROPE AND THE U.N.: TRENDS
　　　AND PROSPECTS. Cambridge, Mass.: Center for International
　　　Studies, M.I.T., 1959. 110 p.

　　　　　An appraisal of the attitudes of West Europeans toward
　　　　　the UN, listed country by country, including the de-
　　　　　tails of UN relations to each country's national interests,
　　　　　domestic politics, and special history with the UN.

321　Cantori, Louis J., and Spiegel, Steven. THE INTERNATIONAL
　　　POLITICS OF REGIONS: A COMPARATIVE APPROACH. Engle-
　　　wood Cliffs, N.J.: Prentice-Hall, 1970. 432 p.

　　　　　A comparative reader on regional politics containing
　　　　　several chapters by Camps, Shulman, Miller, and others
　　　　　on Europe as a regional political system.

322　Cardozo, Michael H. DIPLOMATS IN INTERNATIONAL COOPERA-
　　　TION: STEPCHILDREN OF THE FOREIGN SERVICE. New York:
　　　Cornell University Press, 1962. xxi, 142 p.

　　　　　Focuses upon the development of a new form of diplo-
　　　　　macy in internationally institutionalized cooperation,
　　　　　specifically the relations between national governments
　　　　　and international organizations. Describes several types
　　　　　of diplomats and their political and legal status which
　　　　　have evolved from the experiences of the OEEC, NATO,
　　　　　and the EEC.

323　Claude, Inis L., Jr. EUROPEAN ORGANIZATIONS IN A GLO-
　　　BAL CONTEXT. Enseignement Complementaire, no. 27. Brussels:
　　　Universite Libre de Bruxelles, 1965. 34 p.

324 Council of Europe. Committee of Ministers. PRIVILEGES AND IM-
MUNITIES OF INTERNATIONAL ORGANIZATIONS. By the European Committee on Legal Cooperation. Strasbourg, France: 1970.
91 p.

> Covers the text and commentary on Resolution 89 relat-
> ing to existing agreements and immunities. Also defines
> the procedures used by members of the Council when
> forming new international organizations. Organizations
> used as models for existing arrangements: Council of
> Europe, ELDO, and ESRO, among others.

325 Lafave, Wayne R., and Hay, Peter, eds. INTERNATIONAL TRADE,
INVESTMENT, AND ORGANIZATION. Urbana: University of
Illinois Press, 1967. vii, 306 p.

> Selection of articles introducing discussion of interna-
> tional trade and investment, and regulations put forth
> by regional internal organizations as well as the impact
> that those organizations have on legal norms. Focuses
> on trends and existing problems raised by increased in-
> ternational cooperation.

326 Lawson, Ruth, ed. INTERNATIONAL REGIONAL ORGANIZATIONS:
CONSTITUTIONAL FOUNDATIONS. New York: Frederick A.
Praeger, 1962. 387 p.

> A compendium of the treaties and conventions which
> serve as the legal basis for regional international or-
> ganizations. Six regions considered. The first, the
> Atlantic-Western European region, includes NATO,
> OECD, Council of Europe, Convention on Human Rights,
> ECSC, and EEC treaties and commentary.

327 Luard, Evan, ed. THE EVOLUTION OF INTERNATIONAL OR-
GANIZATIONS. London: Thames and Hudson, 1966. 342 p.

> A series of case studies undertaken by experts in various
> fields and designed to consider changes that have oc-
> curred in important international organizations. Seeks to
> assess the factors influencing or inhibiting change during
> the organization's evolution. The EEC included along
> with the UN, the ILO, and the League of Nations.

328 Nye, Joseph S., Jr., ed. INTERNATIONAL REGIONALISM:
READINGS. Boston: Little, Brown and Co., 1968. 429 p.

> A collection of readings on international regionalism,
> generally, but containing a number of important chap-
> ters on European integration including discussion of the
> EEC and COMECON, theories of integration, and EU-

RATOM. Authors Haas, Scheinman, Mitrany, and Pinder, among others, contribute.

329 Reuter, Paul. INTERNATIONAL INSTITUTIONS. London: George Allen and Unwin, 1958; New York: Frederick A. Praeger, 1961. 316 p.

330 Ropke, W. INTERNATIONAL ORDER AND ECONOMIC INTEGRATION. Dordrecht, Netherlands: D. Reidel Publishing Co., 1959. 280 p.

An evaluation of the relation between economics and peace. Traces the history of ideological conflicts in Europe and other areas, and proposes ideas for economic unification as a means for achieving stability in international relations.

331 Tharp, Paul A., Jr., ed. REGIONAL INTERNATIONAL ORGANIZATIONS: STRUCTURES AND FUNCTIONS. New York: St. Martin's Press, 1971. 278 p.

An assessment of the political processes of several regional international organizations including the activities of the various interest groups in the EEC, political culture and integration in Scandinavia, rule making in the OAS, and U.S. policy towards regional organizations.

## D. NORDIC

332 Anderson, Stanley V. THE NORDIC COUNCIL: A STUDY OF SCANDINAVIAN REGIONALISM. Seattle: published for the American-Scandinavian Foundation by the University of Washington Press, 1967. 194 p.

Seeks to describe and explain Scandinavian regionalism by illuminating its most prominent organ, the Nordic Council. A study in cooperation, not integration or supranationalism.

333 Andren, Nils. GOVERNMENT AND POLITICS IN THE NORDIC COUNTRIES: DENMARK, FINLAND, ICELAND, NORWAY, SWEDEN. Stockholm: Almquist and Wiksell, 1964. 240 p.

An analysis of the Nordic heritage and tradition, national political organization, parties, and so on, as well as their cooperation and integration.

334  Karlstrom, Otto Leroy.  "The Scandinavian Approach to Political Integration."  Ph.D. dissertation, University of Chicago, 1952.

335  Lindgren, Raymond E.  NORWAY-SWEDEN: UNION, DISUNION, AND SCANDINAVIAN INTEGRATION.  Princeton, N.J.: Princeton University Press, 1959.  298 p.

> A case study of Norwegian–Swedish union and subsequent Scandinavian integration which the author makes a part of a broader study of the history of political integration in attempting to develop comparative concepts.

336  Løchen, Einar.  NORWAY'S VIEWS ON SOVEREIGNTY: A REPORT PREPARED FOR UNESCO.  Bergen, Norway: Griegs, 1955.  102 p.

> "A report containing the prevailing legal opinions on Norwegian sovereignty and its responsibilities toward the international community.  Individual studies consider Norway's position in the League of Nations, in the U.N., in NATO, and in the OEEC with respect to state sovereignty."
>
>                    BIBLIOGRAPHIE ZUR EURO-
>                    PAISCHEN INTEGRATION

337  Nelson, George R., ed.  FREEDOM AND WELFARE: SOCIAL PATTERNS IN THE NORTHERN COUNTRIES OF EUROPE.  Copenhagen: Ministries of Foreign Affairs of Denmark, Finland, Iceland, Norway, and Sweden, 1953.  539 p.

> An analysis of the social conditions and social welfare policies of the northern countries, their similarities and differences which provide the basis for a common Nordic approach.

338  Nordic Organizations Committee.  THE ORGANIZATION OF NORDIC CO-OPERATION.  Stockholm: Fritzes Hovbokhandel, 1970. 31 p.

339  Ohlin, Bertil.  NORDIC COOPERATION.  Stockholm: The Nordic Council, 1965.

340  Wendt, Frantz.  THE NORDIC COUNCIL AND COOPERATION IN SCANDINAVIA.  Copenhagen: Munksgaard, 1959.  247 p.

> A history and description of Scandinavian cooperation, especially through the Nordic Council.  Illustrative of a particular type and region of European cooperation.

## Chapter 3

## THE EUROPEAN COMMUNITIES:
## BACKGROUND, POLICIES, AND INSTITUTIONS
### (Excluding Specific Studies on the ECSC listed in 2.B.4)

## A. GENERAL

341  Barber, James, and Reed, Bruce, eds. EUROPEAN COMMUNITY: VISION AND REALITY. London: Croom, Helm, 1973. xiii, 434 p.

> A collection of articles, extracts from newspapers, journals, books and HANSARD's on the objectives and accomplishments of the EEC.

342  Barker, Elisabeth. THE COMMON MARKET. London: Wayland; New York: G.P. Putnam's Sons, 1973. 128 p.

343  Baumann, Carol Edler. WESTERN EUROPE: WHAT PATH TO INTEGRATION? Boston: D.C. Heath and Co., 1967. 156 p.

> A brief collection of essays on the rationale, problems, and alternatives to European integration. Discusses the idea, background, issues, theoretical objectives, and national perspectives relating to integration.

344  Beck, Robert H., et al. THE CHANGING STRUCTURE OF EUROPE: ECONOMIC, SOCIAL AND POLITICAL TRENDS. Minneapolis: University of Minnesota Press, 1970. viii, 286 p.

> Eight essays for the nonspecialist concerning Europe of the mid-sixties and looking into the decade of the seventies. Addresses economic integration, problems of agriculture, education, and cultural trends.

345  Bliss, Howard. THE POLITICAL DEVELOPMENT OF THE EUROPEAN COMMUNITY: A DOCUMENTARY COLLECTION. Waltham, Mass.: Blaisdell Publishing Co., 1970. 316 p.

> Thirty documentary excerpts from several basic documents relating to the creation, structure, and political dynamics of the European Community.

346   Bodenheimer, Susanne J.  "Political Union: A Microcosm of European Politics."  Masters thesis, M.I.T., 1966.

347   Broad, Roger, and Jarrett, Robert.  COMMUNITY EUROPE TODAY. Rev. ed.  London: Oswald Wolff, 1972.  255 p.

> A discussion of the development of the European Communities from the early 1950s to the close of 1971. Outlines the main economic, political, and social trends in the six founding-member countries.  Especially written for Britons entering the EC in 1973.

348   Brooks, John.  THE EUROPEAN COMMON MARKET.  New York: Smith, Keynes and Marshall, 1963.  71 p.

> Anecdotal recounting of the Common Market from observations of its headquarters, staff, and archhero Jean Monnet.  Told by a perceptive layman.

349   Cabot, Thomas D.  COMMON MARKET: ECONOMIC FOUNDATION FOR A UNITED STATES OF EUROPE?  New York: Committee for Economic Development, 1959.  28 p.

> A brief statement describing the advantages of an economically and politically unified Europe.

350   Calmann, John, ed.  THE COMMON MARKET: THE TREATY OF ROME EXPLAINED.  London: Anthony Blond, 1967.  79 p.

> Explication of the principles and practical implications of European Common Market membership.

351   Camps, Miriam.  EUROPEAN UNIFICATION IN THE SIXTIES: FROM THE VETO TO THE CRISIS.  New York: published for the Council on Foreign Relations by McGraw-Hill Book Co., 1966. 267 p.

> A detailed analysis of the European Community during the period January 1963 through spring 1966, including an interpretation of the two crises beginning and ending the period of British entry.  A perspective on the U.S. role in Europe added.

352   _____.  THE FIRST YEAR OF THE EUROPEAN ECONOMIC COMMUNITY.  Princeton, N.J.: Center of International Studies, Princeton University, 1958.  28 p.

> A brief review of the institutions and policies of the EEC after one year.

353 _____. WHAT KIND OF EUROPE? THE COMMUNITY SINCE
DE GAULLE'S VETO. London: published for the Royal Institute
of International Affairs by the Oxford University Press, 1965. 140 p.

> A detailed account of developments in the European
> Community in the eighteen months following de Gaulle's
> veto of British entry which showed how and why the
> Community's style and method of operating changed.

354 Caporaso, James A. THE STRUCTURE AND FUNCTION OF EURO-
PEAN INTEGRATION. Pacific Palisades, Calif.: Goodyear Publishing Co., 1974. 256 p.

> A structural-functional analysis of the patterns of Euro-
> pean integration. Such functions as interest articula-
> tion, aggregation, and rule making examined at the
> community level.

355 Centre d'Etude et Documentation Europeennes. TEN YEARS OF
EUROPEAN INTEGRATION. Papers presented at a colloquy 14-15
March 1968. Montreal: Les Presses de l'Ecole des Hautes Etudes
Commerciales, 1968.

> Analyses of juridical, monetary, fiscal, and economic
> problems as well as a discussion of the role of North
> America in the integration of West Europe by the re-
> spective special counsellors to the Executive Commission
> of the European Community.

356 Constantopoulos, Demetrios. THE EUROPEAN ECONOMIC COM-
MUNITY: A "REAL UNION." Hamburg: Girardet and Co.,
1958. 50 p.

> A study of the concepts of integration relative both to
> qualitative and quantitative views, and also to real and
> partial unions. Seeks to show via analyses of the EEC
> and ECSC that integration has a necessary logic of its
> own which will impel progress.

357 De La Mahotiere, Stuart. THE COMMON MARKET. London:
Hodder and Stoughton, 1961. 192 p.

> Covers a variety of subjects on the European Community:
> British influence and entry, the energy policy, and the
> Common Market's implications for India's third five-year
> plan are included, as are the principal clauses of the
> Rome Treaty.

358 Deniau, J.F. THE COMMON MARKET: ITS STRUCTURE AND
PURPOSE. 2d ed. London: Barrie and Rockliff, 1961. 170 p.

> A broadly descriptive and introductory account of the

ideas behind the Rome Treaty, and a look at its main
provisions, processes, and problems. Also discusses the
theory of economic markets and its application.

359   Ellis, Harry B. THE COMMON MARKET. Cleveland: World
Publishing Co., 1965. 204 p.

A history of the breakdown of national rivalries and the
rise of the Common Market, along with a description of
the EEC, ECSC, NATO, EFTA, OECD, and EURATOM.

360   European Community Information Service. UNITING EUROPE: THE
EUROPEAN COMMUNITY SINCE 1950. London: 1975. 18 p.

A brief, chronological introduction to the major events
in the founding and expansion of European integration.

361   European Economic Community Commission. ACTION PROGRAM:
SECOND STAGE OF THE COMMON MARKET. New York: Commerce Clearing House, 1963. 63 p.

362   _____. THE FIRST STAGE OF THE COMMON MARKET: REPORT
ON THE EXECUTION OF THE TREATY, JANUARY 1958-JANUARY
1962. Brussels: 1962. 115 p.

A report on the internal development of the Community
in terms of a common market and policy, and consideration of the Community's relations as they have evolved
with the outside world.

363   Farr, Walter, ed. DAILY TELEGRAPH GUIDE TO THE COMMON
MARKET. Rev. ed. London: William Collins for the DAILY TELE-
GRAPH, 1973. 190 p.

A general overview of the Common Market directed at
Britons who want information on the debate over British
entry.

364   Fry, Richard, ed. THE COMMON MARKET IN ACTION: ARTI-
CLES REPRINTED FROM THE GUARDIAN. Manchester, Engl.:
Manchester Guardian and Evening News, 1960. 16 p.

365   Galtung, Johan. THE EUROPEAN COMMUNITY: A SUPERPOWER
IN THE MAKING. London: George Allen and Unwin, 1973.
194 p.

A critical view of the EC. Asks what the EC really
means to the world's masses and proletariat.

366  GOVERNMENT AND OPPOSITION 2 (April 1967). Special issue: "The Politics of European Integration."

Devoted to numerous articles on European integration.

367  Graubard, Stephen R., ed. A NEW EUROPE? Boston: Houghton Mifflin Co., 1964. 691 p.

A collection of twenty-six articles on numerous facets of Europe: political integration, economics, the Adenauer era, education, class structures, theology, architecture, and others, written by both European and American scholars.

368  Gurland, Robert, and MacLean, Anthony. THE COMMON MARKET: A COMMONSENSE GUIDE FOR AMERICANS. New York: Paddington Press, 1974. 223 p.

369  Hallstein, Walter. ECONOMIC INTEGRATION AND POLITICAL UNITY IN EUROPE. Community Topics, no. 2. Brussels: European Community, Press and Information Service, 1961.

370  _____. EUROPE IN THE MAKING. Translated by Charles Roetter. London: George Allen and Unwin, 1973. 343 p.

A review of the past fifteen years of European "federal" growth, its institutions and personalities, by the first president of the commission of the EC. Also assesses the successes and gaps yet to be addressed on the path to political union.

371  _____. UNITED EUROPE: CHALLENGE AND OPPORTUNITY. Cambridge, Mass.: Harvard University Press, 1962. 109 p.

Contains three lectures given at the Fletcher School of Law and Diplomacy by the president of the commission of the EEC on the historical, economic, and political aspects of integration. Essentially a functionalist argument on the inexorable logic of economic integration which will lead to political integration.

372  Hamlin, D.L.B., ed. THE NEW EUROPE. The Thirty-first Couchiching Conference. Toronto: published for the Canadian Institute on Public Affairs by the University of Toronto Press, 1962. 106 p.

A selection of essays on Europe and European integration. Covers attitudes, culture, education, labor, industry, and the relationship between Eastern Europe and the European Community.

373    Heilbroner, Robert L.   FORGING A UNITED EUROPE:  THE STORY
       OF THE EUROPEAN COMMUNITY.   New York:  Public Affairs
       Committee, 1961.   28 p.

       A short and very simplified overview of the EC designed
       for public information rather than in-depth reporting of
       issues.


374    Henderson, W.O.   THE GENESIS OF THE COMMON MARKET.
       London:  Frank Cass and Co., 1962.   202 p.

       A history of economic integration in the seventeenth,
       eighteenth, and nineteenth centuries including the Zoll-
       verein and ECSC as antecedents to the EEC.


375    Hodges, Michael, ed.   EUROPEAN INTEGRATION:  SELECTED
       READINGS.  Harmondsworth, Engl.:  Penguin Books, 1972.  462 p.

       A collection of nineteen readings on European integra-
       tion covering its history, theory, process, and external
       support.


376    Hoepli, Nancy L., ed.   THE COMMON MARKET.   New York:
       H.W. Wilson, 1975.   181 p.

       "A compilation of reprinted articles discussing the his-
       tory of the Common Market, its strengths and weak-
       nesses, its relations with the United States, and its future."

                                                         Publisher


377    Inglehart, Ronald [F.].   THE SILENT REVOLUTION:  POLITICAL
       CHANGE AMONG WESTERN PUBLICS.   Lexington, Mass.:  D.C.
       Heath and Co., 1975.

       The results of survey research indicating feelings of na-
       tionalism, regional belonging, awareness of sectoral
       problems like agriculture, opinions on the Common Mar-
       ket, and opinions on the desirability and feasibility of
       a United States of Europe.


378    _____.   "The Socialization of Europeans:  Nation-Building in
       Western Europe."   Ph.D. dissertation, University of Chicago Press,
       1967.


379    Ionescu, Ghita, ed.   THE NEW POLITICS OF EUROPEAN INTE-
       GRATION.   London:  Macmillan and Co., 1972.   278 p.

       Material from a collection of studies published in two
       separate periodicals, the July 1967 issue of the JOUR-
       NAL OF COMPARATIVE POLITICS, and October 1971

issue of GOVERNMENT AND OPPOSITION. Among the topics covered are: Jean Monnet; the British Labour Party's view of Europe; the European Parliament; and EC impact on national policy making.

380 Jensen, Finn B., and Walter, Ingo. THE COMMON MARKET: ECONOMIC INTEGRATION IN EUROPE. Philadelphia: J.B. Lippincott Co., 1965. 278 p.

A general, descriptive survey of economic policy making in the EC with succinct summaries of the policy and problems that arose in each sector or were likely to arise in the future: regional problems, social policy, competition, national taxation, and monetary integration.

381 Junckerstorff, H.K., ed. THE INTERNATIONAL MANUAL ON THE EUROPEAN ECONOMIC COMMUNITY. St. Louis: St. Louis University Press, 1963. 521 p.

Fifteen articles on a variety of EEC topics covering subjects from American appraisals of Europe to the economic and agricultural policies of the EEC.

382 Keesing's Publications. THE EUROPEAN COMMUNITIES: ESTABLISHMENT AND GROWTH. A Keesing's Research Report. New York: Charles Scribner's Sons, 1975. 208 p.

"An up-to-date, systematic guide to the European Community."

EUROPEAN COMMUNITY

383 Kitzinger, Uwe W. THE CHALLENGE OF THE COMMON MARKET. Oxford: Basil Blackwell, 1961. 168 p.

A description of the EEC, the Rome Treaty, the question of sovereignty, Europe's relations with Africa, and the meaning of British entry to both Britain and the EC.

384 _____. THE EUROPEAN COMMON MARKET AND COMMUNITY. London: Routledge and Kegan Paul, 1967. 226 p.

A selection of documents relating to the political motivations for developing the European Community and for British entry to the Community. Included are the motivations of Churchill, Adenauer, de Gaulle, and Harold Wilson.

385 _____. THE POLITICS AND ECONOMICS OF EUROPEAN INTE-

GRATION. New York: Frederick A. Praeger, 1963. 246 p.

A revised and expanded version of an earlier work, THE CHALLENGE OF THE COMMON MARKET. A study of the features of the EC and its lessons for international relations.

386 Kormoss, I.B.F., ed. TOWARDS A COMMUNITY POLICY ON ENVIRONMENT. Bruges, Belgium: De Temple for the College of Europe, 1975. 446 p.

A report of the eleventh "Week of Bruges," a round-table discussion on community policy and the environment.

387 Krassa, Lucie G. THE EUROPEAN ECONOMIC COMMUNITY: A CASE STUDY OF THE NEW ECONOMIC REGIONALISM. Vol. 13, no. 2. College Park: University of Maryland, Bureau of Business and Economic Research, 1959.

388 Lerner, Daniel, and Gorden, Morton. EURATLANTICA: CHANGING PERSPECTIVES OF THE EUROPEAN ELITES. Cambridge, Mass.: M.I.T. Press, 1969. 447 p.

A longitudinal analysis of elite opinion, based on 4,000 interviews, to determine the change in location and attitude over the decade of 1955 to 1965. A measure of integration inferred from these data.

389 Lewis, W.R. ROME OR BRUSSELS? AN ECONOMIST'S COMPARATIVE ANALYSIS OF THE DEVELOPMENT OF THE EUROPEAN COMMUNITY AND THE AIMS OF THE TREATY OF ROME. London: Institute of Economic Affairs, 1971. xxi, 83 p.

390 Lindberg, Leon [Nord], and Scheingold, Stuart A[llen]. EUROPE'S WOULD-BE POLITY: PATTERNS OF CHANGE IN THE EUROPEAN COMMUNITY. Englewood Cliffs, N.J.: Prentice-Hall, 1970. 314 p.

A conceptual analysis of institutional change: the patterns of growth, stabilization, and decline based on case studies of agriculture, transportation, and the question of British entry.

391 Manente, Manfredo. "The Treaty Establishing the European Economic Community and Political Integration of Europe." Ph.D. dissertation, New York University, 1963.

392 Mayne, Richard. THE COMMUNITY OF EUROPE. London: Victor Gollancz, 1962. 192 p.

  A postwar history of the EC, its development and problems, and the implications of Britain's accession.

393 _____. THE INSTITUTIONS OF THE EUROPEAN COMMUNITY. London: Chatham House-Political and Economic Planning, 1968. 82 p.

  A consideration of the EC institutions, their origin, focus, operation, and the effect of new members like Britain.

394 _____. THE RECOVERY OF EUROPE: FROM DEVASTATION TO UNITY, 1945-73. Rev. ed. Garden City, N.Y.: Anchor Books, 1973. 458 p.

  A detailed history of events and their development from the postwar period through 1973. Includes the Schuman Plan, EEC, Britain's role in Europe, and the Atlantic plans of U.S. presidents.

395 Minet, P. FULL TEXT OF THE ROME TREATY AND AN A.B.C. OF THE COMMON MARKET. 3d ed. London: Christopher Johnson, 1962. 218 p.

  A popular edition of the Rome Treaty. Also discusses the background to Britain's decision to join the EEC and sets forth the advantages and disadvantages for the Common Market.

396 Morgan, Roger P. WEST EUROPEAN POLITICS SINCE 1945; THE SHAPING OF THE EUROPEAN COMMUNITY. London: Batsford, 1972. 243 p.

  A history of West European cooperation since 1945. Treats each of the nine countries and the EC in successive periods to give a cross-national and cross-temporal perspective.

397 Mowat, R.C. CREATING THE EUROPEAN COMMUNITY. London: Blandford Press, 1973. 235 p.

  A history of the men, ideals, and institutions which have formed the European Community between World War II and British accession.

398 Nystrom, J. Warren, and Hoffman, George W. THE COMMON MARKET. 2d ed. New York: Van Nostrand Reinhold Co., 1976. 147 p.

  An introductory survey of the European Community in-

cluding national profiles, the steps toward unity taken
by the Community, and an overview of its institutions.

399   Nystrom, J. Warren, and Malof, Peter.  THE COMMON MARKET:
      EUROPEAN COMMUNITY IN ACTION.  Princeton, N.J.:  D.
      Van Nostrand Co., 1962.  134 p.

      A synthesis of materials and insights on Western Europe's
      efforts since World War II at creating a unified commu-
      nity of nations.  For the nonspecialist.

400   Parker, Geoffrey.  THE LOGIC OF UNITY:  AN ECONOMIC
      GEOGRAPHY OF THE COMMON MARKET.  London:  Longman
      Group, 1968; New York:  Frederick A. Praeger, 1968 (Published
      as AN ECONOMIC GEOGRAPHY OF THE COMMON MARKET).
      178 p.

      Parker presents a picture of the distribution of economic
      activity in the Common Market and the nature of Bri-
      tain's relation with the Common Market based on that
      distribution.

401   _____.  THE LOGIC OF UNITY:  A GEOGRAPHY OF THE EU-
      ROPEAN ECONOMIC COMMUNITY.  2d ed.  New York:  Long-
      man, 1975.  210 p.

      "An appraisal of the Common Market in terms of human
      geography."

                    EUROPEAN COMMUNITY

402   Pinder, John, and Pryce, Roy.  EUROPE AFTER DE GAULLE: TO-
      WARDS THE UNITED STATES OF EUROPE.  Harmondsworth, Engl.:
      Penguin Books, 1969.  191 p.

      An examination of contemporary Europe, why it has not
      been effective against the nation-state, and why a full
      federation must be created.  Also considers the economic
      and political consequences of British entry into the EC.

403   Pryce, Roy.  THE POLITICAL FUTURE OF THE EUROPEAN COM-
      MUNITY.  London:  Marshbank for the Federal Trust, 1962.  108 p.

      An examination of the "political content" of Community
      achievements as well as projections of the Community's
      future political development in light of Britain's bid for
      entry.

404   _____.  THE POLITICS OF THE EUROPEAN COMMUNITY.  To-
      towa, N.J.:  Rowman and Littlefield, 1973.  187 p.

      A description and analysis of the EC, its history, decision-

making apparatus, and prospects including British impact
on the Community and the politics of the enlarged EC.

405 Rougemont, Denis de. THE POLITICS OF EUROPEAN INTEGRA-
TION: HOW THEY LED TO THE PRESENT SYSTEM; HOW THEY
WORK WITHIN THE COMMUNITY. London: 1967.

406 Sampson, Anthony. ANATOMY OF EUROPE: A GUIDE TO THE
WORKINGS, INSTITUTIONS, AND CHARACTER OF CONTEMPO-
RARY WESTERN EUROPE. New York: Harper and Row, 1968. 462 p.

American title for no. 407.

407 _____. THE NEW EUROPEANS: A GUIDE TO THE WORKINGS,
INSTITUTIONS, AND CHARACTER OF CONTEMPORARY WESTERN
EUROPE. London: Hodder and Stoughton, 1968. 462 p.

A perceptive, journalistic view of Western Europe and
the manifold areas in which it is approaching integration: press, patterns of travel, students, technocrats,
defense, and others.

408 Savage, Katharine. THE HISTORY OF THE COMMON MARKET.
London: Longman-Young Books, 1969. 129 p.

A historical narrative summarizing briefly the World War II
antecedents to European integration, the Treaty of Rome,
Community institutions, and the first British bid for membership. (Also published as THE STORY OF THE COM-
MON MARKET. New York: Walck, 1970.)

409 Schmitt, Hans A. THE PATH TO EUROPEAN UNION: FROM
MARSHALL PLAN TO THE COMMON MARKET. Baton Rouge, La.:
State University Press, 1962. 272 p.

A description of the movements toward West European
Union including the experience of the Coal and Steel
Community as the first experimental stage of European
integration.

410 Shepherd, Robert J. PUBLIC OPINION AND EUROPEAN INTE-
GRATION. Westmead, Engl.: Saxon House, D.C. Heath, 1975.
xiii, 249 p.

A study of the relationship between public opinion and
European integration, including a discussion of the theories of integration, how public opinion affects each theory, the elements in shaping public opinion towards integration, and the problems created.

411 Shimm, Melvin G., et al., eds. EUROPEAN REGIONAL COM-
MUNITIES: A NEW ERA ON THE OLD CONTINENT. New York:
Oceana Publications, 1962. 242 p.

A compendium from the Duke University School of Law
containing fifteen articles, mostly by prominent Europeans, concerning problems of the three European Communities: EEC, ECSC, and EURATOM. Numerous theoretical questions raised on federalism and supranationalism, on labor and capital movements, and on parliamentary control of the respective communities.

412 Shonfield, Andrew. EUROPE: JOURNEY TO AN UNKNOWN
DESTINATION: AN EXPANDED VERSION OF THE B.B.C. REITH
LECTURES, 1972. London: Penguin Books, 1973. 96 p.

A brief study of a variety of facets of the EC, the nature of its supranationality, the French and British incompatibility, the American connection, third country
relations, and the nature of its technocracy.

413 Spinelli, Altiero. THE EUROPEAN ADVENTURE: TASKS FOR
THE ENLARGED COMMUNITY. London: Charles Knight, 1972.
194 p.

An "agenda" for Europe addressed to politicians, national civil servants, and Eurocrats concerning an over-
haul of the CAP, advanced technology policy, monetary union, and democratization of the Community structure.

414 Tinbergen, Jan. THE EUROPEAN ECONOMIC COMMUNITY:
CONSERVATIVE OR PROGRESSIVE? Stockholm: Social Science
Institute, Stockholm University, 1963. 39 p.

From the 1963 Wicksell Lectures. Considers whether or
not the EC is a progressive or regressive force in shaping the world.

415 _____. THE TREND TOWARDS INTEGRATION. Athens: Center
of Economic Research, 1963. 23 p.

A brief analysis explaining why economic integration is
proceeding in various parts of the world, and the advantages integration, specifically the Common Market,
brings.

416 Walsh, A.E., and Paxton, John. THE STRUCTURE AND DEVELOP-
MENT OF THE COMMON MARKET. 2d ed. London: Hutchinson
and Co., 1972. 244 p.

A general guide to the Common Market and an assess-

ment of the first decade from a customs union to a political union including assessments on agriculture, competition, transport, the ECSC, and EURATOM.

417  Warnecke, Steven J., ed.  THE EUROPEAN COMMUNITY IN THE
1970'S.  New York: Frederick A. Praeger, 1972.  228 p.

A collection of eleven essays concerning the economic
and political integration of Europe, including expansion,
effects of U.S. foreign policy, and Europe's own world
role.

418  Wortmann, Herman R.  ESSAYS ON THE EUROPEAN COMMON
MARKET.  Bloomington: Bureau of Business Research, Graduate
School of Business, Indiana University, 1966.  133 p.

Eleven essays on the economic problems facing the Community as well as the trends in agriculture, developing
countries, tariffs, growth, and taxation.

419  Yondorf, Walter.  "Europe of the Six: Dynamics of Integration."
Ph.D. dissertation, University of Chicago, 1963.

Analysis of the EC institutions and problems including
a description of the Europarliament, political groups and
membership, budgetary problems, and relations with the
executives.

## B. AGRICULTURE

420  Andrews, Stanley.  AGRICULTURE AND THE COMMON MARKET.
Ames: Iowa State University Press, 1973.  183 p.

A series of assessments on the implications of the Common Market's agricultural policies for U.S. agriculture,
including a discussion of EFTA, and British and COME-
CON arrangements.

421  Butterwick, Michael, and Rolfe, Edmund Neville.  AGRICULTURAL
MARKETING AND THE EEC.  London: Hutchinson and Co., 1971.
xi, 287 p.

A study of British and European agricultural marketing
systems and a forecast of the results should Britain join
the EEC.  The respective systems discussed from their
historical, economic, and political perspectives.

422  _____ .  FOOD, FARMING AND THE COMMON MARKET.  London: Oxford University Press, 1968.  255 p.

An analysis of the differences between Britain and the

EEC on agricultural policy. Assesses the effects on Britain of making changes necessary to accede to the EEC.

423 Coppock, John O. NORTH ATLANTIC POLICY: THE AGRICULTURAL GAP. New York: Twentieth Century Fund, 1963. 270 p.

A study of the problems of agriculture arising from the politics and economics of the industrialized countries of the West, and the potential of these agripolicies to block European integration.

424 Dovring, Folke. LAND AND LABOUR IN EUROPE: 1900-1950. 2d ed. The Hague: Martinus Nijhoff, 1960. 480 p.

A study of agriculture, its problems and reforms in Europe during the first half of the twentieth century including countries from Iceland to Greece. A useful background to Europe's CAP.

425 Federal Trust for Education and Research. CURRENT AGRICULTURAL PROPOSALS FOR EUROPE. London: 1970. 57 p.

426 _____. A NEW AGRICULTURAL POLICY FOR EUROPE. London: 1970. 40 p.

427 Hallett, Graham. BRITISH AGRICULTURE AND EUROPE. London: 1961.

428 _____. THE ECONOMICS OF AGRICULTURAL POLICY. London: Basil Blackwell, 1968. ix, 292 p.

Among other topics, examines national and international problems of agricultural policy, including British subsidy policy, the agricultural policy of the EEC, and its implications for British membership.

429 Healey, Derek T. BRITISH AGRICULTURE AND THE COMMON MARKET. London: Britain in Europe, 1962. 145 p.

Concerned specifically with the possible impact of the Common Market on British agriculture. Numerous tables are included. The work is considered an authoritative source.

430 Heathcote, Nina. AGRICULTURAL POLITICS IN THE EUROPEAN COMMUNITY. Canberra: Australian National University, 1971. 49 p.

An analysis of the Common Agricultural Policy of the EC, its political implications for the European Com-

munity, and the implications of the Mansholt Plan for
CAP reform.

431   Knox, Francis. THE COMMON MARKET AND WORLD AGRICUL-
TURE: TRADE PATTERNS IN TEMPERATE ZONE FOODSTUFFS.
New York: Praeger Publishers, 1972. xii, 138 p.

432   Lamartine Yates, Paul. FOOD, LAND AND MANPOWER IN
WESTERN EUROPE. New York: Macmillan Co., 1960. 294 p.

A study attempting to measure and project population
growth trends. Also the commensurate growth in the
labor force, in consumption goods and services, in capital equipment, and in government services necessary to
meet the growth trends assessed. The Common Market
analyzed as one of the components in the overall picture of Europe's future.

433   Lockhart, Jacques. AGRICULTURAL CO-OPERATION IN THE EU-
ROPEAN ECONOMIC COMMUNITY. Brussels: European Economic
Community, 1967. 247 p.

434   McCrone, Gavin. AGRICULTURAL INTEGRATION IN WESTERN
EUROPE. London: Political and Economic Planning, 1963. 47 p.

435   _____. THE ECONOMICS OF SUBSIDIZING AGRICULTURE.
Toronto: University of Toronto Press, 1962. 189 p.

Discusses agriculture in the British economy since 1939
including the larger problems of international speciali-
zation and the relationship between British agriculture
and the Common Market.

436   Marsh, John S. BRITISH ENTRY TO THE EUROPEAN COMMUNITY:
IMPLICATIONS FOR BRITISH AND NORTH AMERICAN AGRICUL-
TURE. Washington, D.C.: National Planning Association, 1971.
xi, 45 p.

A report critical of the likely and negative effects on
British and North American agriculture resulting from
British accession to the EC. Analyzes the CAP and its
effects on Britain, and outlines tentative rules for trade
in agricultural goods--rules necessary to protect British
interests.

437   Marsh, John S., and Ritson, Christopher. AGRICULTURAL POLICY
AND THE COMMON MARKET. London: Royal Institute of International Affairs, 1971. 199 p.

A study of the character and development of the European Community's Common Agricultural Policy and the effects the CAP may have on Britain.

438  Marsh, John S., et al. FARMERS AND FOREIGNERS: IMPACT OF THE COMMON AGRICULTURAL POLICY ON THE ASSOCIATES AND ASSOCIABLES. London: Overseas Development Institute, 1973. 70 p.

439  Megret, Jacques. AGRICULTURE IN THE COMMON MARKET. Common Market Report Series no. 17. New York: Commerce Clearing House, 1965. 60 p.

440  Muth, Hanns P. FRENCH AGRICULTURE AND THE POLITICAL INTEGRATION OF WESTERN EUROPE: TOWARD AN EVER CLOSER UNION AMONG THE EUROPEAN PEOPLES. Leiden, Netherlands: A.W. Sijthoff, 1970. 320 p.

A profile of French agriculture and its political involvement from the Fourth Republic through the first nine years of the Common Market. Emphasizes integration at the bottom (farmers) rather than at the top (elites).

441  _____. "Toward an Ever Closer Union Among European Peoples: French Agriculture and the Political Integration of Western Europe." Ph.D. dissertation, Columbia University, 1970.

442  Newhouse, John. COLLISION IN BRUSSELS: THE COMMON MARKET CRISIS OF 30 JUNE 1965. New York: W.W. Norton, 1967. 195 p.

A descriptive account of the events surrounding the June 30 crisis concerning the EC Commission's attempt to adopt a regulation to finance the agricultural market, and the implications for Franco-German relations. Also assesses Italian and German influence in the EC.

443  Pagoulatos, Emilios. "The Effects of Agriculture and Trade Policies on European Economic Integration." Ph.D. dissertation, Iowa State University, 1973.

444  Papi, Ugo, and Nunn, Charles, eds. ECONOMIC PROBLEMS OF AGRICULTURE IN INDUSTRIAL SOCIETIES. Proceedings of a conference held by the International Economic Society. London: Macmillan and Co., 1969. 671 p.

Discusses conceptual and policy problems raised because of changes in technique, scale, and organization of agriculture in advanced societies. Part 1 emphasizes formation of the EEC's Common Agricultural Policy (CAP). Part 2 concerns general problems and policies in the agricultural sector.

445 Political and Economic Planning. AGRICULTURAL INTEGRATION IN WESTERN EUROPE. PEP Planning Series, vol. 24, no. 470. London: 1963.

446 _____. AGRICULTURAL POLICIES IN WESTERN EUROPE. Occasional Paper no. 3. London: 1959. 31 p.

An outline of the aims and methods of agricultural policies in non-EEC countries. Also includes problems and prospects of harmonization between the EEC and non-EEC countries in the agricultural sector.

447 _____. AGRICULTURAL POLICY IN THE EUROPEAN ECONOMIC COMMUNITY. Occasional Paper no. 1. London: 1958. 26 p.

448 _____. AGRICULTURE, THE COMMONWEALTH AND EEC. Occasional Paper no. 14. 2d ed. London: 1963. 48 p.

Political analysis of contemporary issues raised in the agricultural sector between the Commonwealth of Nations and the EEC, including the adoption of a common agricultural policy.

449 _____. FOOD PRICES AND THE COMMON MARKET. Occasional Paper no. 13. London: 1961. 18 p.

A political look at the economic effects of food prices in the EEC and their relation to the CAP.

450 _____. PROPOSALS FOR A COMMON AGRICULTURAL POLICY IN EEC. Occasional Paper no. 5. London: 1960.

451 Richter, J.H. AGRICULTURAL PROTECTION AND TRADE: PROPOSALS FOR AN INTERNATIONAL POLICY. New York: Frederick A. Praeger, 1964. xi, 148 p.

A study of the agricultural sector from a variety of perspectives: in the EEC; in GATT; as a problem between Britain and the EEC; various responses to it from the EEC; and as a problem for U.S. and EEC relations.

452 Robinson, Alan D. DUTCH ORGANIZED AGRICULTURE IN INTERNATIONAL POLITICS, 1945-60. The Hague: Martinus Nijhoff, 1962. 192 p.

Exploration of the nature and participation of pressure

groups in several foreign issues of European unity.

453 Rogers, S.J., and Davey, B.H. eds. THE COMMON AGRICULTURAL POLICY AND BRITAIN. Farnborough, Engl.: D.C. Heath and Co., 1973. 158 p.

> The factors bearing on agriculture in the context of Britain's entry into the EC, and the effect on price support methods, consumption, and domestic agricultural production.

454 Self, Peter, and Storing, Herbert J. THE STATE AND THE FARMER: BRITISH AGRICULTURAL POLICIES AND POLITICS. London: George Allen and Unwin, 1962; Berkeley and Los Angeles: University of California Press, 1963. 251 p.

> An exploration of the policies and organizations affecting Britain with the aim of demonstrating the importance of the agricultural sector and the problems this sector creates as Britain considers accession to the EEC.

455 Selly, Clifford. ILL FARES THE LAND: FOOD, FARMING AND THE COUNTRYSIDE. London: Andre Deutsch, 1972. 176 p.

456 Tracy, Michael. AGRICULTURE IN WESTERN EUROPE: CRISIS AND ADAPTATION SINCE 1880. New York: Frederick A. Praeger, 1964. 415 p.

> A consideration of European agriculture, country by country, since 1880, detailing policies and objectives which led to the CAP. Part 4: European economic integration, Britain and Europe, and the relationship between Europe and the world in agricultural matters.

457 Trow-Smith, Robert. LIFE FROM THE LAND: THE GROWTH OF FARMING IN WESTERN EUROPE. London: Longman Group, 1967. 238 p.

> A history of the evolution of farming in Western Europe from prehistoric times to the present including the impact of the Common Market on agriculture.

458 Warley, T.K. AGRICULTURE: THE COST OF JOINING THE COMMON MARKET. European Series, no. 3. London: Chatham House and PEP, 1976. 57 p.

> A study of the agricultural problems facing Britain if she were to join the EC, and an attempt to assess whether or not those conditions changed between the first and second accession requests.

459 _____, ed. AGRICULTURAL PRODUCERS AND THEIR MARKETS.
London: Basil Blackwell, 1966. 596 p.

> An astute analysis of the achievements of marketing
> boards on agriculture in Britain and Europe, and in the
> developing countries, among other topics.

## C. BUREAUCRACY AND ADMINISTRATION

460 Brierley, Caroline. THE MAKING OF EUROPEAN POLICY. London: published for the Royal Institute of International Affairs by the
Oxford University Press, 1963. 53 p.

> A description of the functioning of the major institutions
> (Commission, Economic and Social Committee, Parliament,
> Council of Ministers) of the EC and how the decisions
> of these institutions have actually been made.

461 Clark, W. Hartley. THE POLITICS OF THE COMMON MARKET.
Englewood Cliffs, N.J.: Prentice-Hall, 1967. 180 p.

> A discussion of the distribution of power within the Com-
> mon Market, and of institutional decision making and
> actions taken by the Council of Ministers, commission,
> court, and Parliament.

462 Conservative Political Centre. THE NEW EUROPE. By Emile Noel
et al. London: 1962. 54 p.

> A collection of essays on the European idea as well as
> European institutions, trade, and external relations. A
> brief but authoritative account of the relations between
> the Economic Commission for Europe and the EC Coun-
> cil of Ministers. He also compares the commission with
> the ECSC High Authority.

463 Coombes, David. POLITICS AND BUREAUCRACY IN THE EURO-
PEAN COMMUNITY: A PORTRAIT OF THE COMMISSION OF THE
EEC. London: published for PEP by George Allen and Unwin, 1970.
343 p.

> A comprehensive study of the role of the commission of
> the EC as it has evolved, showing the interface be-
> tween the politics of Europe and the bureaucracy of
> the executive function.

464 _____. THE ROLE OF EUROCRATS. London: 1969.

465 _____. TOWARDS A EUROPEAN CIVIL SERVICE. European Series, no. 7. London: published for PEP by Chatham House, 1968. 63 p.

An attempt to find out how far Eurocrats have adopted a truly European style of administration which is distinct from administrative practices in the member states, including selection and appointment.

466 Coombes, David, with Wiebecke, Ilka. THE POWER OF THE PURSE IN THE EUROPEAN COMMUNITIES. London: published for PEP by Chatham House, 1972. 103 p.

A detailed consideration of the procedures by which the EC will fund itself, its budget, and the political ramifications for national sovereignty implied by such procedures.

467 Coombes, David, ed. THE POWER OF THE PURSE: A SYMPOSIUM ON THE ROLE OF EUROPEAN PARLIAMENTS FOR BUDGETARY DECISIONS. New York: Frederick A. Praeger, 1976. 394 p.

Eighteen essays focus upon the interface between parliamentary and budgetary power, and integration. Individual authors look at the budgetary process in various European countries: Britain, France, Germany, Italy, Holland, and Switzerland.

468 Dogan, Mattei, ed. THE MANDARINS OF WESTERN EUROPE: THE POLITICAL ROLE OF TOP CIVIL SERVANTS. New York: Halsted Press, 1975. 314 p.

Explores the relationship between high civil servants and traditional politicians in eleven countries. Seeks to explain how the increasing administrative activities of the modern state result in the decline of parliamentary institutions. Also develops the distinction between the "classical," nonpolitical bureaucrat and the political bureaucrat who is replacing him.

469 Druker, Isaac E. FINANCING THE EUROPEAN COMMUNITIES. European Aspects, Law Series, no. 14. Leiden, Netherlands: A.W. Sijthoff, 1975. 450 p.

"This is a comprehensive study of the evolution of the finance system of the European Communities, since the establishment of the ECSC in 1950 to the accession of the United Kingdom, against the background of finance law . . . . [It] presents an analysis of problems relating to revenue sources, parliamentary control, allocation of resources and audit control. . . ."

Publisher

470 Gaudet, Michel. THE INSTITUTIONAL EXPERIENCE OF THE EU-
ROPEAN COMMUNITIES 1950-71. Paris: Action Committee for
the United States of Europe, February 1970. 40 p.

471 Granick, David. THE EUROPEAN EXECUTIVE. Garden City, N.Y.:
Doubleday and Co., 1962. 384 p.

> Based on interviews. An analysis of executives' and
> businessmen's views in Britain, France, Belgium, and
> Germany on entrepreneurship, the role of the techno-
> crat, trade unionism, and ownership.

472 Kapp, Elfriede. THE MERGER OF THE EXECUTIVES OF THE EU-
ROPEAN COMMUNITIES. Cahier de Bruges, n.s. 10. Bruges,
Belgium: De Temple for the College of Europe, 1964. 113 p.

> "A legally structured analysis of the merger of the ex-
> ecutives of the ECSC, EEC, and EURATOM, and the
> political problems such a merger would cause."
>
> BIBLIOGRAPHIE ZUR EURO-
> PAISCHEN INTEGRATION

473 Lindberg, Leon N[ord]. THE POLITICAL DYNAMICS OF EUROPEAN
ECONOMIC INTEGRATION. Stanford, Calif.: Stanford University
Press, 1963. 367 p.

> A study of the process of political integration, its decision-
> making and systemic functions, as well as selected fea-
> tures of the EEC in its first four years of operation.

474 _____. "The Political Dynamics of European Economic Integration." Ph.D. dissertation, University of California, Berkeley,
1962.

475 Namenwirth, Joseph Zvi. "Bureaucratic Power and European Unification: A Causal Inquiry." Ph.D. dissertation, Harvard University,
1963.

476 Niblock, Michael. THE EEC: NATIONAL PARLIAMENTS IN
COMMUNITY DECISION-MAKING. London: published for PEP
by Chatham House, 1971. 112 p.

> A study of the role of national parliaments in the Com-
> munity's decision-making process, and vice versa. Con-
> centrates specifically on the roles of Germany, the Neth-
> erlands, Belgium, and France.

477 Peterson, Robert L[ouis]. CAREER MOTIVATIONS OF ADMINIS-
TRATORS AND THEIR IMPACT IN THE EUROPEAN COMMUNITY.

Monograph Series in World Affairs, vol. 11, no. 4. Denver: University of Denver, 1974. 42 p.

478 _____. "Perspectives in the Commission of the European Economic Community: Attitudes and Integration." Ph.D. dissertation, Yale University, 1968.

479 Political and Economic Planning. BUDGETARY CONTROL IN THE EUROPEAN ECONOMIC COMMUNITY: A CASE STUDY IN "SUPRANATIONAL" ADMINISTRATION. Occasional Paper no. 6. London: 28 March 1960. 42 p.

An analysis of budgetary control exercised by Community bodies and the annual budgets of the Community.

480 Rosenthal, Glenda Goldstone. THE MEN BEHIND THE DECISIONS: CASES IN EUROPEAN POLICY-MAKING. Lexington, Mass.: D.C. Heath and Co., 1975. 166 p.

A study of decision making in the EC using five case studies on generalized preferences, association agreements, free movement of labor, agriculture, and monetary union. Each of the five case studies analyzed through the lens of each of three conceptual schemes, and the perspectives of Sicco Mansholt, Levi Sandri, and Pierre Werner.

481 Spinelli, Altiero. THE EUROCRATS: CONFLICT AND CRISIS IN THE EUROPEAN COMMUNITY. Baltimore: Johns Hopkins University Press, 1966. 229 p.

An insightful description of European-level bureaucratic and interest group interactions. Also an argument against the functionalist theory of integration which notes that political power-holders ultimately will determine Europe's fate, for instance, the federalist perspective.

## D. ECONOMICS, MONEY, AND COMMERCE

482 Albinowski, Stanislaw. COMMERCIAL POLICY OF THE EUROPEAN ECONOMIC COMMUNITY. Warsaw: Zachodnia Agencja Prasowa, 1965. 175 p.

A study of the economic and political impact of the EEC on the world economy and the consequences for economic relations between the Socialist and capitalist parts of Europe, viewed from a Polish and COMECON (CMEA) perspective.

483   Balassa, Bela, ed.  EUROPEAN ECONOMIC INTEGRATION.  Contributions to Economic Analysis, no. 89.  New York:  American Elsevier Publishing Co., 1975.  416 p.

"An appraisal of the experiences of the European Community and the European Free Trade Association."

EUROPEAN COMMUNITY

484   Cairncross, Alec, et al.  ECONOMIC POLICY FOR THE EUROPEAN COMMUNITY:  THE WAY FORWARD.  London:  Macmillan and Co., 1974.  xxi, 245 p.

By five economists.  Discusses problems of European integration and the policy consequences in the areas of monetary and fiscal integration, regional policy, the Common Agricultural Policy, industrial development and competition, the social environment, and international economic policy.

485   Coffey, Peter, and Presley, John R.  EUROPEAN MONETARY INTEGRATION.  New York:  St. Martin's Press, 1971.  131 p.

A history of European economic integration and an analysis of the theoretical aspects of monetary integration.

486   Collin, F.  THE FORMATION OF A EUROPEAN CAPITAL MARKET.  Brussels:  By the Author, 1964.

A study of intra-European capital movements and their implications for European integration.  Maintains that although there exists intense exchange of goods among European countries, exchange of capital is relatively small.  Also discusses new forms of financing that have appeared in recent years on European capital markets.

487   Cooper, Richard N.  STERLING, EUROPEAN MONETARY UNIFICATION, AND THE INTERNATIONAL MONETARY SYSTEM.  Washington, D.C.:  National Planning Association, 1972.  34 p.

An analysis of the effect of European monetary unification on the world monetary system, specifically how British entry will affect sterling, the British balance of payments, common currency, and how these relate to a world monetary system.

488   Denton, Geoffrey R.  PLANNING IN THE EEC:  THE MEDIUM-TERM ECONOMIC POLICY PROGRAMME OF THE EUROPEAN ECONOMIC COMMUNITY.  European Series, no. 5.  London:  published for PEP by Chatham House, 1967.  55 p.

A study of the political interplay in establishing medium-

term planning and economic policies in the EC. Also
reviews policy both in France and Germany and compares the two to British planning policies.

489 _____, ed. ECONOMIC AND MONETARY INTEGRATION IN
EUROPE. London: Croom, Helm, 1974. 118 p.

490 Dosser, Douglas. BRITISH TAXATION AND THE COMMON MAR-
KET: A VOLUME OF ESSAYS. London: C. Knight, 1973. ix,
180 p.

A technical subject used to show the importance of har-
monizing European policies. Also covers the problems
and advantages Britain faces in acceding to the EC.
Included is a theory of tax harmonization and a discussion of VAT (value-added tax), as well as the British
and Community budgets.

491 Dosser, Douglas, and Han, S.S. TAXES IN THE EEC AND BRIT-
AIN: THE PROBLEM OF HARMONIZATION. European Series,
no. 6. London: published for PEP by Chatham House, 1968. 46 p.

492 Europa Institute of the University of Leiden. EUROPEAN COM-
PETITION POLICY: ESSAYS OF THE LEIDEN WORKING GROUP
ON CARTEL PROBLEMS. Leiden, Netherlands: A.W. Sijthoff for
the Europa Institute, 1973. 265 p.

"A critical compilation of essays on EC competition
policy, Commission decision, and Court of Justice rul-
ings . . . [including] cartel dynamics, restrictive agreements, exclusive agencies, concerted practices, selling
organizations, joint ventures, and Common Market Treaty
Articles 85, 86, and 90."

EUROPEAN COMMUNITY

493 Evans, Douglas. THE POLITICS OF TRADE: THE EVOLUTION
OF THE SUPERBLOC. New York: John Wiley and Sons, 1974.
viii, 128 p.

An analysis of the relationship between power politics
and the drift to protectionism in world trade occasioned
by the development of the four superblocs: the United
States, USSR, EEC, and China.

494 Federal Trust for Education and Research. EUROPEAN MONETARY
INTEGRATION. London: 1972. 28 p.

495 _____. INDUSTRY AND THE COMMON MARKET. London:
1971. 88 p.

> Seven seminar papers covering a number of case studies
> on transnational linkups between companies in West Eu-
> rope and the fiscal and legal obstacles to such ventures,
> including the industrial policy proposals of the EC Com-
> mission designed to accelerate industrial integration in
> Europe.

496 Feld, Werner J. TRANSNATIONAL BUSINESS COLLABORATION
AMONG COMMON MARKET COUNTRIES: ITS IMPLICATION
FOR POLITICAL INTEGRATION. New York: Praeger Publishers,
1970. 139 p.

> A conceptual analysis of the role of business executives
> in member states acting as catalysts for political inte-
> gration.

497 Frank, Isaiah. THE EUROPEAN COMMON MARKET: AN ANAL-
YSIS OF COMMERCIAL POLICY. New York: Frederick A. Praeger,
1961. 314 p.

> Analysis of the development of the EC's commercial pol-
> icy through 1959. Also compares economic regionalism
> to economic internationalism in commercial policy.

498 Hurtig, Serge. THE EUROPEAN COMMON MARKET. International
Conciliation, no. 517. New York: Columbia University Press, 1958.
60 p.

499 Kirschen, Etienne-Sadi, et al. FINANCIAL INTEGRATION IN
WESTERN EUROPE. New York: Columbia University Press, 1969.
144 p.

> A focus on the political significance of regional finan-
> cial arrangements and the extent to which various sys-
> tems of government are responsible for difficulties en-
> countered in obtaining financial integration. Also studies
> the way in which political objectives conflict with ad-
> ministrative and economic objectives.

500 Krause, Lawrence B., ed. THE COMMON MARKET: PROGRESS
AND CONTROVERSY. Englewood Cliffs, N.J.: Prentice-Hall,
1964. 182 p.

> A collection of eleven articles by noted American and
> European supporters of European integration with an em-
> phasis on the economic aspects of integration and the
> issues involved: trade, agriculture, and member and
> nonmember problems.

501 Krause, Lawrence B., and Salant, Walter S., eds. EUROPEAN MONETARY UNIFICATION AND ITS MEANING FOR THE U.S. Washington, D.C.: Brookings Institution, 1973. 322 p.

A detailed analysis of the economic and political problems involved in monetary union, the economic changes that union would bring, and their consequences for the United States.

502 Lundstrom, H.O. CAPITAL MOVEMENTS AND ECONOMIC INTEGRATION. Leiden, Netherlands: A.W. Sijthoff, 1961. 231 p.

A useful compilation of information relative to capital movements in Europe and their effect on European integration.

503 McLachlan, Donald L. [Lord Brand], and Swann, D[ennis]. COMPETITION POLICY IN THE EUROPEAN COMMUNITY: THE RULES IN THEORY AND PRACTICE. New York: Oxford University Press, 1967. 482 p.

A systematic and exhaustive account of competition policy, the goals sought in treaties, the problems encountered, the common policies developed, and their effects.

504 Magnifico, Giovanni. EUROPEAN MONETARY UNIFICATION. New York: Halsted Press, 1973. 227 p.

Four essays by the head of international economic cooperation at the Bank of Italy detailing the economic problems, and to a lesser extent the political implications, of monetary integration for Europe.

505 Oort, C.J. ECONOMIC COORDINATION IN THE EUROPEAN ECONOMIC COMMUNITY. Michigan International Business Studies, no. 9. Ann Arbor: University of Michigan, Business Administration, 1967. 59 p.

Deals with the problems of coordinating and integrating economic policy and planning in the EEC, and analyzes policy coordination in exchange-rate adjustments, in common currency, in capital flows, and in income policies. Also studies policies during the Gaullist era, national sovereignty barriers to achieving full integration, and the goal of full monetary and economic union.

506 Oslizlok, J.S. ECONOMIC AND MONETARY INTEGRATION WITHIN THE EUROPEAN ECONOMIC COMMUNITY. Dublin: Irish Council of the European Movement, 1971. 23 p.

507 Political and Economic Planning. CARTEL POLICY AND THE COM-
MON MARKET. London: 1962. 95 p.

> A political analysis of the development and economic
> effects of the Common Market's cartel policy.

508 Preeg, Ernest H. TRADERS AND DIPLOMATS. Washington, D.C.:
Brookings Institution, 1970. 260 p.

> "Preeg offers an extensive report on the Kennedy Round:
> the issues, and personalities involved in the negotiations,
> as well as a complete background on the creation of GATT
> and previous negotiations, the creation of EEC and Euro-
> pean Free Trade Association, and the commercial relations
> between the United States and the EEC and EFTA. . . ."
>
>                    Carson, Sally.  EUROPEAN INTEGRA-
>                    TION AND U.S.-EUROPEAN RELATIONS

509 Readman, Peter, et al. THE EUROPEAN MONEY PUZZLE. London: Michael Joseph, 1973. 165 p.

> An analysis of financial markets and how they could de-
> velop in an enlarged community, including the financial
> opportunities and problems Britain will face in the EC.
> An economic study which seeks to incorporate the poli-
> tics of financial decision making in the community.

510 Robinson, Derek. INCOMES POLICY AND CAPITAL SHARING
IN EUROPE. London: Croom, Helm, 1973. 223 p.

> The author's various papers on Europe. Some chapters
> quite specialized, others, like those on trade unions and
> multinational corporations, more generally useful in con-
> sidering integration.

511 Study Group on Economic and Monetary Union. EUROPEAN ECO-
NOMIC INTEGRATION AND MONETARY UNIFICATION. Brussels:
Commission of the European Communities, 1973. 311 p.

512 Swann, Dennis. THE ECONOMICS OF THE COMMON MARKET.
3d ed. Harmondsworth, Engl.: Penguin Books, 1975. 267 p.

> A study of the political economy of the European Com-
> munity including a theory of economics which the author
> claims leads to political decision making. Tariff bar-
> riers, industrial policies, and regional and social poli-
> cies also discussed.

513 Swann, Dennis, and McLachlan, D[onald]. L. [Lord Brand]. CON-

CENTRATION OR COMPETITION: A EUROPEAN DILEMMA. London: published for PEP by Chatham House, 1967. 59 p.

An essay on antitrust policy and the quest for a "European-sized" company in the Common Market.

514   Thompson, Dennis. THE PROPOSAL FOR A EUROPEAN COMPANY. London: published for PEP by Chatham House, 1969. 73 p.

A discussion of "European" companies, their development in the EC of the six, relation to the Rome Treaty, and the political implications for supranationalism.

515   Trade Policy Research Center. TOWARDS AN OPEN WORLD ECONOMY. New York: published for the Trade Policy Research Center by Macmillan Co., 1972. 198 p.

A collection of essays from an advisory group of the Trade Policy Research Center detailing proposals for the 1972-73 multilateral commercial negotiations. Several essays on Europe included, one on the political effects of the 1971 monetary crisis, and another on the problems of agriculture and the CAP.

516   Triffin, Robert. THE FUTURE OF THE EUROPEAN PAYMENTS SYSTEM. Stockholm: Almquist and Wicksell, 1958. 43 p.

A series of lectures on the European monetary system. Lectures predate dissolution of the EPU. Concerned principally with the role of regional integration in the monetary policy adopted by the EEC and EFTA.

517   Tulloch, Peter. THE POLITICS OF PREFERENCES: EEC POLICY MAKING AND THE GENERALIZED SYSTEM OF PREFERENCES. London: Croom, Helm in association with the Overseas Development Institute, 1975. 118 p.

518   University of Louvain. Institute for Economic, Social and Political Research. THE MARKET ECONOMY IN WESTERN EUROPEAN INTEGRATION: REPORT OF THE SEVENTH FLEMISH ECONOMIC CONGRESS, LOUVAIN, 8-9 May 1965. Louvain, Belgium: Editions Nauwelaerts, 1965.

Included are several highly informative chapters on the structure of the Common Market, the aims and instruments of European executive organs in market organization, foreign trade and development policies, agricultural policy, and transport policy.

519 Vaughn, William Maurice. "Cartel Policy in the European Economic Community, 1958-70: The Growth of a Regulatory Network." Ph.D. dissertation, University of Washington, 1974.

520 Walter, Ingo. THE EUROPEAN COMMON MARKET 1958-65: GROWTH PATTERNS OF TRADE AND PRODUCTION. London: Pall Mall Press, 1967. 212 p.

> Primarily a study of the volume and direction of intra-community trade, but also helpful in assessing the functionalist's political argument derived from economic integration.

521 Wheatcroft, G.S.A., ed. VALUE-ADDED TAX IN THE ENLARGED COMMON MARKET. New York: John Wiley and Sons, 1973. 140 p.

> A sophisticated description of the value-added tax, its application in the respective, member countries of the EC, and its bearing on economic and social policy.

## E. EDUCATION AND CULTURE

522 Beck, Robert H. CHANGE AND HARMONIZATION IN EUROPEAN EDUCATION. Minneapolis: University of Minnesota Press, 1971. 206 p.

> A study of the harmonization of efforts and practices in European education, focusing especially on European institutions fostering changes. A useful guide to the socialization of "Europe."

523 Corbett, John Patrick. EUROPE AND THE SOCIAL ORDER. Leiden, Netherlands: A.W. Sijthoff, 1959. 188 p.

> By a "rationalist social philosopher." Addresses the normative considerations underlying European unity. Asserts that it is not fear or sentiment, but the need to innovate in scientific, technological, economic, and political areas that will motivate unification.

524 Cornelis, P.A. EUROPEANS ABOUT EUROPE: WHAT EUROPEAN STUDENTS KNOW AND EXPECT OF THE UNIFICATION OF EUROPE; A STUDY IN SOCIAL PSYCHOLOGY. Amsterdam: Swets and Zeitlinger, 1970. 176 p.

> Discussion of the study, methods, and results of a survey research project designed to elicit a degree of support among European students for European unification.

525    Friedrich, Carl J.  EUROPE:  AN EMERGENT NATION?  New
       York:  Harper and Row, 1969.  269 p.

       A description of the informal processes of socialization
       and learning that have brought about integration in agri-
       culture, business, labor, academics, and other areas.

526    Haigh, Anthony.  A MINISTRY OF EDUCATION FOR EUROPE.
       London:  George G. Harrap and Co., 1970.  191 p.

       An inside account of an unfinished experiment, a decade
       of interaction between the conferences of European min-
       isters of education and various international organizations
       like the Council of Europe, OECD, and UNESCO.  Euro-
       pean integration and its possibilities measured by educa-
       tion.

527    Solomon, Rhona Rachel, and Smith, A.M.  HIGHER EDUCATION
       IN THE EUROPEAN ECONOMIC COMMUNITY.  Manchester, Engl.:
       Manchester Polytechnic, 1973.  30 p.

528    Stadler, K.R.  ADULT EDUCATION AND EUROPEAN
       CO-OPERATION.  European Aspects, Series B, no. 5.  Leiden,
       Netherlands:  A.W. Sijthoff, 1963.  184 p.

       An overview of adult education in general and the role
       it has played in international relations and European af-
       fairs in creating an interest in European unity.  Surveys
       each major European country noting techniques of edu-
       cation and the effect on interest in European unity.

## F.  ENERGY AND EURATOM

529    Albonetti, Achille.  EUROPE AND NUCLEAR ENERGY.  Atlantic
       Papers, no. 2.  Paris:  Atlantic Institute, 1972.  74 p.

       A monographic study of nuclear energy both from its
       technical-economic and political-organizational sides,
       including EURATOM.

530    Alting von Geusau, Frans A.M.  ENERGY IN THE EUROPEAN
       COMMUNITIES.  John F. Kennedy Institute Series, no. 9.  Leiden,
       Netherlands:  A.W. Sijthoff, 1975.  200 p.

       Ten essays on EC energy policy and its economic and
       political effects.  The problem of oil and OPEC con-
       sidered at length, as are alternative energy sources and
       their policy implications:  coal, oil and gas from the
       USSR, and nuclear energy.

531 American Committee on United Europe. EURATOM AND THE COM-
MON MARKET: A REPORT ON EUROPEAN UNITY. Prepared by
John D. Blumgart. New York: 1956. 26 p.

532 Baker, Steven Jarrold. "Technology and Politics: The Italian Nuclear Program and Political Integration in Western Europe." Ph.D.
dissertation, University of California, Los Angeles, 1973.

533 Boskey, Bennett, and Willrich, Mason, eds. NUCLEAR PROLIFERA-
TION: PROSPECTS FOR CONTROL. New York: Dunellen Publishing Co., 1971. 191 p.

A series of essays on nuclear proliferation and its problems written for the Brookings Institution. See especially
Lawrence Scheinman's article addressing the problem of
reconciling the International Atomic Energy Agency and
EURATOM.

534 Brinton, George M. "Nuclear Power and the Energy Balance in
the Euratom Countries (1960-75)." Ph.D. dissertation, Claremont
Graduate School, 1963.

535 Couste, Pierre Bernard. EEC AND EURATOM: A DANGER TO
INTERNATIONAL COOPERATION. 1957. 43 p.

536 Droutman, Lawrence Julian. "Nuclear Integration: The Failure of
Euratom." Ph.D. dissertation, Columbia University, 1973.

537 Errera, Jacques. EURATOM. New York: Joint Publications Research Service, 1958. 260 p.

Commentary on the EURATOM treaty by participants in
EURATOM's creation including a history of the research
coordination in atomic energy, a description of the
EURATOM institutions, their financing and their relationship to the nation-states and to other European institutions.

538 Gaudet, Michel. EURATOM. London: Pergamon Press, 1959.

539 Goldschmidt, Bertrand. THE ATOMIC ADVENTURE: ITS POLITI-
CAL AND TECHNICAL ASPECTS. Translated by Peter Beer. Oxford: Pergamon Press; New York: Macmillan Co., 1964. 259 p.

A history of the developments in the field of atomic energy including technical and political cooperation. European collaboration and the developments and activities
of EURATOM also included.

540  Hasson, J.A.  THE ECONOMICS OF NUCLEAR POWER.  London: Longmans, Green and Co., 1965.  160 p.

Develops a methodological framework to study the new industry of nuclear power and its effects on social welfare, including nuclear programs in the United States, Britain, and India.  Relates the study to the development of a European Atomic Energy Community.

541  Knorr, Klaus E.  EURATOM AND AMERICAN POLICY.  Princeton, N.J.:  Center of International Studies, 1956.  22 p.

A report on a conference held at Princeton University concerning EURATOM, its role in Western European integration and America's interest and role in Euratom policy, technically and politically.

542  _____.  NUCLEAR ENERGY IN WESTERN EUROPE AND UNITED STATES POLICY.  Princeton, N.J.:  Center of International Studies, 1956.  35 p.

A recognized study of EURATOM and U.S. policy.

543  Kramish, Arnold.  THE PEACEFUL ATOM IN FOREIGN POLICY.  New York:  published for the Council on Foreign Relations by Harper and Row, 1963.  276 p.

544  McKnight, Allan D.  NUCLEAR NON-PROLIFERATION:  IAEA AND EURATOM.  New York:  Carnegie Endowment for International Peace, 1970.  103 p.

545  Moore, Ben T.  EURATOM:  THE AMERICAN INTEREST IN THE EUROPEAN ATOMIC ENERGY COMMUNITY.  New York:  published for the Twentieth Century Fund by Harper and Row, 1958.  40 p.

An analysis of the EURATOM Treaty in relation to the U.S. atomic energy policies.

546  Nau, Henry R.  NATIONAL POLITICS AND INTERNATIONAL TECHNOLOGY:  NUCLEAR REACTOR DEVELOPMENTS IN WESTERN EUROPE.  Baltimore:  Johns Hopkins University Press, 1974.  278 p.

". . . an investigation of the relations between politics and technology in international relations. . . . An attempt to explain how groups identify primarily along territorial or national lines [and] behave in the common or competitive development of big technologies."

Publisher

547    Polach, Jaroslav G.  "Euratom: A Study in European Integration."
Ph.D. dissertation, American University, 1962.

548    _____. EURATOM: ITS BACKGROUND, ISSUES AND ECONOMIC
IMPLICATIONS.  Dobbs-Ferry, N.Y.:  Oceana Publications, 1964.
232 p.

>    A political assessment of EURATOM's role, and the role
>    of atomic energy in the integration of West Europe.

549    Political and Economic Planning.  AN ENERGY POLICY FOR THE
EEC?  London: 1962.  109 p.  New ed. 1963.  38 p.

>    A study of the arguments for a coordinated European en-
>    ergy policy due to the problems arising from increased
>    dependence on oil imported into Europe.

550    Scheinman, Lawrence.  EURATOM: NUCLEAR INTEGRATION IN
EUROPE.  New York: Carnegie Endowment for Peace, 1967.  66 p.

>    An exploration of EURATOM, national disparities in en-
>    ergy, nuclear nationalism, executive leadership, and bar-
>    gaining in the organization.

## G. LEGAL

## 1. General

551    Bathurst, Maurice Edward, et al., eds.  LEGAL PROBLEMS OF AN
ENLARGED EUROPEAN COMMUNITY.  London: Stevens and Co.,
1972.  369 p.

>    The revised papers given at the 1970 International Con-
>    ference on Expansion of the European Communities held
>    in Dublin.  Included are legal problems of the Irish con-
>    stitution, courts, legislature, foreign relations, company
>    law, transportation, and agriculture.

552    Bebr, Gerhard.  THE RULE OF LAW WITHIN THE EUROPEAN COM-
MUNITIES.  Publication no. 11.  Brussels: Universite Libre, Institute
d'Etudes Europeens, 1965.  33 p.

553    Bergsten, Eric E.  COMMUNITY LAW IN THE FRENCH COURTS:
THE LAW OF TREATIES IN MODERN ATTIRE.  The Hague: Martinus Nijhoff, 1973.  145 p.

>    "An analysis of the interpretation and application of EC
>    law in the various French tribunals.  The question of

the supremacy of Community law and its application to French law is raised in regard to the Conseil d'Etat and the Cour de Cassation."

EUROPEAN COMMUNITY

554   Brinkhorst, L.J.   EUROPEAN LAW AND INSTITUTIONS: EURO-PEAN LAW AS A LEGAL REALITY.   And WHY EUROPEAN INSTI-TUTIONS?   By J.D.B. Mitchell.   2 tracts in 1.   Edinburgh: Edin-burgh University Press, 1969.   58 p.

555   Brinkhorst, L.J., and Schermers, H.G., eds.   JURIDICAL REME-DIES IN THE EUROPEAN COMMUNITIES: A CASE BOOK.   Lon-don: Stevens and Sons, 1969.

556   Campbell, Alan.   COMMON MARKET LAW.   2 vols.   London: Longmans, Green and Co., 1969.   1,274 p.

Addressed to a common law audience.   Detailed and professional references to the principal activities and problems of the EC, including a study of the European Court of Justice.

557   Campbell, Alan, and Thompson, Dennis.   COMMON MARKET LAW: TEXT AND COMMENTARIES.   London: Stevens and Sons; A.W. Sijthoff; and Rothman, 1962.   487 p.   SUPPLEMENT, 1963. xvi, 196 p.

A complete explication of the Rome Treaty and treaty law.

558   Dawson, J.P.   THE ORACLES OF THE LAW.   Ann Arbor: Uni-versity of Michigan Law School, 1968.   520 p.

A historical and comparative study of case law in West Europe.   Discusses the growth and decline of English case law, the heritage from Roman law, Germany's com-mitment to legal science, and the organization of French law.   Also covers the relationships of the courts to po-litical authority and judicial decision making.

559   Donner, Andre[as] M[atthias].   THE ROLE OF THE LAWYER IN THE EUROPEAN COMMUNITIES.   Evanston, Ill.: Northwestern University Press, 1968.   xvi, 89 p.

560   Donner, Andreas Matthias, et al.   LAW AND THE EUROPEAN COMMUNITY.   Brussels and New York: European Community Press and Information Service, 1966.   12 p.

561 Elles, Neil. COMMUNITY LAW THROUGH THE CASES. London:
Sweet and Maxwell-Stevens; New York: Matthew Bender, 1973.
411 p.

562 EUROPEAN LEGISLATION, 1952-72. London: Butterworth and
Co., 1975. 1,463 p.

> Likely to be a legal classic on European Community law.
> The arrangement and terminology of the law are adapted
> for English lawyers. Well indexed.

563 Federal Bar Association, Washington, D.C. PROCEEDINGS OF
THE 1960 INSTITUTE ON LEGAL ASPECTS OF THE EUROPEAN
COMMUNITY. Washington, D.C.: 1960. 218 p.

> An economic and political analysis of the European Com-
> munity to give the American lawyer a broader view of
> it, both long-range and day to day. Views on U.S.-
> EEC relations are legal-political, legal-technical, and
> legal-economic.

564 Gormley, W. Paul. THE PROCEDURAL STATUS OF THE INDI-
VIDUAL BEFORE INTERNATIONAL AND SUPRANATIONAL TRIBU-
NALS. The Hague: Martinus Nijhoff, 1966. xv, 206 p.

565 Kapteyn, P.J.G., and van Themaat, P. Verloren. INTRODUC-
TION TO THE LAW OF THE EUROPEAN COMMUNITIES AFTER
THE ACCESSION OF NEW MEMBER STATES. Translated by C. Dik-
shoorn. Rev. ed. London: Sweet and Maxwell, 1973. xx, 433 p.

566 Lasok, D., and Bridge, J.W. LASOK AND BRIDGE'S INTRODUC-
TION TO THE LAW AND INSTITUTIONS OF THE EUROPEAN COM-
MUNITY. London: Butterworth and Co., 1973. 314 p.

> "An analysis of EC law and institutions and their rela-
> tion to the individual, sovereign member states. . . .
> The book describes the nature of the European Commu-
> nity and its law, its institutional organization, the rela-
> tionship between EC law and member states' municipal
> law, and the 'law of the economy' as one of the EC's
> operational premises."

## EUROPEAN COMMUNITY

567 Lauwaars, R.H. LAWFULNESS AND LEGAL FORCE OF COMMU-
NITY DECISIONS: SOME CONSIDERATIONS ON THE BINDING DE-
CISIONS WHICH THE COUNCIL AND THE COMMISSION CAN TAKE
BY VIRTUE OF THE TREATY ESTABLISHING THE EUROPEAN ECONOM-
IC COMMUNITY. Leiden, Netherlands: A.W. Sijthoff, 1973. 355 p.

> A survey of the legal aspects of institutional decision

making in the European Community, the legal powers of
the commission and council as well as the powers of the
court.

568　Mathijsen, P.S.R.F.　A GUIDE TO EUROPEAN COMMUNITY LAW.
London:　Sweet and Maxwell, 1972.　204 p.

A guide to EC law with the thesis that such law is au-
tonomous and not subservient to national law.　Further,
seeks to show that various types of law are the result
of the type of institutional relationships, for example,
between the commission and the council.　Also discusses
the legal consequences of British entry into the EC.

569　Mezerik, Avrahm G.　COMMON MARKET:　POLITICAL IMPACTS;
UNDERDEVELOPED COUNTRIES, EUROPE, UNITED STATES, UNITED
NATIONS.　New York:　International Review Service, 1962.　62 p.

570　Parry, Anthony, and Hardy, Stephen.　EEC LAW.　London:　Sweet
and Maxwell-Stevens, 1973.　511 p.

A concise picture of all aspects of EEC law before the
enlargement, plus details of the accession agreements.
For use both as a text and a reference.　Indexed and
has an extensive bibliography.

571　Schechter, A.H.　INTERPRETATION OF AMBIGUOUS DOCUMENTS
BY INTERNATIONAL ADMINISTRATIVE TRIBUNALS.　New York:
Frederick A. Praeger, 1964.　183 p.

An analysis of international legal developments since
World War II in the U.N. administrative tribunals, in
the ILO, and in the Court of Justice of the European
Communities in interpreting international rules and regulations.

572　Simmonds, K.R., ed.　SWEET & MAXWELL'S EUROPEAN COM-
MUNITY TREATIES.　2d ed.　London:　Sweet and Maxwell, 1972.
xii, 310 p.

A guide to EC law with the thesis that such law is au-
tonomous and not subservient to national law.　Further,
seeks to show that various types of law are the result
of the type of institutional relationships, for example,
between the commission and the council.　Also discusses
the legal consequences of British entry into the EC.

573　Smith, Munroe.　THE DEVELOPMENT OF EUROPEAN LAW.　New
York:　Columbia University Press, 1928.　316 p.

574  Stein, Eric; Hay, Peter; and Waelbroeck, Michel. EUROPEAN COMMUNITY LAW AND INSTITUTIONS IN PERSPECTIVE. New York: Bobbs-Merrill Co., 1976. 1,132 p.

A casebook on the law of international institutions in Western Europe including treaty, national legislative and court-decision extracts designed as a textbook but useful to the law profession as well. Chapters 2 and 3: the legal institutions and processes of the EC. Other chapters cover trade and commercial policy, antitrust, civil rights, and military and political policy. Includes a volume of documents.

575  Wall, Edward H. THE EUROPEAN COMMUNITIES ACT 1972. London: Butterworth and Co., 1973.

"This book is intended as a short, practical guide to the Act. The author takes the Act's twelve sections and four schedules separately, reproducing and explain - ing them fully."

Publisher

## 2. Legal—Community and Common Law

576  Collins, Lawrence. EUROPEAN COMMUNITY LAW IN THE UNITED KINGDOM. London: Butterworth and Co., 1975. 170 p.

A study of the structural and procedural applications of EC law within the context of the British legal system, how EC law is to be applied by the courts of Britain, the way in which the law works in conjunction with the European court in Luxembourg, and ways to challenge EC acts.

577  Conservative Political Centre. EUROPE AND THE LAW: STUDIES ON THE IMPLEMENTATION OF THE EEC'S COMMON POLICY AND ITS IMPACT ON THE UNITED KINGDOM LAW. By members of the Society of Conservative Lawyers. London: 1969. 96 p.

578  Duke University School of Law. "An Expansion of the Common Market." LAW AND CONTEMPORARY PROBLEMS 37, no. 2 (1972): entire issue.

An assessment of the legal ramifications of an enlarged European Community. Particular attention paid to the question of British entry.

579  Keeton, George W., and Schwarzenberger, Georg, eds. ENGLISH

LAW AND THE COMMON MARKET. London: Stevens and Sons, 1963. 230 p.

> Public lectures of the faculty of law at University College, London, 1962–63, concerning the impact of U.K. membership in the EC on British life and institutions, as well as the practical legal problems facing the EC.

580 Lang, John Temple. THE COMMON MARKET AND COMMON LAW: LEGAL ASPECTS OF FOREIGN INVESTMENT AND ECONOMIC INTEGRATION IN THE EUROPEAN COMMUNITY WITH IRELAND AS A PROTOTYPE. Chicago: University of Chicago Press, 1966. 573 p.

> Seeks to provide a comparative analysis of the legal and economic effects of entry into the EEC on the laws of capital-importing countries. Ireland is the case study. An excellent bibliography included.

581 Lauterpacht, E., and Collins, L[awrence]. LAUTERPACHT AND COLLINS ON EUROPEAN COMMUNITY LAW IN THE UNITED KINGDOM. London: Butterworth and Co., 1973.

> "This work sets out to describe the principles of EEC law in the context of English law, and the problems of the application of and challenge to Community rules, both in English and Community courts."

> Publisher

582 Wortley, B.A., ed. THE LAW OF THE COMMON MARKET. Melland Schill Lecture Series. Dobbs-Ferry, N.Y.: Oceana Publications, 1974. 248 p.

> This collected study is a continuation of Wortley's earlier AN INTRODUCTION TO THE LAW OF THE EUROPEAN ECONOMIC COMMUNITY (1972). Focuses on the impact of EC law upon the law of the U.K. Additional essays on the Yaounde Convention and the Deniau Memorandum, among other topics.

## 3. Legal—European Court of Justice

583 Bebr, Gerhard. JUDICIAL CONTROL OF THE EUROPEAN COMMUNITIES. London: published for the London Institute of World Affairs by Stevens and Sons, 1962. 268 p.

> Based on the case law of the court. A study of the EC Court of Justice, its role, and EUROCOURT'S development in a climate lacking strong political solidarity and the possible influence this may have on the development of the European Communities.

584 Brinkhorst, L.J., and Wittenberg, trans. THE RULES OF PRO-
CEDURE OF THE COURT OF JUSTICE OF THE EUROPEAN COM-
MUNITIES. Leiden, Netherlands: A.W. Sijthoff, 1962.

585 Europa Institute at the University of Leiden. THE RULES OF PRO-
CEDURE OF THE COURT OF JUSTICE OF THE EUROPEAN COM-
MUNITIES. Leiden, Netherlands: 1964.

586 Eversen, H.J., et al., eds. COMPENDIUM OF CASE LAW RELAT-
ING TO THE EUROPEAN COMMUNITIES, 1973. New York: American Elsevier Publishing Co., 1975. 304 p.

> An English version of the 1973 French and German ver-
> sions covering ". . . extracts from judgments of the Court
> of Justice of the European Communities delivered during
> 1973 and summarized decisions of national courts . . . ar-
> ranged in chronological order under the provisions of Com-
> munity law to which they relate."
>
> Publisher

587 _____. COMPENDIUM OF CASE LAW RELATING TO THE EURO-
PEAN COMMUNITIES, 1974. Amsterdam: North Holland Publishing
Co., 1976. 347 p.

> "Extracts from the judgements of the Court of Justice
> of the European Communities delivered during 1974. Al-
> so contains appropriate summarized decisions of national
> courts."
>
> EUROPEAN COMMUNITY

588 Feld, Werner J. THE COURT OF THE EUROPEAN COMMUNITIES:
NEW DIMENSIONS IN INTERNATIONAL ADJUDICATION. The
Hague: Martinus Nijhoff, 1964. 127 p.

> An introduction to the institutional and political facets
> of the Court of Justice of the European Communities
> with an emphasis on economic and political implications
> for evolving the European idea.

589 Lipstein, K. THE LAW OF THE EUROPEAN COMMUNITY. London: Butterworth and Co., 1974. 368 p.

> "An article by article analysis of the EEC Treaty in-
> cluding interpretations by the European Court of Justice
> of each article and the practical measures ensuing from
> the articles and the Court's interpretations."
>
> EUROPEAN COMMUNITY

590  Valentine, David Graham. THE COURT OF JUSTICE OF THE EU-
ROPEAN COMMUNITIES. 2 vols. London: Stevens and Sons,
1965. 1,474 p.

> A translation and detailed commentary on the Rome Treaty
> articles (vol. 1), and the judgments of the court between
> 1954 and 1960 (vol. 2).

591  Wall, Edward H. THE COURT OF JUSTICE OF THE EUROPEAN
COMMUNITIES: JURISDICTION AND PROCEDURE. London: Butterworth and Co., 1966. 321 p.

> A consideration of the central judicial machinery of the
> EC and the legal elements necessary to harmonize in or-
> der for integration to progress.

## 4. Legal—Law and Business

592  Alexandrowicz, Charles Henry, ed. WORLD ECONOMIC AGEN-
CIES: LAW AND PRACTICE. London: Stevens and Sons, 1962.
310 p.

> Discusses the formation and operation of world economic
> agencies and how they influence international law. Em-
> phasizes internal structures of organizations like the EEC,
> ECSC, GATT, and the U.N., as well as distribution of
> power, consequences of membership, law-promoting func-
> tions, and administrative features.

593  Balekjian, W.H. LEGAL ASPECTS OF FOREIGN INVESTMENT IN
THE EUROPEAN ECONOMIC COMMUNITY. Manchester, Engl.:
Manchester University Press, 1967. 356 p.

> An analysis of the legal problems a foreign investor might
> encounter. Also, concerned for EC law generally, the
> way in which it protects against nationalizations and ap-
> plies to business and cartelization. A technical treatise,
> but extremely valuable as an erudite study of EC law.

594  British Institute of International and Comparative Law. COMPARA-
TIVE ASPECTS OF ANTI-TRUST LAW IN THE UNITED STATES, THE
UNITED KINGDOM AND THE EUROPEAN ECONOMIC COMMUNITY.
London: 1963. 153 p.

> Conference papers comparing a variety of legal topics:
> antitrust, mergers, and enforcement policies. Its spe-
> cial concern is business law topics.

595  _____. LEGAL PROBLEMS OF THE EUROPEAN ECONOMIC COM-
MUNITY AND THE EUROPEAN FREE TRADE ASSOCIATION. New

York: Frederick A. Praeger, 1960; London: Stevens and Sons, 1961. 110 p.

Nine conference papers given at the British Institute of International and Comparative Law examining and contrasting the legal structures of the EEC and EFTA generally, and in relation to specific topics like patents and competition.

596    Cawthra, Bruce.  CAWTHRA'S RESTRICTIVE AGREEMENTS IN THE EEC: THE NEED TO NOTIFY.  London: Butterworth and Co., 1972.  xvii, 179 p.

A guide to the rules of notification with the EEC Commission of any agreement possibly infringing on articles 85 and 86 concerning monopolistic practices.  Useful for businessmen and legal advisors.  It is also useful as a guide to European Court of Justice decisions and EEC Commission decisions on monopolies.

597    Deringer, A.  THE COMPETITION LAW OF THE EUROPEAN ECO- NOMIC COMMUNITY.  New York: Commerce Clearing House, 1968.  418 p.

An examination of the law regulating EEC competition. Discusses the concept of invalidity under civil and cartel law, reviews forms of restraints, abuse of power, investigating powers of the EEC, and review by the International Court of Justice.

598    Everling, Dr. Ulrich.  THE RIGHT OF ESTABLISHMENT IN THE COMMON MARKET.  Chicago: Commerce Clearing House, 1964. 219 p.

A comprehensive description of the "right of establishment" in the Common Market.  Also shows how economic power in the Rome Treaty permits major intervention by the EC into the vital spheres of political, legal, and social life of the member states.  Included is an analysis of "legal functionalism" as an integrating concept.

599    Friedman, Wolfgang, ed.  THE PUBLIC CORPORATION: A COM- PARATIVE SYMPOSIUM.  University of Toronto, School of Law, Comparative Law Series, vol. 1.  Toronto: Carswell, 1954. 612 p.

A discussion of the legal status and organization of the public corporation.  Fourteen essays on the public corporation include Australia, Canada, France, Germany, England, India, Israel, Italy, Sweden, and the USSR.

600 Graupner, R. THE RULES OF COMPETITION IN THE EUROPEAN ECONOMIC COMMUNITY: A STUDY OF THE SUBSTANTIVE LAW ON A COMPARATIVE LAW BASIS. The Hague: Martinus Nijhoff, 1965. 283 p.

A thorough treatment of the law covering rules of competition but also an interesting discussion of the way in which a community-wide law filters down into national law, that is, the political osmosis of law.

601 Hauser, Rita E., and Hauser, Gustave M. A GUIDE TO DOING BUSINESS IN THE EUROPEAN COMMON MARKET. Vol. 1: FRANCE AND BELGIUM. New York: Oceana Publications, 1960.

A guide for attorneys, businessmen and government officials concerning the effects of French and Belgian private and public law on business in relation to the European Economic Community.

602 Stein, Eric. HARMONIZATION OF EUROPEAN COMPANY LAWS. Indianapolis: Bobbs-Merrill Co., 1971. 558 p.

A study of company law at the Community level. Emphasizes the method of EC lawmaking and assesses the degree of integration achieved and the politics in developing that integration.

603 Stein, Eric, and Nicholson, Thomas L., eds. AMERICAN ENTERPRISE IN THE EUROPEAN COMMON MARKET: A LEGAL PROFILE. 2 vols. Ann Arbor: University of Michigan Press, 1960. 1,242 p.

A legal analysis by professors and international civil servants in the United States and Europe surveying European integration and the various legal forms available to an enterprise in business operations.

604 Swann, Dennis, and Lees, Dennis. ANTITRUST POLICY IN EUROPE. London: Financial Times, 1973. 106 p.

Primarily a guide for businessmen on Europe's antitrust laws and policies. Includes the EEC's antitrust philosophy, rules and administration, as well as how both the EC Commission and Court of Justice of the European Communities have handled many cases. The landmark Continental Can case covered in appendix.

605 Wortley, B.A., ed. AN INTRODUCTION TO THE LAW OF THE EUROPEAN ECONOMIC COMMUNITY. Manchester, Engl.: Manchester University Press, 1972. 134 p.

Six essays on EC law include monopoly, restrictive practices, and company law. It is intended for the British reader.

## 5. Legal—Law and Political Integration

606  Axline, W[illiam]. Andrew. EUROPEAN COMMUNITY LAW AND ORGANIZATIONAL DEVELOPMENT. Dobbs-Ferry, N.Y.: Oceana Publications, 1968. 214 p.

A study in international organization and law since World War II, including the law of the ECSC, EC, EURATOM, and the way in which it relates to the process of integration. Develops a theory of law, society, and integration.

607  _____. "Legal and Organizational Growth in Europe: An Approach to the Study of Integration." Ph.D. dissertation, Johns Hopkins University, 1967.

608  Green, Andrew Wilson. POLITICAL INTEGRATION BY JURISPRUDENCE: THE WORK OF THE COURT OF JUSTICE OF THE EUROPEAN COMMUNITIES IN EUROPEAN POLITICAL INTEGRATION. Leiden, Netherlands: A.W. Sijthoff, 1969. 847 p.

An evaluation of the political effect of the actions of the Court of Justice of the European Communities on political integration of Western Europe and a comparison of the Court of Justice with American courts.

609  _____. "The Role of the Court of Justice of the European Communities in the Process of European Political Integration: The Federalizing Judiciary of the European Communities." Ph.D. dissertation, University of Pennsylvania, 1968.

610  Grieves, Forest. SUPRANATIONALISM AND INTERNATIONAL ADJUDICATION. Urbana: University of Illinois Press, 1969. 266 p.

A conceptual analysis of supranational assumptions, constitutional bases, and actual practice of five international courts including the Court of Justice of the European Communities, and the European Court of Human Rights.

611  Hay, Peter. FEDERALISM AND SUPRANATIONAL ORGANIZATIONS: PATTERNS FOR NEW LEGAL STRUCTURES. Urbana: University of Illinois Press, 1966. 335 p.

Included are selected topics dealing with law and policy as they relate to supranational organization conceptually, and to the European Community specifically. A formal description of the legal-political role of the EC Court of Justice and a description of the nature, composition, and organization of the Court of Justice which should be helpful to the layman as well as to the lawyer also detailed.

612  Mann, Clarence J. THE FUNCTION OF JUDICIAL DECISION IN EUROPEAN ECONOMIC INTEGRATION. The Hague: Martinus Nijhoff, 1972. 507 p.

An institutional analysis of the role of the European Court of Justice and its effects on the legal, political, and economic sectors of the EC.

613  Pescatore, Pierre. THE LAW OF INTEGRATION: EMERGENCE OF A NEW PHENOMENON IN INTERNATIONAL RELATIONS, BASED ON THE EXPERIENCE OF THE EUROPEAN COMMUNITIES. Leiden, Netherlands: A.W. Sijthoff, 1974. 117 p.

"Collected lectures and essays by the author on the 'law of integration' as opposed to the so-called classical international legal order."

EUROPEAN COMMUNITY

614  Scheingold, Stuart Allen. "Law and Politics in Western European Integration." Ph.D. dissertation, University of California, Berkeley, 1963.

615  _____. THE LAW IN POLITICAL INTEGRATION: THE EVOLUTION AND INTEGRATIVE IMPLICATIONS OF REGIONAL LEGAL PROCESSES IN THE EUROPEAN COMMUNITY. Occasional Papers in International Affairs, no. 27. Cambridge, Mass.: Harvard University Center for International Affairs, 1971. 48 p.

An assessment of the legal processes in the political integration of Western Europe, including a rejection of federalism, and the U.S. federal model for Europe.

616  _____. THE RULE OF LAW IN EUROPEAN INTEGRATION: THE PATH OF THE SCHUMAN PLAN. New Haven, Conn.: Yale University Press, 1965. 331 p.

A nonlegal but sophisticated view of the political role of the Court of Justice of the European Communities, and an assessment of its role after ten years of operation in integrating Europe.

617  Wall, Edward H.  EUROPE: UNIFICATION AND LAW.  Harmondsworth, Engl.: Penguin Books, 1969.  222 p.

> An introduction to European Community law which seeks
> to answer questions about the origins, purpose, and op-
> erations of EC law.

## H.  PARLIAMENT—PARTIES AND ELECTIONS

618  Birke, Wolfgang.  EUROPEAN ELECTIONS BY DIRECT SUFFRAGE:
A COMPARATIVE STUDY OF THE ELECTORAL SYSTEMS USED IN
WEST EUROPE AND THEIR UTILITY FOR THE DIRECT ELECTION
OF A EUROPEAN PARLIAMENT.  European Aspects, Series C, studies
on politics, no. 5.  Leiden, Netherlands:  A.W. Sijthoff, 1961.
124 p.

> A discussion of the advantages of the d'Hondt system of
> proportional representation meant to ensure better repre-
> sentation of the many political parties in Europe.

619  Cocks, Sir Barnett.  THE EUROPEAN PARLIAMENT:  STRUCTURE,
PROCEDURE AND PRACTICE.  London:  Her Majesty's Stationery
Office, 1973.  336 p.

620  College of Europe.  ELECTIONS IN THE COUNTRIES OF THE EU-
ROPEAN COMMUNITIES AND IN THE UNITED KINGDOM.  Ca-
hiers de Bruges.  Bruges, Belgium: 1967.  406 p.

> A comparative study of the electoral results in the six
> founding members of the EC and in the U.K. from 1957
> to 1959.

621  European Movement [Britain].  DIRECT ELECTIONS TO THE EURO-
PEAN PARLIAMENT:  REPORT OF AN ALLPARTY STUDY GROUP
COMMISSIONED BY THE EUROPEAN MOVEMENT.  Rapporteur,
Ben Patterson.  London: Furnival Press, 1974.  83 p.

> A study by a working party from a broad political spec-
> trum of alternative systems under which direct elections
> might be conducted including systems of voting, consti-
> tuency sizes, and the problem of dual mandates.

622  European Parliament.  ELECTIONS TO THE EUROPEAN PARLIA-
MENT BY DIRECT UNIVERSAL SUFFRAGE:  SPECIAL ISSUE BASED
ON PATIJN REPORT.  Working Document 368/74.  Strasbourg,
France: 1975.  63 p.

623  _____.  SYMPOSIUM ON EUROPEAN INTEGRATION AND THE

FUTURE OF PARLIAMENTS IN EUROPE. LUXEMBOURG, 1974.
Summary Report. Strasbourg, France: 1974. vii, 94 p.

624 European Parliament. ELECTIONS TO THE EUROPEAN PARLIA-
MENT BY DIRECT UNIVERSAL SUFFRAGE: SPECIAL ISSUE BASED
ON PATIJN REPORT. Working Document 368/74. Strasbourg,
France: 1975. 63 p.

Selections taken from the texts of government proposals,
policy proposals of member governments, party and leading figure commentary, policy statements of the various
European movements of the most important proposals and
initiatives on direct elections of the European Parliament.

625 _____. THE FIRST TEN YEARS, 1958-68. Strasbourg, France:
Directorate-General for Parliamentary Documentation and Information, 1968. 180 p.

An official and broad description of the European Parliament's role, activities, and achievements during its
first decade of operation.

626 Federal Trust for Education and Research. ELECTING THE EURO-
PEAN PARLIAMENT. London: 1972. 32 p.

627 _____. PARLIAMENTARY ASPECTS OF THE ENLARGED EURO-
PEAN COMMUNITIES. London: June 1972. 37 p.

628 Fitzmaurice, John. THE PARTY GROUPS IN THE EUROPEAN PAR-
LIAMENT. Farnborough, Engl.: Saxon House; Lexington, Mass.:
Lexington Books, 1975. xi, 228 p.

629 Forsyth, Murray. THE PARLIAMENT OF THE EUROPEAN COM-
MUNITIES. London: Political and Economic Planning, 1964. 119 p.

A discussion of the actual political role of the European
Parliament in the decision-making process through 1964
including the EC Commission-Parliament relationship,
the attendance of commissioners at committee meetings,
written and oral questions, and the annual report.

630 Frank, Elke, ed. LAWMAKERS IN A CHANGING WORLD. Englewood Cliffs, N.J.: Prentice-Hall, 1966. 186 p.

See especially the chapter by Lindberg: "The Role of
the European Parliament in an Emerging European Community."

631   Hogan, Willard N.   REPRESENTATIVE GOVERNMENT AND EURO-
PEAN INTEGRATION.   Lincoln:  University of Nebraska Press, 1967.
246 p.

A study of the issues involved in representation beyond
the nation state.  Assumes that transnational activities
are a significant development for the theory and practice of political representation.  Includes a study of the
European Parliament and an argument against direct elections.

632   Hovey, J. Allan, Jr.   THE SUPERPARLIAMENTS:  INTERPARLIA-
MENTARY CONSULTATION AND ATLANTIC COOPERATION.
New York: Frederick A. Praeger, 1966.  202 p.

An assessment of six Atlantic and European parliaments
and their actual and potential roles in public and parliamentary control, and their influence on the integration process.

633   Kerr, Henry Hampton, Jr.   "The European Parliament and European
Integration:  The Effects of Participation in an International Parliamentary Assembly."   Ph.D. dissertation, University of Michigan,
1970.

634   Kitzinger, Uwe W.   BRITAIN, EUROPE AND BEYOND:  ESSAYS
IN EUROPEAN POLITICS.   European Aspects, Series C, studies on
politics, no. 16.  Leiden, Netherlands:  A.W. Sijthoff, 1965.
222 p.

A study of the West European electoral systems most relevant to a future European electoral system and the development of a European polity.

635   Kjekshus, Helge.   "The Parties Against the States:  Prefederal Party
Alignments in the European Community."   Ph.D. dissertation, Syracuse University, 1966.

636   Lindsay, Kenneth.   EUROPEAN ASSEMBLIES:  THE EXPERIMENTAL
PERIOD 1949-59.  New York:  Frederick A. Praeger, 1960.  267 p.

A study of European international assemblies like the
Nordic Council and WEU, their functions, and the attitudes of national parliaments and parliamentarians toward these assemblies.

637   _____.   TOWARDS A EUROPEAN PARLIAMENT.  Strasbourg, France:
Secretariat of the Council of Europe, 1958.  166 p.

An analysis of the Council of Europe, especially of the

assembly, delegates, and delegations as well as issues and achievements of the Council. It includes a critical assessment of Britain's role toward both the Council and Europe.

638  Meynaud, Jean, and Sidjanski, Dusan. INTEREST GROUPS IN THE EEC. 2 vols. Montreal: Montreal University Press, 1969. 503 p.

639  Oudenhove, Guy van. THE POLITICAL PARTIES IN THE EURO-PEAN PARLIAMENT: THE FIRST TEN YEARS, SEPTEMBER 1952-SEPTEMBER 1962. Leiden, Netherlands: A.W. Sijthoff for the Council of Europe, 1965. 268 p.

A study of the politicization of the European Parliament through its political groupings, and an assessment of the effects of these groupings on integration.

640  Political and Economic Planning. DIRECT ELECTIONS AND THE EUROPEAN PARLIAMENT. Occasional Paper no. 10, 24 October 1960. London: 1960. 39 p.

An examination of the effects and implications for Europe of direct elections to the European Parliament. A critical assessment of the adopted draft convention included.

641  _____. THE PARLIAMENT OF THE EUROPEAN COMMUNITIES. Political and Economic Planning, vol. 30, no. 478, 9 March 1964. London: 1964. 119 p.

See no. 629.

642  Schwarz, John Erwin. "Power, Persuasion and the Influence of the European Parliament." Ph.D. dissertation, Indiana University, 1967.

## I. REGIONAL DEVELOPMENT

643  Allen, Kevin, and MacLennan, M.C. REGIONAL PROBLEMS AND POLICIES IN ITALY AND FRANCE. Beverly Hills, Calif.: Sage Publications, 1971. 368 p.

An outline and discussion of national regional policies since World War II and the relation of such policies to national development. This study also analyses regional development in the context of EEC policies for Italy, France, and Britain.

644    Barzanti, Sergio.  THE UNDERDEVELOPED AREAS WITHIN THE
       COMMON MARKET.  Princeton, N.J.:  Princeton University Press,
       1965.  437 p.

       A detailed and scholarly study of the underdeveloped
       areas in the European Community especially in France
       and Italy.  Analyzes the causes, problems and issues
       in underdevelopment and the institutions, both national
       and community-wide, dealing with underdevelopment.


645    Klaasen, L.H.  AREA REDEVELOPMENT POLICIES IN BRITAIN
       AND THE COUNTRIES OF THE COMMON MARKET.  Washington,
       D.C.:  U.S. Department of Commerce, and the Redevelopment As-
       sociation, 1965.


646    Lind, Harold, and Flockton, Christopher.  REGIONAL POLICY IN
       BRITAIN AND THE SIX:  THE PROBLEM OF DEVELOPMENT AREAS
       AND COMMUNITY REGIONAL POLICY.  European Series, no. 15.
       London:  published for PEP by Chatham House, 1970.  76 p.

       Two studies of regional economic policy in Britain and
       the European Community, and the implications for Brit-
       ish entry into the EC.


647    Robertson, B.C.  REGIONAL DEVELOPMENT IN THE EUROPEAN
       ECONOMIC COMMUNITY.  London:  George Allen and Unwin,
       1962.  95 p.

       Research on the principles basic to regional planning in
       general as well as schemes for southern Italy and south-
       west France.  Also discusses ways in which the EEC is
       concerned with regional development through readapta-
       tion and provisions of the ECSC.  Sums up achievements
       and indicates the future of regional policies in the EEC.


648    Robinson, E.A.G., ed.  BACKWARD AREAS IN ADVANCED COUN-
       TRIES.  New York:  St. Martin's Press, 1969.  474 p.

       Proceedings of the International Economic Association at
       Varenna in 1967.  Covers the theoretical background
       and links between location theory and regional develop-
       ment in the U.K., the United States, Wallonia, Frei-
       bourg, Switzerland, West Germany, Italy, and Sweden.


649    Sant, Morgan, ed.  REGIONAL POLICY AND PLANNING FOR
       EUROPE.  Farnborough, Engl.:  Saxon House; Lexington, Mass.:
       Lexington Books, 1974.  xix, 268 p.

## J. SOCIAL POLICY—TRADE UNIONS AND LABOR

650    Balfour, Campbell.  INDUSTRIAL RELATIONS IN THE COMMON
       MARKET.  London:  Routledge and Kegan Paul, 1972.  130 p.

       A study of the industrial relations of the EC and Nor-
       way, including the economic and political background.
       Primarily an introduction to the literature.

651    Beever, R. Colin.  EUROPEAN UNITY AND THE TRADE UNION
       MOVEMENT.  Leiden, Netherlands: A.W. Sijthoff, 1960.  297 p.

       A comprehensive analysis of the role of trade unions in
       European integration, establishing the reasons for their
       consistent support of integration (the communist unions
       excepted) and showing the effects of integration on
       trade unions, and vice versa.

652    _____.  TRADE UNIONS AND FREE LABOR MOVEMENT IN THE
       EEC.  London:  published for PEP by Chatham House, 1969.  50 p.

       An examination of a particular aspect of the EC's social
       policy, the free movement of labor as well as a study
       of trade union organization and representation to the EC,
       the effect of trade unions on the EC, and the EC's ef-
       fect on trade unions.

653    _____.  TRADE UNIONS AND THE COMMON MARKET.  Oc-
       casional Paper no. 461.  London:  Political and Economic Planning,
       1962.

       An analysis of the particular provisions for the labor
       movement entailed in the Rome Treaty.  Also considers,
       specifically, the implications for Britain.

654    Boehning, W.R.  THE MIGRATION OF WORKERS IN THE UNITED
       KINGDOM AND THE EUROPEAN COMMUNITY.  London:  Oxford
       University Press, 1972.  167 p.

       Reviews the historical development of the free movement
       of labor, its present status, and EEC policies.  In addi-
       tion, the British and Swiss policies towards migrant la-
       borers, including topical issues of labor movement, dis-
       cussed.

655    Bouscaren, Anthony Trawick.  EUROPEAN ECONOMIC COMMU-
       NITY MIGRATIONS.  The Hague: Martinus Nijhoff, 1969.  155 p.

       A review of the movement of labor within the EC, and
       the problems and implications of labor migrations.  Con-

siders each member of the EC as well as EC policy in general including the appropriate sections of the Rome Treaty.

656 Bouvard, Marguerite Galembert. "The Labor Movement and the European Communities." Ph.D. dissertation, Harvard University, 1965.

657 _____. LABOR MOVEMENTS IN THE COMMON MARKET COUN- TRIES: THE GROWTH OF A EUROPEAN PRESSURE GROUP. New York: Praeger Publishers, 1972. xxx, 272 p.

A thorough effort to describe the relations between la- bor unions in the several countries and the institutions of the EEC showing how the creation of new institu- tions above nation-states has led labor to carry demands and pressure to a supranational level with essentially negative results.

658 Castles, Stephen, and Kosack, Godula. IMMIGRANT WORKERS AND CLASS STRUCTURE IN WESTERN EUROPE. New York: Ox- ford University Press, 1972. 514 p.

The most comprehensive published survey of data on im- migrants in West Europe including an analysis of their wages and the impact on economic growth and political stability.

659 Collins, Doreen. THE EUROPEAN COMMUNITIES: THE SOCIAL POLICY OF THE FIRST PHASE. Vol. 2: THE EUROPEAN ECO- NOMIC COMMUNITY 1958-72. London: Martin Robertson, 1975. 286 p.

The first part of the work focuses upon the application of the treaty to employment, wages and working condi- tions, population movements, and social services. The second part addresses the development of a common so- cial policy.

660 European Community. Press and Information Service. THE COM- MON MARKET AND THE COMMON GOOD: SOCIAL POLICY AND WORKING AND LIVING CONDITIONS IN THE EUROPEAN COMMUNITY. [5th ed.]. Brussels: [1976]. 33 p.

661 Fitzgerald, Mark J. THE COMMON MARKET'S LABOR PROGRAMS. Notre Dame, Ind.: University of Notre Dame Press, 1966. 256 p.

An analysis of the significant internal changes of the

member countries of the EC resulting from EC labor policy. Also discusses the social conditions of laborers,
labor programs, and industrial relations.

662 Fogarty, Michael P. WORK AND INDUSTRIAL RELATIONS IN
THE EUROPEAN COMMUNITY. London: published for PEP by
Chatham House, 1975. 43 p.

A review of the European Community's social policy.

663 Gorz, Andre. STRATEGY FOR LABOR: A RADICAL PROPOSAL.
Boston: Beacon Press, 1967. 199 p.

An attempt to show that the EC's type of welfare capitalism cannot cope with the problems of the disadvan-
taged because it can never produce real economic planning. Suggests a strategy for unions to regain a hand
in the major changes affecting advanced industrial societies.

664 Industrial Research and Information Service. TRADE UNIONS AND
THE E.E.C. London: published for the Industrial Research and Information Service by Iris Publications, 1973. 35 p.

A political tract showing how and why the British labor
movement is wrong to oppose the EEC, and why the EEC
is in the best interest of both worker and trade union.

665 International Confederation of Free Trade Unions. EUROPEAN RE-
GIONAL ORGANIZATION: EUROPEAN UNIFICATION AND
VARIOUS STATEMENTS REGARDING THE FREE TRADE UNIONS
IN THE WEST EUROPEAN COUNTRIES. A summarized report of
the European Trade Union School held at Egmont-on-Sea, Nether-
lands, at the Trade Union Training Center of the National Free
Trade Organization of the Netherlands, September 1954. Brussels:
European Regional Secretariat, ICFTU, 1955. 157 p.

666 Jacobs, Eric. EUROPEAN TRADE UNIONISM. London: Croom,
Helm, 1973. 180 p.

A clear and informative account of European trade unions,
their strength, organization, and personalities including
a discussion of the way in which they see their role and
the future in Europe.

667 Kindleberger, Charles P. EUROPE'S POSTWAR GROWTH: THE
ROLE OF LABOR SUPPLY. Cambridge, Mass.: Harvard University
Press, 1967. 252 p.

A discussion of the importance of labor supply, rather
than demand, in postwar European economic growth.

Asserts that the large-scale migration from Southern Europe to Western European countries has contributed greatly to establishing a single, cohesive labor market.

668 Klaasen, L.H., and Drewe, P. MIGRATION POLICY IN EUROPE: A COMPARATIVE STUDY. Farnborough, Engl.: D.C. Heath, 1973. 134 p.

An in-depth analysis of the social and economic factors determining interregional labor mobility including the migration policies of France, Britain, the Netherlands, and Sweden, and the consistency of migration policies in comparison to other sector policies, such as housing and regional development.

669 Lawson, Roger, and Reed, Bruce. SOCIAL SECURITY IN THE EUROPEAN COMMUNITY. London: published for PEP by Chatham House, 1975. 70 p.

"An examination of Britain's social security and medical care policies and how they compare to social provisions in other EC member states."

EUROPEAN COMMUNITY

670 Lorwin, Val R. LABOR AND WORKING CONDITIONS IN EUROPE. New York: Macmillan Co., 1967. 160 p.

A broad view of labor in Europe presented in nine articles by leading authorities from Europe. Examines the changing role of labor in European society, conditions of work, and attitudes of labor.

671 Marx, Eli, and Kendall, Walter. UNIONS IN EUROPE: A GUIDE TO ORGANIZED LABOR IN THE SIX. Brighton, Engl.: University of Sussex, Centre for Contemporary European Studies, 1971. 47 p.

A useful short guide to trade unionism in the Common Market.

672 Neirinck, J.D. SOCIAL POLICY OF THE EEC COMMISSION: A GENERAL SURVEY, ACHIEVEMENTS AND TRENDS AT THE END OF 1967. Louvain, Belgium: University of Louvain School of Law, Seminar for Labor Relations, 1967.

673 Rose,. Arnold N. MIGRANTS IN EUROPE: PROBLEMS OF ACCEPTANCE AND ADJUSTMENT. Minneapolis: University of Minnesota Press, 1969. 194 p.

A study of European integration at the "people" level,

cross-national migration of workers, and their subsequent acceptance as a condition of European unity.

674 Stearns, Peter N. EUROPEAN SOCIETY IN UPHEAVAL: SOCIAL HISTORY SINCE 1800. New York: Macmillan Co., 1967. 400 p.

An exploration of aspects common to and affecting the European social structure: the social impact of industrialization, economic development, religion, class structures, social protest, and welfarism.

675 Stewart, Margaret. EMPLOYMENT CONDITIONS IN EUROPE. Essex, Engl.: Gower Press, 1972. 206 p.

A comparative survey of remuneration, allowances, fringe benefits, personal income tax, living costs and conditions, and educational resources in the EC (plus Norway). The EEC Commission's responsibilities in regard to labor and social policies included.

676 TOWARDS A EUROPEAN MODEL OF DEVELOPMENT: REPORTS FROM THE CONFERENCE ON INDUSTRY AND SOCIETY IN THE EUROPEAN COMMUNITY. Brussels: European Bookshop, 1973. 819 p.

Included are twenty-eight reports by trade union, industrial, and independent experts on the major needs and social forces in Europe. Covers three major areas: industrial development and the reduction of regional disparity, collective needs and the equality of life, and the EC and the world.

## K. TECHNOLOGY

677 Armand, Louis, and Drancourt, Michel. THE EUROPEAN CHALLENGE: A DETAILED BLUEPRINT ON HOW EUROPE CAN USE THE TOOLS OF THE NEW TECHNOLOGY TO KEEP PACE WITH THE 1970'S. Translated by P. Evans. London: George Weidenfeld and Nicolson, 1970. 256 p.

A political exhortation to modernize, via the federal approach, the building of a united Europe.

678 Federal Trust for Education and Research. EUROPEAN TECHNOLOGICAL COOPERATION: REPORT OF A TWO-DAY CONFERENCE, 16-17 SEPTEMBER 1969. London: 1970. 125 p.

Ten essays on functional integration, its import for Europe, and the organizations fostering the cooperation, such as CERN in nuclear energy, and ESRO in space research.

679 Foch, Rene. EUROPE AND TECHNOLOGY: A POLITICAL VIEW. Atlantic Papers, no. 2. Paris: Atlantic Institute, 1970. 55 p.

680 Layton, Christopher. EUROPEAN ADVANCED TECHNOLOGY: A PROGRAM FOR INTEGRATION. London: George Allen and Unwin, 1969. 290 p.

> A study of the American leadership in science and technology, and the attempts of European countries to counter it. Also describes ways in which Europe can develop a common science and technology policy.

681 Meyer, Sir Anthony. A EUROPEAN TECHNOLOGICAL COMMUNITY. London: Conservative Political Centre, 1966. 23 p.

682 Moonman, Eric, ed. SCIENCE AND TECHNOLOGY IN EUROPE. Harmondsworth, Engl.: Penguin Books, 1969. 176 p.

683 Reed, Laurance. EUROPE IN A SHRINKING WORLD: A TECHNOLOGICAL PERSPECTIVE. London: Oldbourne Press, 1967. 208 p.

> Discusses the political implications of postwar economic trends and problems and the relevance of a united Europe for their resolution.

684 Williams, Roger. EUROPEAN TECHNOLOGY: THE POLITICS OF COLLABORATION. London: Croom, Helm, 1973. x, 214 p.

> An analysis of the possibilities of technological cooperation and how it has been thwarted by political and administrative problems. Further, suggests how the technology gap between the United States and Europe may be bridged.

## L. TRANSPORT

685 Bayliss, Bryan T. EUROPEAN TRANSPORT. London: Kenneth Mason Publications, 1965. 205 p.

> A wide-ranging discussion of the importance of transport and a common transport policy to customs unions generally and to the EEC specifically.

686 Beran, Kurt. "The Impact of the European Communities' Common Transport Policy and the National Transport Policies of the Member Nations." Ph.D. dissertation, University of Oregon, 1974.

687 Costello, John, and Hughes, Terry. THE BATTLE FOR CONCORDE. Salisbury, Engl.: Compton Press, 1971. 158 p.

> A case study of French-British cooperation in aerospace covering the period of time immediately after de Gaulle's second veto of British entry into the EC.

688 Despicht, Nigel. POLICIES FOR TRANSPORT IN THE COMMON MARKET. Sidcup, Engl.: Lambarde Press, 1964. xii, 308 p.

689 _____. THE TRANSPORT POLICY OF THE EUROPEAN COMMU- NITIES. European Series, no. 12. London: published for PEP by Chatham House, 1969. 85 p.

> A monograph detailing one of the three "common poli- cies" of the EC, transportation. A brief description of the transport systems of the six EC founding members is given, followed by a discussion of the mandate and legis- lation of the EC as well as an assessment of the successes and failures of integration in the transportation area.

690 Trench, Sylvia. TRANSPORT IN THE COMMON MARKET. PEP Pamphlets, vol. 29, no. 473. London: Political and Economic Planning, 1963. 284 p.

691 Verploeg, Elias Alexander Gijsbertus. THE ROAD TOWARDS A EU- ROPEAN COMMON AIR MARKET: CIVIL AVIATION AND EURO- PEAN INTEGRATION. The Hague: Martinus Nijhoff, 1963. 260 p.

# Chapter 4

# EUROPEAN COMMUNITIES

# AND MEMBER-STATE RELATIONS

## A. GENERAL

692    Bodenheimer, Susanne J.   POLITICAL UNION:  A MICROCOSM
OF EUROPEAN POLITICS, 1960-66.  Leiden, Netherlands: A.W.
Sijthoff, 1967.  229 p.

A study of the efforts among the EC's six founding members to extend their collective decision making into foreign and military policy questions.  Centers on the Fouchet negotiations.  Also argues against the notion that
economic integration and political strategy are synony-
mous--that different strategies must be employed.

693    Brinkhorst, L.J.  LOCAL AUTHORITIES AND THE COMMON
MARKET:  AN ANALYSIS OF THE TREATIES OF PARIS AND
ROME.  The Hague:  published for the International Union of
Local Authorities by Martinus Nijhoff, 1966.  68 p.

A study of the most important provisions of the Treaties
of Paris and Rome concerning local government and the
ways in which the three European Communities affect
local government tasks and activities within the member countries.

694    Helms, Andrea Rose Carroll.  "Nation-Building in the European
Community:  Regional Post-National Political Development in Western Europe."  Ph.D. dissertation, University of Connecticut, 1969.

695    Holt, Stephen.  SIX EUROPEAN STATES:  THE COUNTRIES OF
THE EUROPEAN COMMUNITY AND THEIR POLITICAL SYSTEMS.
New York:  Taplinger Publishing Co., 1970.  414 p.

A reference for teachers and students of the six European
political systems of the EC.  The systems treated compara-
tively by institutions and functions, for instance, parties,
interest groups, and parliaments.

696  Layton, Christopher. CROSS-FRONTIER MERGERS IN EUROPE: HOW CAN GOVERNMENTS HELP? Bath, Engl.: Bath University Press, 1971. 107 p.

697  Puissochet, Jean-Pierre. THE ENLARGEMENT OF THE EUROPEAN COMMUNITIES: A COMMENTARY ON THE ACCESSION OF DEN-MARK, IRELAND AND THE UNITED KINGDOM. European Aspects, Law Series, no. 15. Leiden, Netherlands: A.W. Sijthoff, 1975. 480 p.

A comprehensive treatment of the accession of Denmark, Ireland, and the United Kingdom including the broader implications of enlargement, the main features of the instruments of accession, and commentary on the ancil-lary documents.

698  Rhoades, Don Bentley. "European Integration: A View From the Nation-States." Ph.D. dissertation, University of Nebraska, Lincoln, 1972.

699  Wallace, Helen. NATIONAL GOVERNMENTS AND THE EURO-PEAN COMMUNITIES. London: published for PEP by Chatham House, 1973. 103 p.

A study of the patterns of national administrative in-puts into the community process and the effects of that involvement on the national institutions of the original six states and also on the British government.

## B. BENELUX

700  Belgian Government Information Center, New York. BELGIUM AND CURRENT WORLD PROBLEMS. New York: 1953. 63 p.

Speeches by the Foreign Minister and by the Belgian Ambassador to the UN regarding Belgium's position on European integration, especially regarding a European army.

701  Bliss, Howard. "A Process of Federalism: Belgium's participation in the European Community." Ph.D. dissertation, Cornell University, 1967.

702  Meade, James E. NEGOTIATIONS FOR BENELUX: AN ANNO-TATED CHRONICLE 1943-56. Princeton, N.J.: Princeton University Press, 1957. 89 p.

A catalog of the negotiations among the Belgians, Dutch,

and Luxembourgers between 1943 and 1956 showing the problems and processes involved in building a full economic union.

703 Nederlandsh Gennotschap vor Internationale Zaken. EUROPEAN AND ATLANTIC COOPERATION: THE DUTCH ATTITUDE. The Hague: 1965. 259 p.

A volume of articles on European and Atlantic cooperation from the Dutch perspective: Luns on NATO, Beugel on "The U.S. and European Unity," Beyen on federal and supranational modes of cooperation, and Brugmans on de Gaulle.

704 Sexter, Dorothy Achenbaum. "The Belgian Coal Mines in the European Coal and Steel Community." Ph.D. dissertation, University of California, Davis, 1969.

705 Smith, Keith Allen. "Socialization and Multiple Loyalties: The Experience of the Dutch and European Communities." Ph. D. dissertation, Fletcher School of Law and Diplomacy, 1972.

706 Urbscheit, Peter W. "The Dutch-German Borderland Geography and Interaction: A Case Study Within the Framework of West European Integration." Ph.D. dissertation, University of Waterloo, Canada, 1973.

707 Weil, Gordon L[ee]. THE BENELUX NATIONS: THE POLITICS OF SMALL-COUNTRY DEMOCRACIES. New York: Holt, Rinehart and Winston, 1970. 260 p.

Investigates how the BENELUX countries have developed a variety of mechanisms for dealing with the problems of the individual and his culture. Also examines the policies of small nations in international relations and with regard to the European integration movement specifically.

## C. BRITAIN

## 1. General

708 Arnold, David J. BRITAIN, EUROPE AND THE WORLD, 1870-1955. London: Edward Arnold, 1966. 408 p.

709 Barclay, G. St. J. COMMONWEALTH OR EUROPE? St. Lucia,

Australia: University of Queensland Press, 1970. 210 p.

A description and interpretation of official British attitudes towards West European integration since World
War II and the reactions of other Commonwealth governments to Britain's changing views.

710    Barker, Elisabeth. BRITAIN IN A DIVIDED EUROPE, 1945-70.
London: George Weidenfeld and Nicolson, 1971. 316 p.

A history and description of Britain's attitudes toward
Europe and her participation in European activities between 1945 and 1970.

711    Bell, Coral, ed. EUROPE WITHOUT BRITAIN: SIX STUDIES OF
BRITAIN'S APPLICATION TO JOIN THE COMMON MARKET AND
ITS BREAKDOWN. Melbourne: published for the Australian Insti-
tute of International Affairs by F.W. Cheshire, 1963. 120 p.

"The consequences of the collapse of negotiations in
January 1963 in Brussels, seen from the Australian
point of view. The six studies insist more on the dip-
lomatic and political aspects than on the economic
ones."

UNIVERSAL REFERENCE SYSTEM

712    Bellini, James. BRITISH ENTRY: LABOUR'S NEMESIS. Young
Fabian Pamphlet, no. 30. London: Fabian Society, 1972. 25 p.

713    Beloff, Max. THE FUTURE OF BRITISH FOREIGN POLICY. New
York: Taplinger Publishing Co., 1969. 154 p.

An examination of the changing nature of British foreign policy including Britain's relationship with the
United States and with a federated Europe.

714    _____. NEW DIMENSIONS IN FOREIGN POLICY: A STUDY
IN BRITISH ADMINISTRATIVE EXPERIENCE, 1947-59. London:
George Allen and Unwin, 1961. 208 p.

A study of the impact of the EC on Britain's national
administration.

715    Beloff, Nora. THE GENERAL SAYS NO: BRITAIN'S EXCLUSION
FROM EUROPE. Baltimore: Penguin Books, 1963. 181 p.

A detailed discussion of the negotiations in Brussels between the original six members of the EC six and Britain
over the British entry attempt in 1963, the issues and the
rejection. The thrust: Britain must accept the principle

of entry first and argue details later, or she will never get into the EC.

716    Bilgrami, Ashgar H.   BRITAIN, THE COMMONWEALTH AND THE EUROPEAN UNION ISSUE.  Ambilly-Annemasse, France:  Imprimerie "Les Presses de Savoie," 1961.  147 p.

An Indian's view of the British approach to European union as shaped by the Commonwealth influences.  A summary of each Commonwealth country's view of Britain in the EC and an argument for a reconciliation of interests between the Commonwealth and the EEC are included.

717    Boyd, Laslo Victor.  "The Anglo-American Special Relationship and British-European Integration, 1958-70."  Ph.D. dissertation, University of Pennsylvania, 1971.

718    Branston, Ursala.  BRITAIN AND EUROPEAN UNITY.  London: Conservative Political Center, 1953.  52 p.

719    British Council of Churches.  CHRISTIANS AND THE COMMON MARKET.  London:  published for the British Council of Churches and the Conference of British Missionary Societies by SCM Press, 1967.  135 p.

720    Bromley, J.S., and Kossmann, E.H., eds.  BRITAIN AND THE NETHERLANDS IN EUROPE AND ASIA.  New York: St. Martin's Press, 1968.  264 p.

See especially the chapter by A. Davies, "England and Europe 1815-1914," which is an explanation of the inconsistencies of Britain's attitude towards Europe in the nineteenth century which makes understanding of Britain's twentieth-century attitude more comprehensible.

721    Brown, Michael Barratt, and Hughes, John.  BRITAIN'S CRISIS AND THE COMMON MARKET.  London:  1961.

722    Calleo, David P.  BRITAIN'S FUTURE.  New York:  Horizon Press, 1968.  252 p.

A look at the viable alternatives for Britain's future from economic, political, military, and cultural perspectives including ties with the Commonwealth, with Europe, and the United States.

723    Camps, Miriam.  BRITAIN AND THE EUROPEAN COMMUNITY,

1955–63. Princeton, N.J.: Princeton University Press, 1964.
547 p.

A review of the British search for accommodation with
the EEC, the EEC background, and a report on the
negotiations.

724 _____. DIVISION IN EUROPE. Princeton, N.J.: Center of
International Studies, Woodrow Wilson School of Public and International Affairs, Princeton University, 1960. 61 p.

A historical account of the negotiations on European
unity until 1958, the problems in the negotiations,
and problems of future negotiations between Europe
and Britain.

725 _____. FOUR APPROACHES TO THE EUROPEAN PROBLEM.
Occasional Paper, no. 12. London: Political and Economic
Planning, 1961. 26 p.

An analysis of alternative British approaches to Europe:
does not join EC, joins the EC, integrates into an Atlantic Community, or tries the global or GATT approach.

726 Churchill, Winston S. EUROPE UNITE: SPEECHES 1947 AND
1948. Edited by Randolph Churchill. Boston: Houghton Mifflin
Co., 1950. 506 p.

Fifty-two speeches given by Sir Winston Churchill,
several which specifically detail his thinking and policies (as well as Britain's) towards Europe, its institutions, and Britain's role in relation to them.

727 Clark, Colin. BRITISH TRADE IN THE COMMON MARKET. London: Stevens and Sons, 1962. 149 p.

Not only a discussion of Britain joining the EEC, but
also an excellent description of the EC functions regarding: tariffs, quotas, overseas associates, cartels,
and monetary and social policy.

728 _____. THE COMMON MARKET AND BRITISH TRADE. New
York: Frederick A. Praeger, 1962. 149 p.

The American title for no. 727.

729 Confederation of British Industry. BRITAIN IN EUROPE. London:
1970. 72 p.

A second appraisal of Europe and the economic and

political implications of British membership in the Common Market.

730     Coombes, David, et al. WESTMINSTER TO BRUSSELS: THE SIGNIFICANCE FOR PARLIAMENT OF ACCESSION TO THE EUROPEAN COMMUNITY. PEP Broadsheet, no. 540. London: published for the Hansard Society and the Study of Parliament Group by PEP, 1973. iii, 28 p.

731     Davidson, Ian. BRITAIN AND THE MAKING OF EUROPE. London: Macdonald and Co., 1971. 150 p.

A descriptive account of the European Community relating especially to the attempts by Britain to join the EC, and to de Gaulle's reactions.

732     De la Mahotiere, Stuart. TOWARDS ONE EUROPE. Baltimore: Penguin Books, 1970. 331 p.

A chronology of European integration with emphasis on the political aspects of British entry into the EEC, including the original refusal by Britain to enter and the later application to join the EEC. Also monetary cooperation, industry, technology, transport policy, and the future of NATO discussed.

733     Downs, Charles Lowell. "Britain and the Council of Europe." Ph.D. dissertation, University of Georgia, 1969.

734     Economist Intelligence Unit. BRITAIN AND EUROPE: A STUDY OF THE EFFECTS ON BRITISH MANUFACTURING INDUSTRY OF A FREE TRADE AREA AND THE COMMON MARKET. London: 1957. 228 p.

An assessment of EFTA from the perspective of the British economy if the proposed EEC comes into being. Finds that Britain will be forced to join one or the other organization, preferably EFTA, but cannot remain outside both.

735     _____. BRITAIN, THE COMMONWEALTH AND EUROPEAN FREE TRADE. London: 1958. 40 p.

736     Economist Newspaper Ltd. BRITAIN INTO EUROPE. Edited by Andrew Knight. London: 1971. 49 p.

From eleven briefs published in the ECONOMIST between 24 April and 3 July 1971 assessing British entry into the EC.

737     European Economic Community. Commission. REPORT TO THE EUROPEAN PARLIAMENT ON THE STATE OF THE NEGOTIA- TIONS WITH THE UNITED KINGDOM. Brussels: 1963. 112 p.

> A statement by the commission of the results obtained, problems outstanding, and the official opinion of the commission concerning British entry into the European Community.

738     Evans, Douglas, ed. BRITAIN IN THE EEC. London: Victor Gollancz, 1973. 208 p.

> A postaccession view of Britain in the EC contained in ten articles, including industrial effects, regional pol- icy effects, the United States and Britain, and security of Western Europe.

739     Fimmen, Edo. LABOUR'S ALTERNATIVE: THE UNITED STATES OF EUROPE OR EUROPE LTD.? London: Labour Publishing Co., 1924.

740     Frank, Sir Oliver. BRITAIN AND THE TIDE OF WORLD AFFAIRS. London: Oxford University Press, 1955. 71 p.

> A history of British policy towards Europe as well as broader British interests are discussed.

741     Geographical Association [London]. BRITAIN AND THE COM- MON MARKET: TWO PAPERS DELIVERED AT THE ANNUAL CONFERENCE, 1963. London: April 1963.

> See especially Fisher's paper: "The Changing Signifi- cance of the Commonwealth in the Political Geogra- phy of Great Britain."

742     Gishford, Anthony, and Caudery, Victory, eds. FANFARE FOR EUROPE. Introduction by Edward Heath. London: published for Fanfare for Europe by Arrow Books, 1972. 170 p.

> Addresses, essays, and lectures on Britain's entry into "Europe" under the official theme: "Fanfare for Eu- rope."

743     Han, S.S., and Leisner, H.H. BRITAIN AND THE COMMON MARKET: THE EFFECT OF ENTRY ON THE PATTERN OF MANU- FACTURING PRODUCTION. New York: Cambridge University Press, 1971. 116 p.

> An economic assessment of the net effect on home man- ufacturing which entry will have for Britain, and, con-

versely, how British entry into the EC will affect patterns and production there.

744    Headley, Anne Renouf. "National Interests and Supranational Delegation: Discontinuities and Developments in Anglo-French West European Treaty Systems During the 1920's." Ph.D. dissertation, Yale University, 1966.

745    Hene, Derek H. DECISION ON EUROPE: AN EXPLANATION OF THE COMMON MARKET. London: Jordan and Sons, 1970. 239 p.

   Written for the general reader. An assessment of the implications for Britain of joining the EC.

746    _____. WHAT THE COMMON MARKET REALLY MEANS. London: Jordan and Sons, 1967. 198 p.

   A description and discussion for the general reader detailing the EC and its various organs and activities as well as the question of its importance to Britain and the question of British entry.

747    Holt, Stephen. THE COMMON MARKET: THE CONFLICT OF THEORY AND PRACTICE. London: Thomas Nelson and Sons, 1967. 207 p.

   A description of the Common Market, its origins, development, and operations. An explanation of the framework within which Britain's foreign business competitors operate, and the extent to which they are affected by the EEC also included.

748    Horn, David Bayne. GREAT BRITAIN AND EUROPE IN THE EIGHTEENTH CENTURY. Oxford: Clarendon Press, 1967. xi, 411 p.

   A treatment of Britain's eighteenth-century relations with Europe on a country-by-country basis in order to show the length and variety of cross-national issues which are yet today important in the context of Britain's accession to the EC.

749    Hugo, Grant. BRITAIN IN TOMORROW'S WORLD: PRINCIPLES OF FOREIGN POLICY. London: Chatto and Windus, 1969. 256 p.

   Outlines the choices open to Britain in the field of foreign policy, especially towards Europe.

750     Huizinga, Jakob Herman. CONFESSIONS OF A EUROPEAN IN
ENGLAND. London: Heineman Group, 1958. 296 p.


751     Johnson, Maurice Glen. "British Political Parties and the Unification of Europe." Ph.D. dissertation, University of North Caro-
lina, Chapel Hill, 1966.


752     Johnstone, Kenneth. BRITAIN AND THE COMMON MARKET:
A CHRISTIAN VIEW. London: British Council of Churches, 1971.
24 p.


753     Kitzinger, Uwe W. THE CAMPAIGN FOR EUROPE. London:
Oxford University Press, 1973.


754     _____. DIPLOMACY AND PERSUASION: HOW BRITAIN JOINED
THE COMMON MARKET. London: Thames and Hudson, 1973.
433 p.

> A description of the events preceding and culminating
> in British accession, from both the British perspective
> and the EC viewpoint.


755     _____. THE SECOND TRY: LABOUR AND THE EEC. Oxford:
Pergamon Press, 1968. 353 p.

> Selected documents relating to Britain's second bid to
> enter the Common Market. Includes speeches of the
> prime minister, British Parliamentary addresses, and
> journalistic accounts as well as the positions of the
> political parties, the trade unions, and the public.


756     Lambert, John. BRITAIN IN A FEDERAL EUROPE. London:
Chatto and Windus, 1968. 208 p.

> Written for the nonexpert. A description of the Euro-
> pean Community, de Gaulle's struggle to stem federal-
> ism, and the issues of British entry into the EC.


757     Lamfalussy, A. THE UNITED KINGDOM AND THE SIX: AN
ESSAY ON ECONOMIC GROWTH IN WESTERN EUROPE. London: Macmillan and Co., 1963. 147 p.

> An analysis of the causes of economic growth in the
> six and the development of the Common Market to de-
> termine if British entry will benefit Britain.


758     Lerner, Daniel. AS BRITAIN FACES THE CONTINENT: HOW
ITS LEADERS WEIGH THEIR CHOICES. Cambridge, Mass.: M.I.T.
Center for International Studies, 1962.

759     Lieber, Robert J[ames]. BRITISH POLITICS AND EUROPEAN UNITY: PARTIES, ELITES, AND PRESSURE GROUPS. Berkeley and Los Angeles: University of California Press, 1970. 317 p.

> A comprehensive account of the role of pressure groups and parties in forming British policy towards European unity, especially towards EFTA and the EEC.

760     _____ . "British Politics and European Unity: Parties, Elites and Pressure Groups." Ph.D. dissertation, Harvard University, 1968.

761     Macmillan, Harold. RIDING THE STORM: 1956-59. New York: Harper and Row, 1971. 786 p.

> The memoirs of Harold Macmillan, former British prime minister, which cover, in part, the initial British negotiations with the EEC. A useful perspective on Britain's role and the way in which government policy toward the EEC evolved.

762     Mally, Gerhard. BRITAIN AND EUROPEAN UNITY. London: Hansard, 1966. 156 ,p.

763     May, John. BRITAIN IN EUROPE. Birmingham, Engl.: Clearway Publishing Co., 1973. 64 p.

> Written especially for young people.

764     Meade, James E. UNITED KINGDOM, COMMONWEALTH AND COMMON MARKET: A REAPPRAISAL. London: Institute of Economic Affairs, 1970. 72 p.

> A discussion of British entry, the conditions Britain must demand from the EEC, and the likely effects of membership on the Commonwealth, on the balance of payments, on farmers, and on EFTA.

765     Meerhaeghe, M.A.G. van, ed. ECONOMICS: BRITAIN AND THE EEC. By Harry Johnson et al. London: Longmans, Green and Co., 1969. 104 p.

> A collection of papers from a symposium at the University of Ghent in 1969 focusing on problems of British entry: economic, financial and monetary, and technological.

766     Moncrieff, Anthony, ed. BRITAIN AND THE COMMON MARKET, 1967: SEVEN B.B.C. BROADCASTS EDITED AND PRO-

DUCED BY ANTHONY MONCRIEFF. Introduction by Uwe Kitzinger. London: B.B.C. Publications, 1967. viii, 154 p.

> A series of BBC broadcasts on the theme of Britain and
> the Common Market. Includes such topics as agricul-
> ture, the effect on sterling, economic prospects, and
> sovereignty.

767    Monte, H. THE UNITY OF EUROPE. London: 1943. 196 p.

768    Moran, Mary Charles. "A Study of the Developing Idea of European Integration and British Response in the Twentieth Century."
Ph.D. dissertation, St. John's University, 1957.

769    Moustafa, Ezz-El-Din-Ali. "British Participation in European Organizations, 1945-56." Ph.D. dissertation, University of Minnesota, 1957.

770    Palmer, Michael. THE NEGOTIATIONS ON POLITICAL UNION.
Planning, vol. 28, no. 465, 1 October 1962. London: Political
and Economic Planning, 1962.

771    Pfaltzgraff, Robert L[ouis]., Jr. THE BRITISH COMMON MAR-
KET DECISION AND BEYOND. Philadelphia: University of
Pennsylvania, Foreign Policy Research Institute, 1962. 52 p.

> Assesses the attitudes of British citizens both before
> and after Britain's first unsuccessful bid for member-
> ship in the EEC.

772    _____. "Great Britain and the European Economic Community:
A Study of the Development of British Support for Common Market
Membership Between 1956 and 1961." Ph.D. dissertation, Univer-
sity of Pennsylvania, 1964.

773    Pinder, John. BRITAIN AND THE COMMON MARKET. London:
Cresset Press, 1961. 134 p.

> A well-balanced picture, in broad strokes, of the ori-
> gins, development, and implications of the Common
> Market. Also seeks to answer the obvious questions
> a novice would ask about each important development
> in the Common Market. A readable, general intro-
> duction to the subject.

774    _____, ed. THE ECONOMICS OF EUROPE: WHAT THE COM-
MON MARKET MEANS FOR BRITAIN. London: published for

the Federal Trust by C. Knight, 1971. viii, 222 p.

> An assessment of the economic effects on the British
> resulting from membership in the European Community,
> the topics discussed include: trade, industry, agri-
> culture, and capital and taxation.

775    Pisani, Edgar, et al. PROBLEMS OF BRITISH ENTRY INTO THE
EEC: REPORTS TO THE ACTION COMMITTEE FOR THE UNITED
STATES OF EUROPE. London: published for PEP by Chatham
House, 1969. 108 p.

> Five analyses concerning the problems and solutions to
> Britain's entry into the EC in the monetary, agricul-
> tural, technological, and institutional fields.

776    Political and Economic Planning. DIVISION IN EUROPE. Occasional Paper no. 8. London: 1960. 66 p.

777    _____. WESTMINSTER TO BRUSSELS: THE SIGNIFICANCE FOR
PARLIAMENT OF ACCESSION TO THE EUROPEAN COMMUNITY.
London: published for the Study of Parliament Group, PEP, and
the Hansard Society, 1973. 28 p.

> A detailed examination of how the British Parliament
> might handle questions relating to the EC.

778    Political and Economic Planning. Institut de Science Economique
Appliquee. ASPECTS OF EUROPEAN INTEGRATION: AN ANGLO-
FRENCH SYMPOSIUM. London and Paris: 1962. 140 p.

> A collection of papers by Pierre Uri, Miriam Camps,
> and others concerning the negotiations and the prob-
> lems involved in Britain's joining the EEC, written
> by both French and British authors and commented up-
> on each by the other. Also included are the projected
> effects of British entry into the EEC on Associated Over-
> seas Territories, the Commonwealth, agricultural pol-
> icy, competition policy, and other topics.

779    THE POUND INTO EUROPE?: STERLING, THE CITY, AND
EEC ENTRY. By Raymond Barre et al. London: Banker Ltd.,
1971. 52 p.

780    Price, John Wilber. "British Attitudes Toward European Unity As
Reflected by the Participation of the United Kingdom in the Council of Europe." Ph.D. dissertation, University of Michigan, 1957.

781    Reader's Digest Association [London]. PRODUCTS AND PEOPLE. London: 1963.

> "Contains 54 talks comparing the material possessions and attitudes of the Community countries and the U.K."
>
> A GUIDE TO THE STUDY OF THE EUROPEAN COMMUNITY

782    Roth, Andrew. CAN PARLIAMENT DECIDE ABOUT EUROPE OR ABOUT ANYTHING? London: Macdonald and Co., 1974. 229 p.

> An essay on the decision by Prime Minister Heath to join Europe, how the British Parliament was used in the decision, its power and role in decision making, and the likely future of the institution.

783    Royal Institute of International Affairs, ed. IMPLICATIONS OF THE BRUSSELS BREAKDOWN. By Kenneth Younger et al. A Chatham House Memorandum. Oxford: Oxford University Press for the Royal Institute, 1963. 46 p.

> See especially the three lectures by Younger, Shonfield, and Beaton on the political, economic, and strategic implications of the failure of the Brussels negotiations between Britain and the EC. The fourth lecture, by Dorthy Pickles, concerns France's role in the breakdown.

784    Schroeder, Robert George. "Britain and the European Common Market." Ph.D. dissertation, University of California, Berkeley, 1959.

785    Scottish Conservative Central Office, ed. SCOTLAND AND EUROPE: SEVEN VIEWPOINTS. By Jock Bruce-Gardyne et al. Edinburgh: 1971. 45 p.

786    Shanks, Michael, and Lambert, John. BRITAIN AND THE NEW EUROPE: THE FUTURE OF THE COMMON MARKET. London: Chatto and Windus, 1962. 253 p.

> The British title for no. 787.

787    _____. THE COMMON MARKET TODAY AND TOMORROW. New York: Frederick A. Praeger, 1962. 253 p.

> An overview of the EC, its background, common policies, African relations, and the meaning of Britain's accession. Also published as BRITAIN AND THE NEW EUROPE, by Chatto and Windus, London. See no. 786.

788    Sisson, C.H.  THE SPIRIT OF BRITISH ADMINISTRATION AND
       SOME EUROPEAN COMPARISONS.  New York: Frederick A.
       Praeger, 1959.  162 p.

       A detailed study of British administration and adminis-
       trators, and a comparison of their training and compe-
       tence with their European counterparts in Germany,
       France, and Sweden.


789    Sohler, Katherine B.  "Britain's Position in Europe, 1848-1871."
       Ph.D. dissertation, Yale University, 1950.


790    Spanier, David.  EUROPE, OUR EUROPE.  London:  Martin Secker
       and Warburg, 1972.  194 p.

       A journalistic narrative of the negotiations in Brussels
       and the political maneuvering in London which cul-
       minated in the British accession to the Rome Treaty
       and to the EC.


791    Strange, Susan.  THE STERLING PROBLEM AND THE SIX.  Lon-
       don:  Political and Economic Planning, 1967.  70 p.


792    Sullivan, Nicholas J.  "Britain and the Union of Europe, 1919-
       39."  Ph.D. dissertation, Fordham University, 1954.


793    Swift, William J., ed.  GREAT BRITAIN AND THE COMMON
       MARKET, 1957-69.  New York: Facts on File, 1970.  430 p.

       A comprehensive chronology of events and a journalis-
       tic account of Britain's confrontation with the EEC.


794    Thomas, Hugh.  EUROPE: THE RADICAL CHALLENGE.  New
       York:  Harper and Row, 1973.  211 p.

       For the general audience.  A primer on the European
       Economic Community, its problems, institutions, exter-
       nal relations, and defense arrangements.  The social
       and economic policy of the Community also covered.
       All this is against the backdrop of Britain's decision
       to enter the EC, and the consequences to be expected.


795    Times Publishing Co.  [London].  BRITAIN AND EUROPE: THE
       FUTURE; A BRITISH AND GERMAN VIEW OF THE POLITICAL
       AND ECONOMIC PROSPECTS.  First Published in the TIMES in
       England and DIE WELT in Germany on 28 October 1966.  London:
       1967.  74 p.

796       . COMMON MARKET AND COMMONWEALTH: A NEW
SURVEY. London: 1962. 160 p.

> A monograph for the British public describing the in-
> stitutions, policies, and implications of accession.

797 Torelli, M. GREAT BRITAIN AND THE EUROPE OF THE SIX.
Montreal: Annals of the Centre d'Etudes et de Documentation
Europeen, 1969.

> A brief consideration of British Prime Minister Harold
> Wilson's Labour Government and its attitudes toward
> Europe.

798 Van Der Stoel, M. THE BRITISH APPLICATION FOR MEMBER-
SHIP OF THE EUROPEAN COMMUNITIES, 1963-68. Paris:
Western European Union, General Affairs Committee, 1968. 101 p.

799 Vital, David. THE MAKING OF BRITISH FOREIGN POLICY.
New York: Frederick A. Praeger, 1968. 132 p.

> Analyzes constitutional, political, institutional, and
> sociological influences on the determination of British
> foreign policy, and the problems facing foreign policy
> analysis, including the Common Market decision, EFTA,
> and the Commonwealth.

800 Watt, D.C., ed. DOCUMENTS ON INTERNATIONAL AFFAIRS
1962. London: Chatham House and the Royal Institute of International Affairs, 1962. 938 p.

> A selection of documents on international affairs in-
> cluding the European Communities. Two themes cov-
> ered in the European section: the negotiations con-
> cerning British accession from the British perspective;
> and the negotiations from the French perspective in-
> cluding the Fouchet drafts and de Gaulle's January
> 1963 press conference. A useful research tool.

801 Williams, Shirley. BRITAIN AND THE FREE TRADE AREA. Research Series 202. London: Fabian International Bureau, 1958.
33 p.

> A Socialist's perspective on Britain's plan to join a
> free trade area, what it might consist of, other coun-
> tries' perspectives on integration, and the special prob-
> lems for Britain in joining an FTA. The second part
> of a two-part analysis.

802       . THE COMMON MARKET AND ITS FORERUNNERS.

London:  Fabian International Bureau, 1958.  41 p.

> Part of a two-part Fabian analysis on an integrated
> Europe and Britain's participation.

803  Wood, G.E.  EUROPEAN MONETARY UNION AND THE U.K.:
A COST-BENEFIT ANALYSIS.  Guildford, Engl.:  University of
Surrey, 1973.  23 p.

804  Wrinch, Pamela N.  "Sir Winston Churchill on Britain's Role Towards Europe: Detachment and Combination."  Ph.D. dissertation,
Yale University, 1954.

## 2. Britain—Pro-Market

805  Beddington-Behrens, Edward.  IS THERE ANY CHOICE?  BRITAIN
MUST JOIN EUROPE.  Harmondsworth, Engl.:  Penguin Books,
1966.  141 p.

806  Beesley, M.E., and Hague, D.C., eds.  BRITAIN IN THE COM-
MON MARKET: A NEW BUSINESS OPPORTUNITY.  London:
Longman's Group, 1974.  xii, 298 p.

807  Bow Group.  BRITAIN INTO EUROPE.  London:  Bow Group for
the Conservative Political Centre, 1962.  71 p.

> An argument for British entry into the EEC aimed at
> the Conservative Party.  A clear and insightful dis-
> cussion of EC structures as well as a consideration of
> the problem of parliamentary sovereignty and EC mem-
> bership.

808  Carter, W. Horsfall.  SPEAKING EUROPEAN: THE ANGLO-
CONTINENTAL CLEAVAGE.  London:  George Allen and Unwin,
1966.  223 p.

> An impressionistic account of General de Gaulle's pol-
> icies towards Europe, and the British reaction.  Argues
> that Britain should join Europe, reject the United States,
> and seek to become a world leader in her own right.

809  Douglas-Home, Sir Alec.  BRITAIN'S ATTITUDE TOWARDS A
UNITED EUROPE.  Heule, Belgium: Uitgerverij voor Gemeente-
administratie, 1967.  18 p.

> A monograph expressing the Opposition's strong and
> favorable position towards joining the European Com-
> munity.

810     European Movement [Britain].  EUROPE:  THE CASE FOR GOING
        IN.  London:  published for the European Movement (British Coun-
        cil) by George G. Harrap and Co., 1971.  136 p.

> Four essays supporting British entry into the EC:  the
> economic case, the political case, the natural partner-
> ship, and European democracy.

811     Heath, Edward.  OLD WORLD, NEW HORIZONS:  BRITAIN,
        THE COMMON MARKET AND THE ATLANTIC ALLIANCE.  Lon-
        don:  Oxford University Press, 1970.  89  p.

> By the leader of the Conservative party.  Expresses
> Britain's commitment to the European Community in
> the 1967 Godkin Lectures at Harvard University.

812     Jebb, Gladwyn [Lord Gladwyn].  THE EUROPEAN IDEA.  New
        York:  Frederick A. Praeger, 1966.  159 p.

> Sets forth the case for a united Europe which includes
> Britain.

813     Jensen, Walter Godfried William.  THE COMMON MARKET.
        London:  G.T. Foulis and Co., 1967.  215 p.

> A polemic tracing the development of "supranational-
> ity" from Roman times to the present British bid for
> entry into the EC.  Argues for Britain's accession.

814     Mackay, R.W.G.  HEADS IN THE SAND:  A CRITICISM OF
        THE OFFICIAL LABOUR PARTY ATTITUDE TO EUROPEAN UNITY.
        Oxford:  Basil Blackwell, 1950.  43 p.

> A Labour M.P.'s criticism of the Labour Party's ac-
> tions sabotaging the Council of Europe while officially
> remaining a member of that body.

815     _____.  TOWARDS A UNITED STATES OF EUROPE:  AN ANALY-
        SIS OF BRITAIN'S ROLE IN EUROPEAN UNION.  London:  Hutch-
        inson and Co., 1961.  160 p.

> An argument for England's role in a federated union
> and the author's plan for a United States of Europe.

816     _____.  WHITHER BRITAIN?  Oxford:  Basil Blackwell, 1953.
        46 p.

> Seeks to show that the United States and the USSR
> are strong because they have a large area, large pop-
> ulation, a balanced economy, and are self-supporting.
> To attain these strength-factors, Britain should join a
> European federation.

817     \_\_\_\_. YOU CAN'T TURN THE CLOCK BACK. Chicago: Ziff-Davis Publishing Co., 1948. 367 p.

An analysis of the postwar era in terms of the necessity of a European or Atlantic federation, including Britain's history and her role in such a federation.

818   Mander, John. GREAT BRITAIN OR LITTLE ENGLAND? London: Martin Secker and Warburg, 1963. 206 p.

An inquiry into Britain's power and position in the world vis-a-vis America, Europe, and the Soviet Union. Argues for European ties but is not anti-American.

819   Middleton, Drew. THE SUPREME CHOICE: BRITAIN AND THE EUROPEAN COMMUNITY. London: Martin Secker and Warburg, 1963. 287 p.

A polemic urging Britain both to lead Europe and to remain coordinated with the United States. Includes a bit of prophecy about a new political role for the monarch in government affairs and the dangers of nationalism. Also offers insights on de Gaulle's view of Britain, and on Africa and Europe.

820   Nutting, Anthony. EUROPE WILL NOT WAIT: A WARNING AND A WAY OUT. London: Hollis and Carter, 1960. 122 p.

An indictment of Britain for refusing to accept the leadership of Europe when both France and Germany were eager to thrust it upon her after World War II. More of an introduction to the subject than an analysis, however.

821   Pfaltzgraff, Robert L[ouis]., Jr. BRITAIN FACES EUROPE. Philadelphia: University of Pennsylvania Press, 1969. 228 p.

A perceptive study of the development of a "European" concensus in Britain, and of the shift in British foreign policy from a global to a regional perspective. A study of the process by which government leaders and other relevant elites decided to join the EEC.

822   Watson, George. THE BRITISH CONSTITUTION AND EUROPE. Leiden, Netherlands: A.W. Sijthoff, 1959. 79 p.

A succinctly written essay arguing for a joint European capital and other measures which would make Britain's accession to a supranational institution more appealing.

823    Zaring, J.L. DECISION FOR EUROPE: THE NECESSITY OF BRITAIN'S ENGAGEMENT. Baltimore: Johns Hopkins Press, 1969. 221 p.

> A history of the EEC and the political and economic importance of Britain to the Community. Argues for a nonhegemonial Europe, though French and German elitism seem to be rising.

## 3. Britain—Anti-Market

824    Bow Group. NO TAME OR MINOR ROLE. A Bow Group Pamphlet. Tonbridge, Engl.: Bow Publications for the Conservative Political Centre, 1963. 55 p.

> A clear and forceful statement by the British antimarket forces discussing the terms Britain got in 1963 in Brussels, and why Common Market entry was an ill-fated policy.

825    Bryant, Arthur. A CHOICE FOR DESTINY: COMMONWEALTH AND THE COMMON MARKET. London: William Collins Sons and Co., 1962. 63 p.

> Follows argument of Edmund Burke. Expresses the opinion that if Britain joins the EC without the Commonwealth, the eighteenth-century terror of alienating the citizens will follow. Feels that electors of Britain and fellow British nations should both be consulted on the issue of being separated from each other.

826    Catlin, George E.G. THE ATLANTIC COMMONWEALTH. Baltimore: Penguin Books, 1969. 116 p.

> An "indictment" of British Prime Minister Heath's policy of unconditional entry into the European Common Market and the exclusively "European" anti-Atlantic framework of European union.

827    Communist Party of Great Britain. KEEP OUT OF THE COMMON MARKET. London: 1967. 16 p.

> A polemic expressing the British Communist Party's position and reasons for opposing Britain's entry into the European Common Market.

828    Corbet, R. Hugh, ed. BRITAIN, NOT EUROPE: COMMONWEALTH BEFORE COMMON MARKET. London: Anti-Common Market League, 1962. 72 p.

829    Einzig, Paul. THE CASE AGAINST JOINING THE COMMON
       MARKET. New York: St. Martin's Press, 1971. 132 p.

       An argument against Britain's joining the EEC based on
       the similarity between the economic philosophy of the
       EEC and the "Funk Plan."

830    Evans, Douglas, ed. DESTINY OR DELUSION: BRITAIN AND
       THE COMMON MARKET. London: Victor Gollancz, 1971. 207 p.

       A study of the issues facing British entry by twelve au-
       thors, covering the domestic implications as well as
       global and Commonwealth implications. Skeptical of
       Britain's entry.

831    Gelber, Lionel Morris. THE ALLIANCE OF NECESSITY: BRIT-
       AIN'S CRISIS, THE NEW EUROPE AND AMERICAN INTERESTS.
       New York: Stein and Day, 1966. 192 p.

       An analysis of Britain's world position and an argument
       against entry into the EC. Urges a reappraisal of Brit-
       ain's role in the American arsenal.

832    Hedges, Barry, and Jowell, Roger. BRITAIN AND THE EEC: RE-
       PORT ON A SURVEY OF ATTITUDES TOWARDS THE EUROPEAN
       ECONOMIC COMMUNITY. London: Social and Community Plan-
       ning Research, 1971. 104 p.

       An in-depth exploration of the structure of attitudes
       towards the EEC among the British. Finds five of ten
       Britons opposed to entry.

833    Heiser, H.J. BRITISH POLICY WITH REGARD TO THE UNIFICA-
       TION EFFORTS ON THE EUROPEAN CONTINENT. Leiden, Nether-
       lands: A.W. Sijthoff, 1959. 121 p.

       An examination of Britain's lack of desire or political
       will to join the EC. A selective guide to discussions
       in HANSARD's and in some White Papers included.

834    Jay, Douglas. AFTER THE COMMON MARKET: A BETTER AL-
       TERNATIVE FOR BRITAIN. Harmondsworth, Engl.: Penguin Books,
       1968. 126 p.

       Analyzes Britain's position toward the Common Market
       and outlines an alternate policy based on a wider free
       trade area including the Commonwealth, EFTA, and
       North America.

835    Pickles, William. BRITAIN AND EUROPE: HOW MUCH HAS

CHANGED? Oxford: Basil Blackwell, 1967. 119 p.

Part of the debate concerning British entry into the
EEC. An examination of the prospect, and an objec-
tion, based on the changes that have taken place in
Europe since 1962 because of the EEC.

836 _____. NOT WITH EUROPE: THE POLITICAL CASE FOR STAY-
ING OUT. Fabian Tract 336. London: Fabian Society, 1962.
40 p.

An analysis of the EEC and its machinery concluding
that Britain should stay out. Opposes the EEC's lack
of central authority, its laissez-faire philosophy, and
its bureaucracy.

837 Powell, J. Enoch. THE COMMON MARKET: THE CASE AGAINST.
Surrey, Engl.: Paperfronts, 1971. 121 p.

A polemic and discussion of the advantages and disadvantages of British entry into the EEC.

838 _____. THE COMMON MARKET: RENEGOTIATE OR COME
OUT. Kingswood, Engl.: Elliot Right Way Books, 1973. 123 p.

839 Strauss, Erich. COMMON SENSE ABOUT THE COMMON MAR-
KET: GERMANY AND BRITAIN IN POST-WAR EUROPE. London:
George Allen and Unwin, 1958. 168 p.

A polemic against British entry into the EC on the as-
sumption that EC is an instrument of German and Continental domination. Britain must reject the EC both
on economic and on political grounds.

840 _____. EUROPEAN RECKONING: THE SIX AND BRITAIN'S
FUTURE. London: George Allen and Unwin, 1962. 177 p.

Part 1: a brief recapitulation of the first four years
of the EEC, its successes, failures, and methods for
coping. Part 2: an argument against Britain's enter-
ing the EEC on the terms officially promulgated.

841 Walker-Smith, Derek, and Walker, Peter. "A Call to Commonwealth: The Constructive Case." London: 1962. 34 p. Mimeographed.

842 Young, Simon Z. TERMS OF ENTRY: BRITAIN'S NEGOTIATIONS
WITH THE EUROPEAN COMMUNITY, 1970-72. London: William
Heinemann, 1973. xv, 220 p.

A study of the effects on British accession to the EC,

including a review of the history of the exchange, a
look at budgetary procedures, agriculture, industry,
the Commonwealth, and sterling. Finds the effects
probably not great, and probably not good.

## D. DENMARK AND IRELAND

843     Coughlan, Anthony. THE COMMON MARKET: WHY IRELAND
        SHOULD NOT JOIN! 2d ed. Dublin: Common Market Study
        Group, 1972. 32 p.

844     Denmark. Ministry for Foreign Affairs. DENMARK AND THE
        MARSHALL PLAN: FINAL SURVEY OF THE DANISH GOVERN-
        MENT OF THE OPERATION AND PROGRESS UNDER ERP. Copen-
        hagen: 1953. 53 p.

        A summary of Marshall Plan aid and its results in Den-
        mark, why Denmark decided to join, her defense posi-
        tion, and relations with the Atlantic Community.

845     Government Stationery Office [Dublin]. THE ACCESSION OF
        IRELAND TO THE EUROPEAN COMMUNITIES. Dublin: 1972.
        214 p.

        The Irish government's White Paper on entry into the
        Common Market and the Treaty of Accession contain-
        ing a history of the negotiations, terms, political im-
        plications, and expectations.

846     Irish Council of the European Movement. OPPORTUNITY: IRE-
        LAND AND EUROPE. Dublin: 1972. 48 p.

847     Johnston, Joseph. WHY IRELAND NEEDS THE COMMON MAR-
        KET. Cork, Ireland: Mercier Press, 1962. 120 p.

        A treatment of agriculture and the problems it raises
        for Ireland were Ireland to join the Common Market.

848     Nielsson, Gunnar Preben. "Denmark and European Integration:
        A Small Country at the Crossroads." Ph.D. dissertation, Uni-
        versity of California, Los Angeles, 1966.

849     Sorensen, Max, and Haagerup, Niels J. DENMARK AND THE
        UNITED NATIONS. New York: Manhatten Publishing Co.,
        1956. 154 p.

        A collaborative effort by a group of Danish professors
        and students published for the Carnegie Endowment for

International Peace. Though focused on the UN, includes Danish attitudes on regional organizations like NATO and the EC and is useful for an understanding of Danish attitudes toward regional organizations. Helps explain the Danish accession to the EC.

850    Tuairim Pamphlet. THE EUROPEAN CHALLENGE: ITS SOCIAL, LEGAL AND POLITICAL PROSPECTS. Belfast: 1964. 36 p.

An outline of some of the most important problems facing Ireland in considering whether or not to join the EC, especially constitutional problems for the Irish, and also political problems for the EC.

## E. FRANCE

851    Ardagh, John. THE NEW FRENCH REVOLUTION: A SOCIAL AND ECONOMIC SURVEY OF FRANCE 1945–68. New York: Harper and Row, 1969. 501 p.

A lively and anecdotal description of many facets of French life and culture, its industry and planners, relation to the Common Market, regionalism, agriculture, and other topics.

852    Aron, Raymond. FRANCE AND EUROPE. Translated by G.F. Sheldon. Human Affairs Pamphlets no. 41. Hinsdale, Ill.: Henry Regnery Co., 1949. 24 p.

A brief analysis of the shaping of France's convictions and attitudes on Europe after World War II, how France views Britain, Germany, and the United States, and why these attitudes persist.

853    Aron, Robert. AN EXPLANATION OF DE GAULLE. Translated by Marianne Sinclair. New York: Harper and Row, 1966. 210 p.

An insightful biography of de Gaulle and Gaullism which helps to interpret de Gaulle's views on Europe and his contemporaries.

854    Cameron, Rondo E. FRANCE AND THE ECONOMIC DEVELOPMENT OF EUROPE, 1800–1914. Princeton, N.J.: Princeton University Press, 1961. 586 p.

A useful and detailed historical study of France's economic base, the ties between her and other European states, and the functional basis for French participation in a European Common Market.

855   Carasso, Roger Clyde Andrew.  "Ideological Consideration in the French Rejection of the European Defense Community."  Ph.D. dissertation, Princeton University, 1964.

856   Carmoy, Guy de.  THE FOREIGN POLICIES OF FRANCE, 1944-68. Chicago:  University of Chicago Press, 1970.  510 p.

> An analysis of French foreign policy toward the EC arguing that the Fourth Republic followed a rational policy towards NATO and the EC, while de Gaulle did just the opposite and was bound to fail.

857   Charlton, Sue Ellen M.  "The Attitudes and Policies of the French Socialist Party (SFIO) Regarding European Integration."  Ph. D. dissertation, University of Denver, 1968.

858   _____.  THE FRENCH LEFT AND EUROPEAN INTEGRATION. Monograph Series on World Affairs.  Denver:  University of Denver, 1972.  111 p.

> An exploration of some of the ideological and electoral problems of the French Left, as they relate to European integration.

859   Chopra, H.S.  DE GAULLE AND EUROPEAN UNITY.  Columbia, Mo.:  South Asia Books, 1974.  347 p.

> An analysis of de Gaulle's European plans and policies as well as an apology for him.  Details the Fouchet Plan, the Franco-German Cooperation Treaty, French and British conflict, and French nuclear policy in an attempt to show de Gaulle's policies as both well founded and generally misunderstood.

860   Colebrook, M.J.  "Dialog of the Deaf:  Franco-British Relations and European Integration, 1945-50."  Ph.D. dissertation, University of Geneva, 1968.

861   Crawley, Aidan.  DE GAULLE.  Indianapolis:  Bobbs-Merrill Co., 1969.  510 p.

> Written by an English politician and Minister.  Presents a biographical study of de Gaulle's life and career including his efforts to become leader of France, his domination of the Common Market and European nations.

862   Criddle, Byron.  SOCIALISTS AND EUROPEAN INTEGRATION: A STUDY OF THE FRENCH SOCIALIST PARTY.  London:  Rout-

ledge and Kegan Paul, 1969. 116 p.

An examination of the nature and development of the
French Socialist Party's policy towards European insti-
tutions, integration, and internationalism since World
War II.

863 Crozier, Brian. DE GAULLE. New York: Charles Scribner's
Sons, 1974. 726 p.

A complete biography of de Gaulle, his personality as
well as his politics, role, and achievements. Includes
a considerable portion of de Gaulle's view of Europe
and Britain, and his actions regarding them.

864 De Gaulle, Charles. MEMOIRS OF HOPE: RENEWAL, 1958-62;
ENDEAVOR, 1962. Translated by T. Kilmartin. New York: Simon and Schuster, 1972. 392 p.

De Gaulle's autobiographical description of his role
and the role of France in Europe, and why he kept
Britain out of the EC, as well as comments on the
world leaders with whom he dealt, including Nixon,
Kennedy, Eisenhower, and Macmillan.

865 _____. WAR MEMOIRS. 2 vols. London: George Weidenfeld
and Nicolson, 1960. 319 p., 378 p.

De Gaulle's own expression of the way his attitudes
were shaped towards Britain, Germany, the United
States, and the USSR. Provides an indispensable background to an understanding of de Gaulle's postwar attitudes towards France's role in Europe. Volume 1
covers 1942-44; volume 2, 1944-46.

866 De Launay, Jacques. DE GAULLE AND HIS FRANCE: A PSY-
CHOLOGICAL AND HISTORICAL PORTRAIT. Translated by D.
Albertyn. New York: Julian Press, 1968. 316 p.

An examination of the man and the image to discover
subtle relationships between his policy and personality
including his concept of nation-states, NATO, the
American alliance, and currency reform.

867 Deutsch, Karl, et al. FRANCE, GERMANY, AND THE WESTERN
ALLIANCE: A STUDY OF ELITE ATTITUDES ON EUROPEAN IN-
TEGRATION AND WORLD POLITICS. New York: Charles Scrib-
ner's Sons, 1967. 324 p.

A study of selected French and German leaders and

their opinion on European integration. The core issue
is arms control and disarmament.

868    Fisher, Sydney Nettleton, ed. FRANCE AND THE EUROPEAN
COMMUNITY. Columbus: Ohio State University Press, 1964.
viii, 176 p.

A compendium of topics discussed by various authors
all concerned with the theme of France and the European Community: culture, law, security, and agriculture.

869    Furniss, Edgar S., Jr. FRANCE, TROUBLED ALLY: DE GAULLE'S
HERITAGE AND PROSPECTS. New York: Frederick A. Praeger,
1960. 543 p.

A full-scale study of France in world politics. Chapters 2, 11, 12, and 21 deal specifically with France
and with President de Gaulle's concept of Europe, the
formation of those ideas, and their policy consequences.
Also included are de Gaulle's view of the United States
and NATO, and the way in which these affected European integration.

870    Gilpin, Robert. FRANCE IN THE AGE OF THE SCIENTIFIC
STATE. Princeton, N.J.: Princeton University Press, 1968.
474 p.

A political analysis of the incompatibility of the traditional European nation-state and the new role of
scientific technology in human affairs, including a
discussion of the impact of the technology gap on
transatlantic and intra-European, eco-political relations.

871    Grosser, Alfred. FRENCH FOREIGN POLICY UNDER DE GAULLE.
Translated by Lois Pattison. Boston: Little, Brown and Co., 1965.
175 p.

A scholarly and penetrating analysis of the strands of
de Gaulle's policy towards the United States, Europe,
and the USSR, which helps to focus upon France's peculiar role in the EC and de Gaulle's shaping of that
focus.

872    Haritos, Jeremy G. "Nationalism and European Integration:
French Community Leaders' Opinion and Attitudes Towards Western
European Supranational Political Integration." Ph.D. dissertation,
Fordham University, 1974.

873    Harlow, J.S.  FRENCH ECONOMIC PLANNING: A CHALLENGE
       TO REASON.  Iowa City:  University of Iowa Press, 1966.  200 p.

       Examines the French economic planning process and its
       relationship to the political structure.  Maintains that
       understanding of French planning is necessary to a com-
       prehension of the political and economic course of Eu-
       rope.


874    Hess, John L.  THE CASE FOR DE GAULLE: AN AMERICAN
       VIEWPOINT.  New York:  William Morrow and Co., 1968.  154 p.

       A journalistic account of French-American relations
       and an attempt to assess why de Gaulle acted towards
       the United States, Europe, and Britain as he did.


875    Hoffmann, Stanley.  DECLINE OR RENEWAL?  FRANCE SINCE
       THE 1930'S.  New York:  Viking Press, 1973.  663 p.

       A wide-ranging view of French history, events, and
       persons.  Several chapters deal with de Gaulle's view
       of the United States, of Britain, the world, and Eu-
       rope.


876    Isenberg, Irwin, ed.  FRANCE UNDER DE GAULLE.  New York:
       H.W. Wilson, 1967.  189 p.

       Included are various aspects of Gaullism, what it is,
       and what it means.  Twenty-nine articles excerpted
       from books and magazines, and addresses by de Gaulle
       illustrate his views on  the Atlantic Alliance, Britain
       and the Common Market, as well as on China and the
       USSR.


877    Jebb, Gladwyn [Lord Gladwyn].  DE GAULLE'S EUROPE: OR,
       WHY THE GENERAL SAYS NO.  London:  Martin Secker and
       Warburg, 1969.  168 p.

       Traces the development of General de Gaulle's idio-
       syncratic European policy and urges Britain to ready
       herself for entry into the European Community.


878          .  EUROPE AFTER DE GAULLE.  New York:  Taplinger
       Publishing Co., 1969.  169 p.

       A discussion of the goals and strategies of Charles de
       Gaulle's foreign policy and an examination of de Gaulle's
       wish to keep Britain from joining the European Community,
       his position against supranational controls, and the reason
       why he pursued a unity of Europe "From the Atlantic to the
       Urals."  Presents Europe's possible future after de Gaulle.

879     Kennedy, John Hopkins. "New France and the European Con-
science." Ph.D. dissertation, Yale University, 1942.

880     Kindleberger, Charles P. ECONOMIC GROWTH IN FRANCE
AND BRITAIN, 1851-1950. Cambridge, Mass.: Harvard University Press, 1964. 378 p.

> A trenchant review of the series of factors, resources,
> capital, population, social structures, attitudes, en-
> trepreneurship, technology, and so forth, which distin-
> guish France and Britain and which make their different
> needs and desires from the EC more understandable.

881     Kulski, W.W. DE GAULLE AND THE WORLD: THE FOREIGN
POLICY OF THE FIFTH FRENCH REPUBLIC. Syracuse, N.Y.:
Syracuse University Press, 1966. 428 p.

> An analysis of internal political factors, personality
> factors, and public opinion that shaped de Gaulle's
> foreign policy. Included are his policies toward NATO,
> Britain, and the EEC.

882     Leites, Nathan. THE "EUROPE" OF THE FRENCH. Santa Monica,
Calif.: RAND Corp., 1965. xi, 41 p.

883     _____. ON THE GAME OF POLITICS IN FRANCE. Stanford,
Calif.: Stanford University Press, 1959. 190 p.

> A study of the major domestic political strategy during
> the second phase of the Fourth Republic. Emphasizes
> factions, individuals and organizations, including the
> European Defense Community and the Common Market.

884     Luethy, Herbert. FRANCE AGAINST HERSELF. Translated by
Eric Mosbacher. New York: Frederick A. Praeger, 1955. 476 p.

> A Swiss journalist's interpretation of the "personality
> of France" in which he includes a study of French
> foreign policy and, specifically, her "European" pol-
> icy.

885     Macridis, Roy C. DE GAULLE: IMPLACABLE ALLY. New York:
Harper and Row, 1966. 248 p.

> A guide to the outlook and policies of President de
> Gaulle towards Europe, Britain, the United States,
> and Germany. Addresses an American audience and
> includes pronouncements and several official texts of
> de Gaulle's addresses.

886    Morse, Edward L. FOREIGN POLICY AND INTERDEPENDENCE
       IN GAULLIST FRANCE. Princeton, N.J.: Princeton University
       Press, 1973. xiv, 336 p.

       See especially chapter 6 which examines the preva-
       lence of crisis diplomacy in the EEC, evaluates its
       significance for intra-European and international poli-
       tics, and assesses the political costs and benefits for
       France of crisis precipitation and management within
       the EC.

887    Newhouse, John. DE GAULLE AND THE ANGLO-SAXONS.
       New York: Viking Press, 1970. 370 p.

       A study of de Gaulle's policies and attitudes towards
       the United States and Britain during the general's pres-
       idency.

888    Padover, Saul K., et al. FRENCH INSTITUTIONS: VALUES
       AND POLITICS. Stanford, Calif.: Stanford University Press,
       1954. 102 p.

       A study of the basic values of French civilization
       which gave rise to her foreign policy and other at-
       titudes towards Europe, towards her European partners
       like Germany and Britain, and towards organizations
       like the European Defense Community.

889    Pickles, Dorthy. THE UNEASY ENTENTE: FRENCH FOREIGN
       POLICY AND FRANCO-BRITISH MISUNDERSTANDING. London:
       Royal Institute of International Affairs, 1966. 108 p.

       An essay on, and a description of, the French and
       British differences in their respective approaches to
       Europe, to defense, and to the world since World
       War II. Written from a British perspective.

890    Pinder, John. EUROPE AGAINST DE GAULLE. London: Pall
       Mall Press for the Federal Trust, 1963. 160 p.

       Seeks to show the clash between the ideas of de
       Gaulle (anti-European) and Jean Monnet
       (pro-European). Also seeks to give the rationale,
       and makes proposals for, a federal Europe in which
       Britain must share and cooperate.

891    Political and Economic Planning. FRANCE AND THE EUROPEAN
       COMMUNITY. Occasional Paper no. 11. London: 1961. 42 p.

       A hard look at France's political role in the EC.

892    Reynaud, Paul. THE FOREIGN POLICY OF CHARLES DE GAULLE: A CRITICAL ASSESSMENT. Translated by M. Savill. New York: Odyssey Press, 1964. 160 p.

A critical assessment and attempt to explain de Gaulle's policies of opposition toward the United States and Britain by one who disagreed with those policies.

893    Ritsch, Frederick F[ield, Jr.]. THE FRENCH LEFT AND THE EUROPEAN IDEA, 1947-49. New York: Pageant Press, 1967. 277 p.

A study of the French Left gleaned from the political press of the SFIO and Communist parties in an attempt to assess their views toward a concept of "Europe."

894    _____. "The French Political Parties of the Left and European Integration, 1947-49." Ph.D. dissertation, University of Virginia, 1962.

895    Schoenbrun, David. THE THREE LIVES OF CHARLES DE GAULLE. New York: Atheneum Publishers, 1966. 373 p.

An accounting of de Gaulle's three careers, his person, and his whims which made him so significant to France and for European integration.

896    Serfaty, Simon Henry. "An Ascendant France? French Policy Toward Europe Since World War II." Ph.D. dissertation, Johns Hopkins University, 1967.

897    _____. FRANCE, DE GAULLE AND EUROPE: THE POLICY OF THE FOURTH AND FIFTH REPUBLICS TOWARD THE CONTINENT. Baltimore: Johns Hopkins Press, 1968. 176 p.

An analysis of the image and reality of the decline and ascendance of French power since World War II.

898    Servan-Schreiber, Jean-Jacques, and Albert, Michel. THE RADICAL ALTERNATIVE. Translated by H.A. Fields. London: Macdonald and Co., 1970. 207 p.

A philosophic look at the French and the EC's role in shaping the destiny of the future.

899    Silj, Alessandro. EUROPE'S POLITICAL PUZZLE: A STUDY OF THE FOUCHET NEGOTIATIONS AND THE 1963 VETO. Cambridge, Mass.: Harvard University Press, 1967. 178 p.

Traces the course of the Fouchet negotiations and tries to account for the positions taken and to explain why

respective attitudes were shaped. An important analysis of de Gaulle who, rebuffed, turned away from interest in political union.

900     Silver, Jacob. "France and European Integration: An Inquiry
into the Elements of Political Loyalty." Ph.D. dissertation, Ohio
State University, 1971.

901     Slotta, Peter Luis. "France, Germany and European Unification:
A Formal Analysis." Ph.D. dissertation, University of Pennsylvania, 1968.

902     Toussaint, Donald Ray. "French Policy Toward the Political Unification of Europe, 1944-54." Ph.D. dissertation, Stanford University, 1956.

903     Trunzo, Judith Diane. "Eurafrica: Counterpart or Counterpoint?
A Study of French Views on Regional Integration." Ph.D. dissertation, University of Virginia, 1973.

904     Willis, F. Roy. FRANCE, GERMANY AND THE NEW EUROPE,
1945-67. New York: Oxford University Press, 1968. 431 p.

A history and analysis of the Franco-German rapproche-
ment and the institutions established by the Bonn-Paris
Axis, and the way in which they underlie the European
Community. Includes descriptions of domestic deter-
minants of unity, parties, interest groups, and private
groups like Jean Monnet's Action Committee for the
United States of Europe.

905     Wills, George Robert. "The European Policies of General de
Gaulle." Ph.D. dissertation, Duke University, 1967.

## F. GERMANY

906     Adenauer, Konrad. MEMOIRS, 1945-53. Chicago: Henry Regnery Co., 1966. 477 p.

The first of three volumes (only one in English) in
which Adenauer's view of Germany's role in West European political integration is clearly delineated. Adenauer shows himself to be a "European," pluralist,
devout Christian, and a supranationalist.

907     Birnbaum, Karl E. EAST AND WEST GERMANY: A MODUS

VIVENDI. Farnborough, Engl.: D.C. Heath and Co., 1973. 157 p.

Specifically concerned with the negotiations between the German Federal Republic and the German Democratic Republic between 1970 and 1972. Also concerned with the broader implications for Europe of the agreements and the possibility of closer relations between East and West Europe.

908    Brentano, Heinrich von. GERMANY AND EUROPE: REFLECTIONS ON GERMAN FOREIGN POLICY. New York: Frederick A. Praeger, 1964. 223 p.

Covers three major topics: the economic amalgamation of the three Western zones of occupation in Germany, the problems of consolidating the European countries which have signed the Rome Treaty, and the strengthening of NATO.

909    Deutsch, K[arl]. W., and Edinger, Louis J. GERMANY REJOINS THE POWERS: MASS OPINION, INTEREST GROUPS, AND ELITES IN CONTEMPORARY GERMAN FOREIGN POLICY. Stanford, Calif.: Stanford University Press, 1959. 320 p.

A national study, based on elite opinions and polling studies, concerned with foreign policy and its actors. Focuses on German policy and policymakers concerned with the European arena.

910    Federal Republic of Germany. Press and Information Office. THE EUROPEAN COMMUNITY: FROM THE SUMMIT CONFERENCE AT THE HAGUE TO THE EUROPE OF THE TEN. Bonn: 1972. 136 p.

A collection of statements, addresses, interviews, and miscellaneous communications by officials of the West German government, as well as documents and protocols on the accession of Britain, Ireland, and Denmark to the EC.

911    Freund, Gerald. GERMANY BETWEEN TWO WORLDS. New York: Harcourt Brace, 1961. 296 p.

An attempt to shed light on contemporary Germany caught between the Germanophiles and Germanophobes. Included are Adenauer's policies toward Europe and NATO, towards France and de Gaulle, and Germany's position between East and West.

912    Holborn, Hajo. GERMANY AND EUROPE: HISTORICAL ESSAYS.
       Garden City, N.Y.: Doubleday and Co., 1970. 327 p.

       A history of German culture and ideas from Bismarck's
       era to post-World War II which shows how German
       views toward Europe were shaped.

913    Kiep, Walther Leisler. A NEW CHALLENGE FOR WESTERN EU-
       ROPE: A VIEW FROM BONN. New York: Mason and Lipscomb,
       1974. 217 p.

       "A view of the shifting international balance of power,
       particularly that of the United States, a superpower,
       from the perspective of Germany, a medium-sized
       power. . . . The author . . . questions the conse-
       quences of an ever-diminishing U.S. role in Europe . . .
       [and] sees the need for increased effort to bring about
       Western Europe's political unification."

                              EUROPEAN COMMUNITY

914    McInnis, Edgar, et al. THE SHAPING OF POST-WAR GERMANY.
       New York: Frederick A. Praeger, 1960. 195 p.

       Four essays summarize and analyze the factors involved
       in the possible reunification and integration of Ger-
       many into Europe. Also a study of the present inter-
       national situation and Germany's place in it.

915    Majonica, Ernst. EAST-WEST RELATIONS: A GERMAN VIEW.
       New York: Frederick A. Praeger, 1969. 240 p.

       By a leader in the CDU. Analyzes three issues criti-
       cal to German foreign policy: German reunification,
       European unification, and a strong Atlantic alliance.
       Compares the present to the Adenauer era, and Ger-
       many's relations to the East and to the West.

916    Morgenthau, Hans J., ed. GERMANY AND THE FUTURE OF
       EUROPE. Chicago: University of Chicago Press, 1951. 179 p.

       A collection of essays concerning reunification and
       other problems Germany faces as it integrates into
       Europe.

917    Paterson, William E. THE SPD AND EUROPEAN INTEGRATION.
       Lexington, Mass.: Lexington Books, 1974. 177 p.

       A study of the domestic forces shaping the SPD's poli-
       cies on European integration toward the Council of Eu-
       rope, the Schuman Plan, the EDC and WEU, and the
       EEC and EURATOM.

918     Saar Informationsamt. THE SAAR: KEY TO EUROPEAN UNITY. Saarbruecken, Germany: 1953. 66 p.

> An official publication expressing the position of the Saar on European union, why the Saar is important to Europe, and why it favors European unification.

919     Schroeder, Gerhard. DECISION FOR EUROPE. Translated by D.D. Thompson. London: Thames and Hudson, 1964. 248 p.

920     Shears, Ursala H. "The Social Democratic Party of Germany: Friend or Foe of European Unity?" Ph.D. dissertation, Fletcher School of Law and Diplomacy, 1960.

921     Stolper, Wolfgang F. GERMANY BETWEEN EAST AND WEST. Washington, D.C.: National Planning Association, 1960. xi, 80 p.

> A short economic analysis of Germany's situation relative to reunification and its consequences on European integration.

922     Strauss, Franz-Josef. THE GRAND DESIGN: A EUROPEAN SOLUTION TO GERMAN REUNIFICATION. Translated by B. Connell. New York: Frederick A. Praeger, 1966. 105 p.

> An argument for a European federation, including Eastern Europe, which would eliminate the border problems between East and West Germany as well as reintegrate Germany into her proper role as a European leader.

923     Taussig, Andrew John. "The Impact of the European Communities Upon German Ministries." Ph.D. dissertation, Harvard University, 1971.

924     Wadbrook, William Pollard. WEST-GERMAN BALANCE-OF-PAYMENTS POLICY: THE PRELUDE TO EUROPEAN MONETARY INTEGRATION. New York: Frederick A. Praeger, 1972. 358 p.

> A clear and persuasive explanation of the politico-economic basis for Germany's international monetary policy and the gains Germany could expect to receive from European monetary integration.

## G. ITALY

925     Blackmer, Donald L.M. UNITY IN DIVERSITY: ITALIAN COM-

MUNISM AND THE COMMUNIST WORLD. Cambridge: M.I.T.
Press, 1968. xiii, 434 p.

See especially chapter 9: "The Common Market Controversy," an exposition of the position of the PCI towards Europe and the EEC, and also Masconi's role in
shaping that policy.

926    Divita, James J. "The Role of the Italian Government in the
Formation of an Integrated Western Europe, 1953–68." Ph.D.
dissertation, University of Chicago, 1972.

927    Kogan, Norman. THE POLITICS OF ITALIAN FOREIGN POLICY.
New York: Frederick A. Praeger, 1963. 178 p.

An analysis of the backgrounds and sources of political
power which influence Italian foreign policy. Also
discusses the relation of Italy to Europe and how and
why this policy has evolved.

928    Lamont, Douglas F. MANAGING FOREIGN INVESTMENT IN
SOUTHERN ITALY: U.S. BUSINESS IN DEVELOPING AREAS
OF THE EEC. New York: Frederick A. Praeger, 1973. 170 p.
170 p.

"A case study of the socio-cultural factors involved in
overseas investments. Following a historical sketch of
southern Italy, the book examines economic development in the area as a question of infrastructure and
relative to human factors."

EUROPEAN COMMUNITY

929    Lutz, Vera. ITALY: A STUDY IN ECONOMIC DEVELOPMENT.
London: Oxford University Press for the Royal Institute of International Affairs, 1962. 342 p.

An intensive study of Italy's economic and political
integration between north and south, and traditional
and modern sectors. Also concerned for the theory
of economic integration and development. A superb
background for understanding Italy's role in the European Community.

930    Saville, Lloyd. REGIONAL ECONOMIC DEVELOPMENT IN
ITALY. Durham, N.C.: Duke University Press, 1967. 191 p.

A comparative examination of seven diverse regions of
Italy and their economic development since World War
II. Analyzes unique aspects of each region by study-

ing in detail a representative province of each. Seeks
to show that the same economic policy cannot be applied to all regions. Italy also compared to other
Common Market partners, and the role of the EEC in
regional development assessed.

931    Vannicelli, Primo. ITALY, NATO, AND THE EUROPEAN COM-
MUNITY: THE INTERPLAY OF FOREIGN POLICY AND DOMES-
TIC POLITICS. Cambridge, Mass.: Center for International Af-
fairs, Harvard University, 1974. 67 p.

932    _____. "Lilliput's Response: Interactions Between the Atlantic
Alliance, the European Community, and the Italian Political System." Ph.D. dissertation, Harvard University, 1971.

933    Willis, F. Roy. ITALY CHOOSES EUROPE. New York: Oxford
University Press, 1971. 373 p.

An analysis of the policies and people, the interest
groups, and organizations in Italy which pressured Italy
into joining the Common Market, as well as an assessment of the effects that relationship has brought.

# Chapter 5

# EUROPEAN COMMUNITIES AND EXTERNAL RELATIONS

## A. GENERAL

934     Allen, James J. THE EUROPEAN COMMON MARKET AND THE
GATT. Washington, D.C.: University Press of Washington, D.C.,
1960. 244 p.

> A detailed legal analysis of the compatibility of the
> EEC Treaty and policies with GATT and with U.S.
> trading interests and policies. Analyzes Euro-American
> trade reform in the framework of GATT and OECD as
> well.

935     Alting von Geusau, Frans A.M. EUROPEAN ORGANIZATIONS
AND THE FOREIGN RELATIONS OF STATES: A COMPARATIVE
ANALYSIS OF DECISION-MAKING. Leiden, Netherlands: A.W.
Sijthoff for the Council of Europe, 1962. 290 p.

> A comparison of the decision-making structure of states
> in the conduct of foreign relations with that of Euro-
> pean organizations to ascertain the impact of the lat-
> ter on the former.

936     _____, ed. THE EXTERNAL RELATIONS OF THE EUROPEAN
COMMUNITY: PERSPECTIVE, POLICIES, AND RESPONSES.
Lexington, Mass.: D.C. Heath and Co., 1974. 132 p.

> "The book provides a comprehensive analysis of Europe's
> search for a world role following its postwar economic in-
> tegration. Early chapters stress Europe's pursuit of policies
> reflecting an independence from the United States, while
> other chapters examine the responses of China, the Soviet
> Union, the United States, and Eastern Europe to the en-
> larged Community in light of the present international sys-
> tem."

EUROPEAN COMMUNITY

937     Bailey, Richard. THE EUROPEAN COMMUNITY IN THE WORLD.
        London: Hutchinson and Co., 1973. 200 p.

> A broad look at the EC's external relations with south-
> ern Europe, the Commonwealth, the United States, the
> developing world, and with Eastern Europe.

938     European League for Economic Cooperation. Economic Commission.
        EUROPE AND THE WORLD: THE EXTERNAL RELATIONS OF THE
        COMMUNITY. London: European League, British Section, 1972.
        79 p.

939     Everts, Ph. P., ed. THE EUROPEAN COMMUNITY IN THE
        WORLD: THE EXTERNAL RELATIONS OF THE ENLARGED COM-
        MUNITY. Proceedings of the Conference for International Studies
        and the Europe Institute, University of Leiden. Rotterdam: Rot-
        terdam University Press, 1972. 211 p.

> Assesses the impact of an enlarged (nine or ten mem-
> ber) European Community on the original six members,
> on the developing countries, and on East Bloc coun-
> tries.

940     Feld, Werner J. THE EUROPEAN COMMON MARKET AND
        THE WORLD. Englewood Cliffs, N.J.: Prentice-Hall, 1967.
        184 p.

> A study of the EC's external policy formulation, its
> competence to engage in relations with nonmember
> states and international organizations, and its policies
> toward nonmembers including the socialist bloc and de-
> veloping countries.

941     _____. THE EUROPEAN COMMUNITY IN WORLD AFFAIRS:
        ECONOMIC POWER AND POLITICAL INFLUENCE. Port Wash-
        ington, N.Y.: Alfred Publishing Co., 1976. 300 p.

> Recounts the impact the EC has had, and is having,
> on economic and political relations in the world to-
> wards other developed areas, the Communist countries,
> and with the developing countries. More of a des-
> criptive and historical analysis than a theoretical one.

942     Gorell Barnes, Sir William. EUROPE AND THE DEVELOPING
        WORLD: ASSOCIATION UNDER PART IV OF THE TREATY OF
        ROME. European Series no. 2. London: published for PEP by
        Chatham House, 1967. 46 p.

> A brief monograph considering the origins and nature
> of relations between the EEC and the developing world,

and the implications the EEC's policy toward developing countries has had for British entry into the EC and
future Commonwealth relations.

943   Hassner, Pierre.   EUROPE IN THE AGE OF NEGOTIATION.
Beverly Hills, Calif.: Sage Publications, 1973.   82 p.

A study of West Europe's relationship to the United
States on the one hand, and to Eastern Europe on the
other.   Seeks to assess the transformation of power
and its implications for a unified West European foreign policy.

944   Henig, Stanley.   EXTERNAL RELATIONS OF THE EUROPEAN
COMMUNITY: ASSOCIATIONS AND TRADE AGREEMENTS.
London:  Political and Economic Planning, 1971.   145 p.

An inquiry into the EC's attempts to establish close
relations, especially bilateral relations, with third-
world countries in order to assess if external policy
is, or can be, a type of developing EC foreign policy.

945   Kohnstamm, Max.   THE EUROPEAN COMMUNITY AND ITS ROLE
IN THE WORLD.   Columbia:  University of Missouri Press, 1964.
82 p.

The Green Foundation lectures analyzing the development of the European Community, U.S. and British relations with the EC, and a European view of foreign
relations.

946   Kohnstamm, Max, and Hager, Wolfgang, eds.   A NATION WRIT
LARGE: FOREIGN POLICY PROBLEMS BEFORE THE EUROPEAN
COMMUNITY.   London:  Macmillan and Co., 1973.   275 p.

Ten articles surveying the main problems facing nations
of the EC: foreign policy issues, the internal issues of
a monetary system, agriculture, and energy.

947   Lippmann, Walter.   WESTERN UNITY AND THE COMMON MAR-
KET.   Boston:  Little, Brown and Co., 1962.   51 p.

A compendium of six articles by a journalistic observer of Europe at the period of Britain's first entry bid.
Includes such topics as the meaning of the EC to Britain, to the United States, and to Europe.

948   Mally, Gerhard.   THE EUROPEAN COMMUNITY IN PERSPEC-

TIVE: THE NEW EUROPE, THE UNITED STATES, AND THE WORLD. Lexington, Mass.: Lexington Books, 1973. 349 p.

> An overview of the European Community, its development, and future. Also a critique of the theoretical approaches to integration, and a look at the relations between the EC and nonmembers, especially the United States. Includes an excellent bibliography.

949   Morgan, Roger P. HIGH POLITICS, LOW POLITICS: TOWARD A FOREIGN POLICY FOR WESTERN EUROPE. Beverly Hills, Calif.: Sage Publications, 1973. 65 p.

> A study of the intentions and of the effects of the nine members of the EC acting as a unit in external or foreign relations both towards the Soviet bloc and towards the United States.

950   Stingelin, Peter, ed. THE EUROPEAN COMMUNITY AND THE OUTSIDERS. Don Mills, Ontario: Longman Canada, 1973. 168 p.

> Papers from a symposium on the Common Market at Waterloo Lutheran University on EC relations with nonmember states, focusing on a developing "foreign policy" of the EC towards Canada, Scandinavia, and Eastern Europe.

951   Twitchett, Kenneth J., ed. EUROPE AND THE WORLD: THE EXTERNAL RELATIONS OF THE COMMON MARKET. London: Europa Publications, 1976. 210 p.

> Seven essays focusing on varying aspects of the EC's external relations--trans-Atlantic, the East bloc, Mediterranean policy, and Africa, among others.

952   Weil, Gordon L. A FOREIGN POLICY FOR EUROPE? THE EXTERNAL RELATIONS OF THE EUROPEAN COMMUNITY. Bruges, Belgium: College of Europe, 1970. 324 p.

> An assessment of the problems and prospects of an EC foreign policy, and its effects on the unity of the members. Included is a framework for such a policy and for policy of association status for the developing countries.

## B. DEVELOPING AREAS

## 1. General and Other

953   Camps, Miriam. THE MANAGEMENT OF INTERDEPENDENCE:

A PRELIMINARY VIEW. New York: Council on Foreign Relations, 1974. 104 p.

"An essay contemplating the future direction of the international system. . . . Her special concern is with the institutions--not only the formal structure, but also the informal rules, practices and associations--that will be necessary to manage, . . . relationships stemming from increasing interdependence among modernized and modernizing societies."

EUROPEAN COMMUNITY

954   De Garmo, Peter Henry. "Beyond the Pyrennes: Spain and Europe since World War II." Ph.D. dissertation, University of California, Davis, 1971.

955   Dinwiddy, Bruce, ed. AID PERFORMANCE AND DEVELOPMENT POLICIES OF WESTERN COUNTRIES: STUDIES IN U.S., U.K., EEC, AND DUTCH PROGRAMS. New York: Praeger Publishers, 1973. 139 p.

Written for the Overseas Development Institute. A collection of essays assessing the type of aid and the politics of that aid in the respective countries. Also useful as a study of EEC foreign policy.

956   _____. EUROPEAN DEVELOPMENT POLICIES: THE UNITED KINGDOM, SWEDEN, FRANCE, EEC AND MULTILATERAL ORGANIZATIONS. New York: Praeger Publishers, 1973. 119 p.

"The Overseas Development Institute's sixth annual review of European aid programs. The book examines and evaluates the record of British, French and Swedish aid performance [as well as] multinational organizations in development aid."

EUROPEAN COMMUNITY

957   Friedmann, Wolfgang. METHODS AND POLICIES OF PRINCIPAL DONOR COUNTRIES IN PUBLIC INTERNATIONAL DEVELOPMENT FINANCING: PRELIMINARY APPRAISAL. New York: Columbia University Law School, 1962. iii, 49 p.

An analysis of foreign aid machinery in the United States, Britain, West Germany, and France as well as the EEC showing there is agreement on the need for technical assistance, but disagreement on the concept and principles of capital aid.

958    Jones, David.  EUROPE'S CHOSEN FEW:  POLICY AND PRAC-
       TICE OF THE EEC AID PROGRAMME.  London:  Overseas De-
       velopment Institute, 1973.  70 p.

           "Analyzes the merits and demerits of the present sys-
           tem of aid for Yaounde Associates and projects its
           likely terms and conditions if and when the Common-
           wealth countries in Africa, the Caribbean and the
           Pacific join the association."

                                                        Publisher


959    Lipton, Michael, et al.  AN ENLARGED EUROPEAN COMMU-
       NITY AND THE LESS DEVELOPED COUNTRIES:  A REPORT OF A
       CONFERENCE HELD BY THE INSTITUTE OF DEVELOPMENT STUD-
       IES AND THE CENTER FOR CONTEMPORARY EUROPEAN STUDIES
       AT THE UNIVERSITY OF SUSSEX, JULY 1970.  Brighton, Engl.:
       University of Sussex, Centre for Contemporary European Studies,
       1973.  41 p.


960    Pan American Union.  THE EFFECTS OF THE EUROPEAN ECO-
       NOMIC COMMUNITY ON THE LATIN AMERICAN ECONOMIES.
       Washington, D.C.:  1963.  93 p.

           An analysis of the EEC's impact on Latin American im-
           ports.  Summarizes the policy implications of the EEC's
           charter and its implementation.


961    Ramazani, Rouhollah K.  THE MIDDLE EAST AND THE COM-
       MON MARKET.  Charlottesville:  University Press of Virginia,
       1964.  152 p.

           A study of the adverse effect of the EEC on major
           Middle Eastern exports such as petroleum, grains, and
           fruit.  Also explores positive and negative reactions to-
           ward the EEC, the attempts at cooperation by non-Arab
           countries, and opposition by Arab countries.


962    Salvi, Parasharam Ganapatarao.  THE WEST EUROPEAN MAR-
       KET.  Bombay:  Lalvani Publishing House, 1967.  vi, 88 p.

           A detailed account of the commercial policies of both
           the EEC and EFTA and the impact of these two organi-
           zations on the developing countries.


963    Society for International Development, and Overseas Development
       Institute.  BRITAIN, THE EEC AND THE THIRD WORLD:  REPORT
       OF AN INTERNATIONAL CONFERENCE JOINTLY SPONSORED
       BY THE SOCIETY FOR INTERNATIONAL DEVELOPMENT AND

THE OVERSEAS DEVELOPMENT INSTITUTE AT THE ROYAL SO-
CIETY, 26-27 APRIL 1971. By Lord Campbell et al. New York:
Praeger Publishers, 1972. 95 p.

> A collection of essays, some by officials of the EC
> Commission, detailing the EC's Third World policy,
> the British view, and the meaning for Britain in join-
> ing the EC.

964    Uri, Pierre, ed. ISRAEL AND THE COMMON MARKET. Jeru-
salem: George Weidenfeld and Nicolson, 1971. xiv, 680 p.

> An analysis of the economic effects of association by
> Israel with the EC, the advantages and disadvantages
> in the areas of income tax, the value-added tax, Is-
> rael's capital market, and its labor market.

## 2. Africa

965    Adams, Gordon M. "Political Integration in Europe: the Africa
Association to the European Economic Community." Ph.D. dissertation, Columbia University, 1971.

966    Atlantic Institute. EUROPE AND THE MAGHREB: A SERIES OF
PAPERS. By C. Gasteyger et al. Paris: 1972. 72 p.

967    Carrington, C.E. "The Commonwealth in Africa." N.p., 1962.
Mimeographed.

> Reports on a conference held by African Commonwealth
> nations in 1962 concerning the cold war, Pan-Africanism,
> Britain's desire to join the Common Market, and the
> future of the Commonwealth in Africa.

968    Cordier, Andrew W., ed. COLUMBIA ESSAYS IN INTERNATIONAL
AFFAIRS. Vol. 6, THE DEAN'S PAPERS, 1970. New York: Columbia University Press, 1971.

> See especially the chapter by Rosenthal, "The EEC
> and the Maghreb," an analysis of how Tunisian, Mo-
> roccan, and Algerian membership in the EEC could aid
> those economies.

969    Doimi di Delupis, Ingrid. THE EAST AFRICAN COMMUNITY
AND THE COMMON MARKET. London: Longman Group, 197
184 p.

> An analysis of the functioning of the East African Com-
> munity and its Common Market, as well as the EEC

and its association agreements with the African countries. A discussion of the Yaounde Convention and
the agreement with Nigeria are included.

970    Green, R.H., and Seidman, A.  UNITY OR POVERTY?  THE
       ECONOMICS OF PAN AFRICANISM.  Baltimore:  Penguin Books,
       1968.  364 p.

       Focuses on the theme that Pan-Africanism has been a
       dream but is now crystalizing into an economic neces-
       sity.  Covers factors of economic dependence and in-
       terdependence, relations with other nations, and eco-
       nomic organizations including the EEC.

971    Keeton, George W., and Schwarzenberger, Georg, eds.  THE
       YEARBOOK OF WORLD AFFAIRS, 1971.  New York:  Frederick
       A. Praeger, 1971.

       See the chapter by Curzon and Curzon:  "Neo-Colonialism
       and the European Economic Community."  The Yaounde
       Convention and the association of eighteen African
       states with the EEC, the constitutional provisions for
       the association, and the status of the African states
       after independence covered.

972    Konwea, Robert Chuba.  "European Economic Integration and Afri-
       can States."  Ph.D. dissertation, University of Southern California,
       1969.

973    Mazrui, Ali.  THE ANGLO-AFRICAN COMMONWEALTH:  POLI-
       TICAL FRICTION AND CULTURAL FUSION.  New York:  Pergamon
       Press, 1967.  163 p.

       Examines the development and impact of the EEC on
       Commonwealth Africa as well as British influence on
       the African Commonwealth countries.

974    _____.  TOWARDS A PAX AFRICANA:  A STUDY OF IDEOLOGY
       AND AMBITION.  Chicago:  University of Chicago Press, 1967.
       ix, 287 p.

       A study of contemporary African ideas, and the impact
       of the EEC on  those ideas and their shaping.

975    Ndegwa, Philip.  THE COMMON MARKET AND DEVELOPMENT
       IN EAST AFRICA.  East African Studies, no. 22.  Nairobi:  pub-
       lished for the East African Institute of Social Research by the East
       African Publishing House, 1965.  150 p.

976     Okigbo, P.N.C. AFRICA AND THE COMMON MARKET. Evanston, Ill.: Northwestern University Press, 1967. 183 p.

> A study by the Nigerian who negotiated his country's relations with the EEC. The outgrowth of Okigbo's experiences and reflections during the negotiations, and based on his subsequent university lectures in Nigeria and at Princeton University. Considers the Yaounde Convention and the general problems of African association in a common market of its own, as well as Nigeria's relations with the EEC.

977     Owosekun, Akinola Apeniyi. "Nigerian Cocoa and Petroleum Exports to the Common Market Countries: Demand Elasticities and Prospects." Ph.D. dissertation, Claremont Graduate School, 1974.

978     Rivkin, Arnold. AFRICA AND THE EUROPEAN COMMON MARKET: A PERSPECTIVE. ?d ed. Denver: University of Denver, 1966. 67 p.

> A monograph tracing the salient African national relationships to the EEC, it also considers an alternative African common market.

979     _____. AFRICA AND THE WEST: ELEMENTS OF FREE-WORLD POLICY. New York: Frederick A. Praeger, 1962. 241 p.

> A study of African political and economic development in relation to Western Europe, the EEC, the United States, and Israel.

980     Velyaminov, G. AFRICA AND THE COMMON MARKET. New York: G. Velyaminov, 1964. 20 p.

> A brief monograph on the advantages and disadvantages Africa gets from association with the European Common Market. Expresses basically a negative view towards the EEC and advocates separation from it.

981     Zartman, I. William. THE POLITICS OF TRADE NEGOTIATIONS BETWEEN AFRICA AND THE EUROPEAN ECONOMIC COMMUNITY: THE WEAK CONFRONT THE STRONG. Princeton, N.J.: Princeton University Press, 1971. 243 p.

> A process analysis of trade negotiations between Africa and the EEC, the weak and the strong, respectively, to show negotiating strategies. Also provides a comparative framework for the analysis of specific negotiations.

## 3. India and Asia

982    Billerbeck, Klaus. PROBLEMS AND APPROACHES FOR SOLU-
       TION OF AN ASSOCIATION BETWEEN FIJI/TONGA/WESTERN
       SAMOA AND THE EUROPEAN COMMUNITY. Berlin: German
       Development Institute, 1974. 71 p.


983    Dharma, Kumar. INDIA AND THE EUROPEAN ECONOMIC COM-
       MUNITY. London: published for the Indian Council of World Af-
       fairs by the Asia Publishing House, 1967. 272 p.

       A study of India's relations with the EEC and the ef-
       fect British entry into the EEC will have on India.


984    Ghai, Dharam P. THE ENLARGEMENT OF THE EEC AND THE
       ASIAN COMMONWEALTH COUNTRIES. London: Commonwealth
       Secretariat, 1973. vi, 57 p.


985    Gowda, K. Venkatagiri. THE EUROPEAN COMMON MARKET
       AND INDIA: BASIC ISSUES REEXAMINED. Mysore, India:
       Rao and Raghavan, 1962. 206 p.

       An examination of issues posed by Britain's entry into
       the EEC and the implications for India.


986    Kumar, Dharma. INDIA AND THE EUROPEAN ECONOMIC COM-
       MUNITY. London: published for the Indian Council of World Af-
       fairs by the Asia Publishing House, 1967. 272 p.

       See no. 983.


987    Nigam, R.S. A STUDY OF THE EUROPEAN COMMON MARKET
       AND ITS IMPACT ON INDIA'S FOREIGN TRADE. Delhi: S.
       Chand and Co., 1964. 196 p.

       An assessment of the impact of various measures under
       the EEC plan on India's foreign trade, especially on
       exports.


988    Rangnekar, D.K. INDIA, BRITAIN, AND THE EUROPEAN COM-
       MON MARKET. New Delhi: published for the National Institute
       of Public Affairs by R and K Publishing House, 1963. 236 p.

       Analyses of the impact of European integration on In-
       dia, including Britain's failure to join the EEC in 1962.


989    Sovani, N.V. THE EUROPEAN ECONOMIC COMMUNITY. Dha-
       war, India: J.J.S. Institute of Economic Research, n.d. 51 p.

       A study of the EEC as an experiment in economic and

political integration relating to the Indian experience.

## C.  EFTA AND THE COMMONWEALTH (European Free Trade Area)

990   Bachman, Hans. THE EUROPEAN ECONOMIC COMMUNITY AND THE THREE NEUTRALS: AUSTRIA; SWEDEN; SWITZERLAND. Brussels: European League for Economic Cooperation, 1962. 34 p.

A monograph concerning association of the three neutral members of EFTA with the EEC, the types of agreements possible, and methods of affiliating.

991   Benoit, Emile. EUROPE AT SIXES AND SEVENS: THE FREE TRADE ASSOCIATION AND THE UNITED STATES. New York: Columbia University Press, 1961. 271 p.

A descriptive interpretation of the economic relations among the EEC, EFTA countries, and the United States as well as a discussion of the economic and political importance of European integration to each.

992   Biggs-Davison, John. THE WALLS OF EUROPE: COMMONWEALTH/COMMON MARKET. London: Johnson Publications, 1962. 90 p.

A short historical survey of the European idea, both prewar and post-World War II.

993   Bluhm, William T. BUILDING AN AUSTRIAN NATION: THE POLITICAL INTEGRATION OF A WESTERN STATE. New Haven, Conn.: Yale University Press, 1973. xii, 265 p.

A case study of Austrian integration, but also a comparative theoretical study of integration which challenges some theories like Deutsch's, and affirms other theories, like Etzioni's.

994   Camps, Miriam. THE EUROPEAN COMMON MARKET AND FREE TRADE AREA. Princeton, N.J.: Center of International Studies, Princeton University, 1957. 30 p.

A summary of events and progress concerning the formulation of a free trade area in the period following the signing of the Rome Treaty.

995        . THE EUROPEAN FREE TRADE ASSOCIATION: A PRELIMINARY APPRAISAL. Occasional Paper no. 4. London: Political and Economic Planning, 1959. 38 p.

A review of the background to the decision to form EFTA, and the main features of the plan.

996       _____. THE FREE TRADE AREA NEGOTIATIONS. Occasional Paper no. 2. London: Political and Economic Planning, 1959. 51 p.

> A chronology and analysis of the EFTA negotiations, of their failure, and the implications.

997     Casey, R.G. THE FUTURE OF THE COMMONWEALTH. London: Frederick Muller, 1964. 187 p.

> A discussion of the future of the Commonwealth in light of possible British entry into the EC.

998     Cook, Philip Charles. "EFTA: The Origins and History of the European Free Trade Association." Ph.D. dissertation, University of Georgia, 1968.

999     Corbet, R. Hugh, and Robertson, David, eds. EUROPE'S FREE TRADE AREA EXPERIMENT: EFTA AND ECONOMIC INTEGRATION. London: published for the Graduate School of Contemporary European Studies, University of Reading, and the Trade Policy Research Centre by Pergamon Press, 1971. 268 p.

> A collection of essays by a European team of specialists concerned with EFTA, reappraising its achievements and perspectives for development. A study of Nordic integration included as well.

1000    Cowen, Zelman. THE BRITISH COMMONWEALTH OF NATIONS IN A CHANGING WORLD. Evanston, Ill.: Northwestern University Press, 1965. 117 p.

> Traces the development of the British Commonwealth and its institutions, particularly in legal and structural perspectives. Examines recent changes and inquiries into the politics and prospects of the Commonwealth working in league with the EEC.

1001    Cunningham, W.B., ed. CANADA, THE COMMONWEALTH AND THE COMMON MARKET. Montreal: McGill University Press, 1962. 142 p.

> A report of a seminar at McGill University on the future relations of Canada with the EC, Britain, and the Commonwealth, and the way in which these will be affected by British entry into the EC.

1002    Curzon, Victoria. THE ESSENTIALS OF ECONOMIC INTEGRATION: LESSONS OF EFTA EXPERIENCE. London: published for the Policy Research Centre by St. Martin's Press, 1974. 319 p.

"The author provides a history of the European Free Trade Association (1960-72) with emphasis upon the arrangements whereby the EFTA member countries resolved their differences and liberalized trade among themselves. These arrangements . . . should prove instructive in future regional and global attempts to liberalize trade."

CHOICE

1003 Derry, T.K. A HISTORY OF MODERN NORWAY, 1814-1972. London: Oxford University Press, 1973. 503 p.

A chronicle of Norway which includes a section on Norway's 1972 referendum rejecting membership in the European Community.

1004 Economist Intelligence Unit. THE COMMONWEALTH AND EUROPE. London: 1960. 606 p.

A collection and analysis of data relating to patterns of trade in the Commonwealth and EEC. Included are chapters on production and trade of foodstuffs, raw materials, and manufactures. Also analyzed are trade systems in the "older dominions" of the Commonwealth, Asian members, tropical Africa, and the West Indies.

1005 English, Harry Edward. TRANSATLANTIC ECONOMIC COMMUNITY: CANADIAN PERSPECTIVES. Toronto: published for the Private Planning Association of Canada by the University of Toronto Press, 1968. 70 p.

An assessment of Canada's place in economic cooperation and integration among Atlantic countries, and the impact of closer European Community ties on Canada. Discusses also the goals and organization of the EEC and EFTA, taking into account the political background of East-West relations.

1006 European Free Trade Association. REGIONAL DEVELOPMENT POLICIES IN EFTA. Geneva: 1965. 78 p.

A detailed discussion of principles, objectives, and experiences in relation to problems of regional development in Austria, Denmark, Finland, Norway, Portugal, Sweden, and Britain. Also, underdeveloped, industrialized, and overdeveloped areas are defined and analyzed.

1007   Gelber, H.G.   AUSTRALIA, BRITAIN, AND THE EEC, 1961–63.
London:  Oxford University Press, 1966.  xii, 296 p.

> An in-depth study of a very brief period analyzing
> Australia's reaction to the British reaction to the Com-
> mon Market.  A view of diplomacy, Australian poli-
> tics, and agricultural economics included.

1008   Geneva, Graduate Institute of International Studies.  THE EURO-
PEAN FREE TRADE ASSOCIATION AND THE CRISIS OF EURO-
PEAN INTEGRATION:  AN ASPECT OF THE ATLANTIC CRISIS.
Geneva:  published for the Graduate Institute by Michael Joseph,
1968.  323 p.

> An analysis of the reasons why Europe is still divided
> along lines of the late 1950s and why integration is
> proving so difficult to achieve.  The position of each
> EFTA member is analyzed, and the contribution of
> EFTA toward European integration is presented.

1009   Government Stationery Office [London].  NEGOTIATIONS FOR
A FREE TRADE AREA:  DOCUMENTS RELATING TO THE NEGO-
TIATIONS FROM JULY 1956 TO DECEMBER 1958.  Command 641.
London:  1959.  237 p.

> "This 'command paper' contains the most important docu-
> ments concerning the deliberations on creating a Euro-
> pean Free Trade Area which were published by the Coun-
> cil of the OEEC."
>
>                         BIBLIOGRAPHIE ZUR EURO-
>                         PAISCHEN INTEGRATION

1010   Hughes, William.  CANADA AND THE EUROPEAN COMMON
MARKET.  Vancouver:  University of British Columbia, 1962.
35 p.

> An occasional paper considering primarily Canada's
> economic relations to the EC and questions about the
> result of British entry, while noting similar problems
> for some other Commonwealth countries.

1011   Ingram, Derek.  THE COMMONWEALTH CHALLENGE.  London:
George Allen and Unwin, 1962.  291 p.

> See especially chapter 12 on the Common Market chal-
> lenge.

1012   _____.  PARTNERS IN ADVENTURE:  A NEW LOOK AT THE
COMMONWEALTH TODAY.  London:  Pan Books, 1960.  188 p.

1013    Jervis, James Ashbel. "The Commonwealth and the British Appli-
        cation for Membership of the European Economic Community, 1961-
        63." Ph.D. dissertation, Columbia University, 1969.


1014    Lambrinidis, John S. THE STRUCTURE, FUNCTION, AND LAW
        OF A FREE TRADE AREA: THE EUROPEAN FREE TRADE ASSO-
        CIATION. London: Stevens and Sons, 1965. 303 p.

        A study of the institutional and structural aspects of
        EFTA as well as the substantive provisions of its con-
        vention which seek to establish the legal framework in
        which EFTA is intended to operate.


1015    Løchen, Einar. NORWAY IN EUROPEAN AND ATLANTIC CO-
        OPERATION. Oslo: Universitets Forlaget, 1964. 88 p.


1016    Matthews, Roy A. BRITAIN'S MOVE INTO EUROPE: THE IM-
        PLICATIONS FOR CANADA. Ottawa: The Canadian Institute
        of International Affairs, 1972. 15 p.

        A short but penetrating economic study of the nega-
        tive implications for Canada if Britain joins the EC.


1017    Meyer, Frederick Victor. THE EUROPEAN FREE TRADE ASSO-
        CIATION: AN ANALYSIS OF "THE OUTER SEVEN." New York:
        Frederick A. Praeger, 1960. 140 p.

        The American title for no. 1018.


1018    _____. THE SEVEN: A PROVISIONAL APPRAISAL OF THE EU-
        ROPEAN FREE TRADE ASSOCIATION. London: Barrie and Rock-
        liff, 1960. 140 p.

        The British title for no. 1017.


1019    Orvik, Nils, ed. FEARS AND EXPECTATIONS: NORWEGIAN
        ATTITUDES TOWARD EUROPEAN INTEGRATION. Oslo: Uni-
        versitets Forlaget, 1972. 371 p.

        An analysis of Norwegian attitudes toward European
        integration, sovereignty, and EFTA. Includes politi-
        cal party reactions to the prospect of EC entry, and
        the debates held in Norway over EC membership.


1020    Piquet, Howard S. THE EUROPEAN FREE TRADE ASSOCIATION:
        IMPLICATIONS FOR U.S. EXPORTS. New York: American Man-
        agement Association, 1960. 56 p.

        A critical look at EFTA and the problems its founding
        creates for the United States vis-a-vis the EEC.

1021    Salis, Jean Rodolphe de.  SWITZERLAND AND EUROPE:  ES-
        SAYS AND REFLECTIONS.  Translated by A. and E. Henderson.
        London:  Oswald Wolff, 1971.  319 p.

            A series of essays on facets of the relationship of this
            neutral country with its "Community" European sister-
            states.  Covers a variety of topics, including foreign
            policy and Norwegian relations with the League of
            Nations, the United Nations, and the European Com-
            munity.


1022    Schiff, Martin.  "Swedish Neutrality and European Integration."
        Ph.D. dissertation, Rutgers University, 1969.


1023    Scott, John.  THE NEW EUROPE:  CAN SIX AND SEVEN MAKE
        ONE?  New York:  Time, 1961.  95 p.


1024    Sinclair, Sol.  THE COMMON AGRICULTURAL POLICY OF THE
        EEC AND ITS IMPLICATIONS FOR CANADA'S EXPORTS.  Mon-
        treal:  Canadian Trade Committee, and Private Planning Associa-
        tion of Canada, 1964.  101 p.


1025    Soper, Tom.  COMMONWEALTH AND COMMON MARKET: THE
        ECONOMIC IMPLICATIONS.  London:  Fabian Commonwealth
        Bureau, 1962.  29 p.

            Anti-Market commentary on the Commonwealth and the
            European Community, showing the unity of the former
            and the laxity of the latter.


1026    _____.  EVOLVING COMMONWEALTH.  New York:  Pergamon
        Press, 1965.  141 p.

            An essay on the history and development of the British
            Empire and Commonwealth from colonialism to the pres-
            ent, including the structure of the Commonwealth,
            laws regulating the group, and the role of the Com-
            monwealth in the European Community.


1027    _____, ed.  EUROPE AND THE COMMONWEALTH:  A SYM-
        POSIUM.  By E. Salin et al.  London:  Friends of Atlantic Union,
        1960.  68 p.


1028    Streeten, Paul, and Corbet, Hugh, eds.  COMMONWEALTH POL-
        ICY IN A GLOBAL CONTEXT.  Toronto:  University of Toronto
        Press, 1971.  232 p.

            A collection of essays on the Commonwealth and Brit-

ain's role in it, including the question of the effects
on Britain and the Commonwealth if Britain were to
join the European Community.

1029   Tornudd, Klaus, ed. "Nordic Studies in International Politics."
COOPERATION AND CONFLICT 4, no. 1 (1969): entire issue.

Devoted to Scandinavian and West European integration. Includes articles on Norway, Sweden, Denmark,
and Finland and their relation to the European Economic Community.

1030   Trainer, Orvel. "The Scandinavian Approach to the European
Common Market." Ph.D. dissertation, University of Colorado,
1960.

1031   Tulloch, Peter. THE SEVEN OUTSIDE: COMMONWEALTH ASIA'S
TRADE WITH THE ENLARGED EEC. London: Overseas Development
Institute, 1973. vi, 67 p.

"Measures the effect on exports by India, Bangladesh,
Pakistan, Sri Lanka, Malaysia, Singapore, and Hong
Kong of the phasing out of Commonwealth preference
and its replacement by a Community GSP."

Publisher

1032   Uri, Pierre, ed. FROM COMMONWEALTH TO COMMON MAR-
KET. London: Penguin Books for the Atlantic Institute, 1968.
176 p.

Details the current attitudes in Canada, Australia, New
Zealand, Asia, and Africa towards the prospect of
Britain's entry into the Common Market and seeks to
assess the likely effects of the change in those areas.

1033   Waldheim, Kurt. THE AUSTRIAN EXAMPLE. Translated by Ewald
Osers. New York: Macmillan Co., 1973. 230 p.

Written by the UN Secretary-General before he held
that office. Offers an analysis of Austria's neutral role
in world politics. Also includes several chapters on
the relationship between Austria and the EC, and why
Austria refused full membership.

1034   Wiseman, H.V. BRITAIN AND THE COMMONWEALTH. New
York: Barnes and Noble Publications, 1967. 157 p.

Discusses the Commonwealth in a world context with

an emphasis on British influence. Compares the social and political systems of members with the British model, and projects future political and economic relationships among members, the strength of the ties, and the causes of the weakening of the integrated structure.

## D. GREECE

1035    Hitiris, Theodore. TRADE EFFECTS OF ECONOMIC ASSOCIA-TION WITH THE COMMON MARKET: THE CASE OF GREECE. New York: Praeger Publishers, 1972. 172 p.

A consideration of Greece specifically, both before and after association with the EEC. General concern also given for the theory and practice of relations between the EC and developing countries.

1036    Plessas, Demetrius John. "The Decentralization Aspects of European Regional Policy and Development with Special Reference to Greece." Ph.D. dissertation, University of Michigan, 1969.

1037    Triantis, S.G. COMMON MARKET AND ECONOMIC DEVELOP-MENT: THE EEC AND GREECE. Athens: Center of Planning and Economic Research, 1965. 232 p.

An economic analysis of the effects of Greece's development resulting from association with the EEC.

1038    Yannopoulos, George N. GREECE AND THE EUROPEAN ECO-NOMIC COMMUNITIES: THE FIRST DECADE OF A TROUBLED ASSOCIATION. Sage Research Papers in the Social Sciences, ser. no. 90-021, Contemporary European Studies. Beverly Hills, Calif.: Sage Publications, 1975. 35 p.

## E. SOVIET UNION AND EAST BLOC

1039    Atlantic Institute. THE ATLANTIC COMMUNITY AND EASTERN EUROPE: PERSPECTIVES AND POLICY. Paris: 1967. 108 p.

Presentations from the 1966 Atlantic Institute Conference in Rome by specialists on Eastern Europe. Includes a variety of topics relating to East-West relations: evolution in the USSR and the Balkans, trade, and military and political aspects of East-West trade.

1040    Birnbaum, Karl E. PEACE IN EUROPE: EAST-WEST RELATIONS

1966–68 AND THE PROSPECTS FOR A EUROPEAN SETTLEMENT.
London: Oxford University Press, 1970. 159 p.

> An investigation of official thinking in East and West
> about the relationship between politics and defense in
> Europe during the late 1960s; its immediate policy re-
> quirements and long-range potentialities; effects on
> NATO and defense arrangements; on West European in-
> tegration; and relations between Eastern Europe, the
> USSR, and Western Europe.

1041 Collier, David S., and Glaser, Kurt, eds. BERLIN AND THE
FUTURE OF EASTERN EUROPE. Chicago: Henry Regnery, 1963.
251 p.

> See especially Herman Gross's article: "The Common
> Market and Eastern Bloc Integration," a detailed com-
> parison of the Common Market and COMECON.

1042 _____. WESTERN INTEGRATION AND THE FUTURE OF EAST-
ERN EUROPE. Chicago: Henry Regnery, 1964. 207 p.

> Twelve essays from the 1963 Wiesbaden Conference of
> the Chicago Foundation For World Affairs cover various
> facets of the economic, political, and military rela-
> tionships between East and West Europe, and the in-
> fluence of those relations on East Europe, the United
> States, and on West European integration.

1043 _____. WESTERN POLICY AND EASTERN EUROPE. Chicago:
Henry Regnery, 1966. 245 p.

> Included are the papers delivered at a conference in
> Wiesbaden, Germany, March 1965, on East and West
> Europe sponsored by the Chicago Foundation for Foreign
> Affairs. See especially chapters 12 through 14 for ar-
> ticles relating to West European integration and Eastern
> Europe, and the influence of the one on the other.

1044 Council of Europe. Consultative Assembly. FOCUS ON EAST/
WEST RELATIONS: A POLICY FOR EUROPE. Strasbourg, France:
1956. 252 p.

1045 De Gara, John P. TRADE RELATIONS BETWEEN THE COMMON
MARKET AND THE EASTERN BLOC. Bruges, Belgium: De Temple,
1964. 102 p.

> A study of trade relations between the Common Market
> and the East Bloc countries in an attempt to assess the ef-
> fect of the Common Market as a vehicle for functional in-
> tegration.

1046    European League for Economic Cooperation. ECONOMIC, INDUS-
        TRIAL, SCIENTIFIC AND TECHNICAL COOPERATION BETWEEN
        THE COUNTRIES OF EASTERN AND WESTERN EUROPE. Brussels:
        1967. 117 p.

1047    Free Europe Committee [New York]. EUROPE: NINE PANEL
        STUDIES BY EXPERTS FROM CENTRAL AND EASTERN EUROPE;
        AN EXAMINATION OF THE POST LIBERATION PROBLEM OF
        THE POSITION OF CENTRAL AND EASTERN EUROPEAN NA-
        TIONS IN A FREE EUROPEAN COMMUNITY. New York: 1954.
        146 p.

    Panel studies by scholars from the "satellite countries"
    concerning, specifically, the functional advantages
    and disadvantages of cooperation between the satellite
    countries, once free, and Western Europe.

1048    Galtung, Johan, ed. COOPERATION IN EUROPE. New York:
        Humanities Press, 1971. 371 p.

    An analysis of the cooperation between East and West
    Europe in various fields, including security. Presents
    proposals for furthering that cooperation.

1049    Gorgey, Laszlo. BONN'S EASTERN POLICY, 1964-71: EVO-
        LUTION AND LIMITATIONS. Hamden, Conn.: published for
        the Institute of International Studies, University of South Carolina,
        by Archon Books, 1972. 191 p.

    Bonn's Eastern policy (Ostpolitik) under scrutiny, with
    a discussion of the way in which that policy affects
    her NATO commitments and relations with EURATOM,
    the ECSC, and the EEC.

1050    Institute for Strategic Studies. WESTERN AND EASTERN EUROPE:
        THE CHANGING RELATIONSHIP. London: 1967. 57 p.

    Seven papers from a conference held by the Institute
    covering a variety of problems between East and West
    Europe, the future of Germany, China's impact, and
    the small countries, among others.

1051    John, Ieuan, ed. EEC POLICY TOWARDS EASTERN EUROPE.
        Hants, Engl.: Saxon House; Lexington, Mass.: D.C. Heath and
        Co., 1975. 149 p.

    A series of eight papers by European and American
    scholars addressing East-West relations in economic
    and security policy, and the effect of the relation-
    ship on the international environment.

1052    Kaser, Michael. COMECON: INTEGRATION PROBLEMS OF
THE PLANNED ECONOMIES. London: published for Chatham
House by Oxford University Press, 1966. 215 p.

A detailed description of the economics and politics
of COMECON, useful either as a study of COMECON
integration in East Europe, or as a contrast to the EEC.

1053    London, Kurt, ed. EASTERN EUROPE IN TRANSITION. Baltimore: Johns Hopkins Press, 1966. 364 p.

See especially Hassner's paper "Polycentrism, West
and East: Implications of the Western Debates," which
develops the thesis that until Europe unites it will be
subject to the two superpowers.

1054    Mensonides, Louis J., and Kuhlman, James A., eds. THE FU-
TURE OF INTER-BLOC RELATIONS IN EUROPE. New York:
Praeger Publishers, 1974. 234 p.

"A broad, interdisciplinary view of a changing Europe,
covering three general problem areas: analysis of
change, projection of military and economic problems
in bloc relations, and probable political configurations
in the future. Includes the impact of resource [and]
energy problems on political relationships in Europe,
and emphasizes both Eastern and Western perspectives."

Publisher

1055    Radio Free Europe Research. THE COMMUNISTS AND THE COM-
MON MARKET, 1957-67. Munich: 1967. 88 p.

1056    Ransom, Charles. THE EUROPEAN COMMUNITY AND EASTERN
EUROPE. Totowa, N.J.: Rowman and Littlefield, 1973. 112 p.

Considers some possible effects of the enlargement of
the EC upon the relations between Western and Eastern
Europe, especially between the EEC and COMECON,
and the possibilities of a wider European system.

1057    Schoepflin, George, ed. THE SOVIET UNION AND EASTERN
EUROPE: A HANDBOOK. New York: Praeger Publishers, 1970.
xii, 614 p.

See the chapter "The EEC and Eastern Europe" by
Schoepflin tracing the response of East Europe and
the USSR to the EEC, as well as the EEC response
to Eastern Europe—which is not seen as propitious.

1058    Sinanian, Sylva, et al., eds. New York: Praeger Publishers, 1972. 260 p.

        A compilation of papers from a conference at Columbia University on Eastern Europe. Especially useful studies of East European economic integration and relations with integrated Western Europe, particularly with West Germany in chapters 6 and 8.

1059    SOME APSECTS OF EAST-WEST TRADE IN BRITAIN, GERMANY AND THE COMMON MARKET. Washington, D.C.: 1966.

        Studies in law and economic development.

1060    Waterlow, Charlotte, and Evans, Archibald. EUROPE 1945 TO 1970. London: Methuen and Co., 1973. 316 p.

        A cultural history of both East and West Europe, including a discussion of two important topics: Western Europe unifying behind liberal humanism; Eastern Europe being integrated behind Marxism.

## F. UNITED STATES AND ATLANTIC COMMUNITY (nonsecurity)

## 1. Political and General

1061    Allen, H.C. THE ANGLO-AMERICAN PREDICAMENT: THE BRITISH COMMONWEALTH, THE UNITED STATES AND EUROPEAN UNITY. New York: St. Martin's Press, 1960. 241 p.

        An argument for a federal Atlantic union rather than a narrower association of Britain with Europe. Includes the British position towards Europe and also towards the United States and Atlantic union.

1062    American Academy of Political and Social Science. THE NEW EUROPE: IMPLICATIONS FOR THE UNITED STATES. Special editor James C. Charlesworth. Vol. 348. Philadelphia: 1963. 238 p.

        A collection of articles on European integration including the economic effects of the EC, cultural development, military and political integration, power blocs in the EC, and American relations with the EC.

1063    Atlantic Institute. ATLANTIC PAPERS ANNUAL. Vol. 1, by L.W. Martin et al. New York: Dunellen Publishing Co., 1970. 197 p.

        The first of an annual series on Atlantic affairs from

the Atlantic Institute. Includes three articles on issues facing NATO states: the problem of ballistic mis-
siles, the fate of the pound sterling, and forms of defense cooperation.

1064 _____. THE TECHNOLOGY GAP: THE UNITED STATES AND
EUROPE. New York: published for the Atlantic Institute by
Praeger Publishers, 1970. 170 p.

A study of technological and managerial discrepancies
between the United States and Europe, its causes and
effects on Atlantic cooperation.

1065 Baudry, Bernard. EURO-AMERICA. Paris: Plon, 1962. 212 p.

Examines the conditions for a genuine community between Europe and America. Asserts that the conditions are spiritual-cultural in nature and should revolve
around a grand strategy of the United States, Britain,
and France. Also examines the OECD in the light of
the proposed strategy.

1066 Beloff, Max. THE UNITED STATES AND THE UNITY OF EU-
ROPE. Washington, D.C.: Brookings Institution, 1963. 124 p.

An essay on U.S. foreign policy and U.S. attempts to
persuade European countries of the advantages to them
of close political and economic integration. Also studies the effects on U.S. policy of an integrated Europe.

1067 Beugel, Ernst H. van der. FROM MARSHALL AID TO ATLAN-
TIC PARTNERSHIP: EUROPEAN INTEGRATION AS A CONCERN
OF AMERICAN FOREIGN POLICY. New York: American El-
sevier Publishing Co., 1966. 480 p.

A retracing of American cold war policy and Europe's relation to it. Asserts that the economic redevelopment of Europe as well as its involvement in
the Atlantic alliance were conceived not as ends,
but as means to contain Soviet power.

1068 Birrenbach, Kurt. THE FUTURE OF THE ATLANTIC COMMU-
NITY: TOWARD EUROPEAN-AMERICAN PARTNERSHIP. New
York: Frederick A. Praeger, 1963. 94 p.

A text for the intelligent layman. A comprehensive
but compact survey of problems in building the Atlantic community, economically, militarily, politically,
culturally, including the EC, NATO, and OECD.

1069    Bowie, Robert, and Geiger, Theodore. THE EUROPEAN ECO-
        NOMIC COMMUNITY AND THE UNITED STATES. Washington,
        D.C.: Government Printing Office for the Subcommittee on
        Foreign Economic Policy of the Joint Economic Committee of the
        U.S. Congress, 1961. 60 p.

1070    Brewer, Thomas Lee. "Issue Type and Context in American Foreign
        Policy-Making: An Analysis of Elite Behavior in Sixty-five Euro-
        pean Integration and Atlantic Alliance Cases, 1949-68." Ph.D.
        dissertation, State University of New York at Buffalo, 1971.

1071    Brzezinski, Zbigniew. ALTERNATIVE TO PARTITION: FOR A
        BROADER CONCEPTION OF AMERICA'S ROLE IN EUROPE. New
        York: McGraw-Hill Book Co., 1965. 202 p.

        A consideration of America's critical role in promoting
        elimination of the European partition between East and
        West.

1072    Bundy, McGeorge. THE AMERICANS AND EUROPE: RHETORIC
        AND REALITY. The eighth foundation lecture, 18 July 1969. Ox-
        ford: Ditchley Foundation, 1969. 20 p.

1073    Burgess, W. Randolph, and Huntley, James Robert. EUROPE AND
        AMERICA: THE NEXT TEN YEARS. New York: Frank R. Walker
        Co., 1970. 232 p.

        Within the context of the tendency towards isolationism
        during the last decade, examines the urgent political
        and social issues which face the Atlantic community
        today. Also, seeks to detail the most advantageous
        form of community and the possibilities for progress
        toward that end.

1074    Calleo, David P. THE ATLANTIC FANTASY: THE UNITED
        STATES, NATO AND EUROPE. Baltimore: Johns Hopkins Press,
        1970. 192 p.

        Continues the theme of "Atlantic Fantasy." Argues
        that the United States ought to cease trying to gov-
        ern the Atlantic alliance from Washington and restore
        European responsibilities to Europe.

1075    Calleo, David P., and Rowland, Benjamin M. AMERICA AND THE
        WORLD POLITICAL ECONOMY: ATLANTIC DREAMS AND NATIONAL
        REALITIES. Bloomington: Indiana University Press, 1973. 371 p.

        A survey of the ideological, economic, and political con-
        cerns governing successful U.S. trade policy in recent

years, and an attempt to show why U.S. policy has
failed both in Europe (in the EC) and in Japan.

1076    Camps, Miriam. THE EUROPEAN COMMON MARKET AND
AMERICAN POLICY. Princeton, N.J.: Center of International
Studies, Princeton University, 1956.  30 p.

A concise study of the favorable and unfavorable aspects of the European Economic Community in American eyes, and a statement meant as encouragement
for cooperation between the two blocs.

1077    Catlin, George E.G. THE ATLANTIC COMMUNITY.  London:
Coram Publishers, 1959.  146 p.

An essay and a proposal for an Atlantic federation,
based on an Anglo-American union at its core.

1078    _____. THE GRANDEUR OF ENGLAND AND THE ATLANTIC
COMMUNITY.  London: Pergamon Press, 1966.  217 p.

Voices the doctrine of organic union of Europe, the
Commonwealth, and the United States in an Atlantic
Community.  Includes a survey of the events and in-
stitutions concerned with the Atlantic Community.

1079    Cerami, Charles A. ALLIANCE BORN OF DANGER: AMERICA,
THE COMMON MARKET AND THE ATLANTIC PARTNERSHIP.
New York: Harcourt, Brace and World, 1963.  181 p.

A journalistic account of U.S. and Common Market
relations.

1080    _____. CRISIS, THE LOSS OF EUROPE.  New York:  Harcourt
Brace Jovanovich, 1975.  182 p.

1081    Cleveland, Harold Van Buren, and Cleveland, Joan B.  THE AT-
LANTIC ALLIANCE: PROBLEMS AND PROSPECTS.  New York:
Foreign Policy Association, 1966.  63 p.

A brief analysis of the Atlantic alliance, NATO, weap-
onry, and the issues facing Europe and the European
Community.

1082    Connery, Robert H. THE "ATLANTIC COMMUNITY" REAPPRAISED.
New York: The Academy of Political Science, 1968.  156 p.

1083    Cottrell, Alvin J., and Dougherty, James E.  THE POLITICS OF

THE ATLANTIC ALLIANCE. New York: Frederick A. Praeger, 1964. 264 p.

A political "guide" to NATO, its role, and implications for the United States and for European integration.

1084 Council of Europe. Consultative Assembly. A POLICY FOR EUROPE TODAY: DEBATE AT THE CONSULTATIVE ASSEMBLY, SEPTEMBER 3, 1953. Strasbourg, France: 1953. 247 p.

1085 Cromwell, William C. POLITICAL PROBLEMS OF ATLANTIC PARTNERSHIP: NATIONAL PERSPECTIVES. Bruges, Belgium: College of Europe, 1969. 458 p.

A painstaking analysis of the results of a symposium on Atlantic relations. Claims that while Atlantic relations were stable in the early 1960s, they changed rapidly in the late 1960s. Also discusses the preoccupations with Britain's entry into the EC, de Gaulle's Europe, and U.S.-USSR relations.

1086 De Raeymaeker, Omer, and Bowman, Albert, eds. AMERICAN FOREIGN POLICY IN EUROPE: A COLLOQUIUM ON ASPECTS OF THE AMERICAN PRESENCE IN BELGIUM, THE FEDERAL REPUBLIC OF GERMANY, FRANCE AND ITALY. Louvain, Belgium: published for the Catholic University of Louvain by Nauwelaerts, 1969. 110 p.

A collection of eight articles on the effects and influence of the United States on national decision making in four West European countries. The issues dealt with include European integration.

1087 Deutsch, Harold C. THE NEW EUROPE, THE COMMON MARKET, AND THE UNITED STATES. Foreign Relations Series. River Forest, Ill.: Laidlaw Brothers, 1964. 67 p.

A brief profile of the post-World War II era in European integration and its relation to the United States. Monograph designed as a teaching aid by the North Central Association of College and Secondary Schools.

1088 Drummond, Roscoe, and Coblentz, Gaston. DUEL AT THE BRINK: JOHN FOSTER DULLES' COMMAND OF AMERICAN POWER. New York: Doubleday and Co., 1960. 240 p.

A history of the role of Dulles in shaping U.S. policy towards Europe 1953-59 based on responses of statesmen who knew and worked with him. Offers rich in-

sights into Dulles's relations with Adenauer, Monnet,
Eden, Macmillan, and other "fathers of Europe."

1089    European Movement. EUROPEAN-AMERICAN SURVEY: A PUBLI-
CATION DEVOTED TO BETTER UNDERSTANDING BETWEEN UNITED
EUROPE AND THE UNITED STATES OF AMERICA. Brussels: 1957.
144 p.

A collection of essays. Seeks to foster better understanding betweeen a united Europe and the United
States. By eminent spokesmen like Paul-Henri Spaak
and Robert Schuman. Covers the European political
community, European economic community, defense of
Europe, and U.S.-EC relations.

1090    Gasteyger, Curt. EUROPE AND AMERICA AT THE CROSSROADS.
Paris: Atlantic Institute, 1972. 50 p.

1091    Geiger, Theodore. TRANSATLANTIC RELATIONS IN THE PROS-
PECT OF AN ENLARGED COMMUNITY. London: British-North
American Committee, 1970. 61 p.

An argument for restructuring the Atlantic Community
in light of the progress of European integration; a functionalist argument recognizing the "myth" of Atlantic
union.

1092    Gelber, Lionel Morris. AMERICA IN BRITAIN'S PLACE: THE
LEADERSHIP OF THE WEST AND ANGLO-AMERICAN UNITY.
New York: Frederick A. Praeger, 1961. 356 p.

1093    Godson, Joseph, ed. TRANSATLANTIC CRISIS: EUROPE AND
AMERICA IN THE SEVENTIES. London: Alcove, 1974. 148 p.

"A reproduction with later additions and revisions, of
a series of articles published in the INTERNATIONAL
HERALD TRIBUNE during April and May 1974."

EUROPEAN COMMUNITY

1094    Goodman, Eliot R. THE FATE OF THE ATLANTIC COMMUNITY.
New York: published for the Atlantic Council by Praeger Publishers, 1975. 603 p.

A study of, and an argument for, a closer Atlantic
union. Surveys the various concepts proposed for
union, as well as the problems to be surmounted; Gaullism, NATO, divided Germany, multilateral nuclear
sharing, among others.

1095    Gordon, Kermit, ed. AGENDA FOR THE NATION. Washington,
        D.C.: Brookings Institution, 1968. 620 p.

>    See especially the chapter by Bator, "The Politics of
>    Alliance: The United States and Western Europe,"
>    which is a discussion of policies for defense and nu-
>    clear arms, economic growth between the United States
>    and Europe, and general political trends in Germany,
>    Britain, and France.

1096    Hanrieder, Wolfram F., ed. THE UNITED STATES AND WEST-
        ERN EUROPE: POLITICAL, ECONOMIC AND STRATEGIC PER-
        SPECTIVES. Cambridge, Mass.: Winthrop Publishing Co., 1974.
        xiii, 311 p.

>    Twelve essays dealing with diverse political, economic,
>    military concerns between the United States and Eu-
>    rope. Includes authors like Morgenthau, Waltz, Calleo,
>    Hoffmann, and Diebold, among others.

1097    Hartley, Livingston. ATLANTIC CHALLENGE. Dobbs Ferry, N.Y.:
        Oceana Publications, 1965. xii, 111 p.

>    A history of the Atlantic movement and the way its
>    development compares with the move for unification
>    in the United States, in NATO, and in the EEC. In-
>    cludes a future Atlantic Community modelled on the
>    institutions of the EEC with a parliament, council,
>    and commission.

1098    Hassner, Pierre, and Newhouse, John, eds. DIPLOMACY IN
        THE WEST: OUT FROM PARADOX. A paper on European-
        American relations with an introduction by August Hecksher.
        Tocqueville Series, no. 1. Rev. ed. New York: Twentieth
        Century Fund, 1966. ix, 67 p.

>    A brief study of four problems common to the foreign
>    policies of Britain, France, Germany, Italy, and the
>    United States: the "German Problem," Europe's po-
>    litical development, Atlantic alliance politics, and arms
>    control.

1099    Haviland, H. Field, Jr. THE ATLANTIC COMMUNITY: PROGRESS
        AND PROSPECTS. New York: Frederick A. Praeger, 1963. 294 p.

>    An examination of the cooperative relations among the
>    Atlantic nations as well as relations with the under-
>    developed world, towards the European Community,
>    and towards Eastern Europe.

1100    Herter, Christian A.   TOWARD AN ATLANTIC COMMUNITY.
        New York: published for the Council on Foreign Relations by
        Harper and Row, 1963.  105 p.

> A " . . . statement of the background and develop-
> ment of the steps toward economic and political inte-
> gration of Europe paralleling the military alliance in
> NATO.  He shows that the European Economic Com-
> munity (EEC) . . . is more revolutionary than its pre-
> decessors."
>
> LIBRARY JOURNAL quoted
> in BOOK REVIEW DIGEST

1101    Hodson, H.V., ed.   THE ATLANTIC FUTURE:  THE RECORD OF
        A CONFERENCE HELD AT DITCHLEY PARK FROM 6 TO 8 MAY
        1963.  London: Longman, 1964.  xi, 129 p.

> Included here are five essays dealing with the future
> of the Atlantic Community and its integrated focus,
> including the problem of nuclear arms.

1102    Hoffmann, Stanley.   GULLIVER'S TROUBLES OR THE SETTING
        OF AMERICAN FOREIGN POLICY.   New York:  McGraw-Hill
        Book Co., 1967.  556 p.

> Analyzes American foreign policy towards the Atlantic
> alliance.  Begins with the world of the 1960s and an-
> alyzes America's response to the "new" environment of
> trouble.  A useful guide to a better understanding of
> U.S. policy towards Europe.

1103    Holborn, Hajo.   THE POLITICAL COLLAPSE OF EUROPE.  New
        York: Alfred A. Knopf, 1958.  207 p.

> A history of Europe following the decline of its world
> power.  Finds the Atlantic community inevitable, bring-
> ing with it European cooperation, but not unification.

1104    Jenkins, Roy.  AFTERNOON ON THE POTOMAC?  A BRITISH
        VIEW OF AMERICA'S CHANGING POSITION IN THE WORLD.
        New Haven, Conn.:  Yale University Press, 1972.  60 p.

> A prominent Briton's view of America's role as a super-
> power vis-a-vis Europe and Britain.  Suggests that Brit-
> ain join Europe, and as a result U.S. influence in Eu-
> rope will diminish.

1105    Jones, Alan M., ed.   U.S. FOREIGN POLICY IN A CHANG-
        ING WORLD: THE NIXON ADMINISTRATION, 1969-73.  New

York: David McKay Co., 1973. 379 p.

> See especially Lieber's article "Britain Joins Europe," an analysis of the meaning to the United States of Britain's accession to the EC. Asserts that the intimate U.S.-British relationship will end.

1106 Kaiser, Karl. EUROPE AND THE UNITED STATES: THE FUTURE OF THE RELATIONSHIP. Washington, D.C.: Columbia Books, 1973. 150 p.

> A discussion of the issues and problems in the economic and political relationship between the United States and Western Europe, and a look at the future of those relationships.

1107 Kleiman, Robert. ATLANTIC CRISIS: AMERICAN DIPLOMACY CONFRONTS A RESURGENT EUROPE. New York: W.W. Norton and Co., 1963. 158 p.

> Concerned with Kennedy's "grand design" to create an Atlantic partnership and the setback that design received by de Gaulle's veto in 1963. Also examines why de Gaulle vetoed Britain's entry as well as President Johnson's position on Atlantic Community.

1108 Kraft, Joseph. THE GRAND DESIGN: FROM COMMON MARKET TO ATLANTIC PARTNERSHIP. New York: Harper and Brothers, 1962. 122 p.

> A lengthy essay on the virtues of the Atlantic alliance and the mutual advantages and problems facing the United States and Europe in creating such an alliance.

1109 Lerche, Charles O., Jr. LAST CHANCE IN EUROPE: BASES FOR A NEW AMERICAN POLICY. Chicago: Quadrangle Books, 1967. 221 p.

> An analysis of U.S.-European relations in the post-World War II era and how conditions have changed, though the assumptions about those conditions have not.

1110 Lichtheim, George. EUROPE AND AMERICA: THE FUTURE OF THE ATLANTIC COMMUNITY. London: Thames and Hudson, 1963. 256 p.

> A discussion of European integration and the Atlantic community, including the importance of not building Europe outside the Atlantic Community.

1111      . THE NEW EUROPE: TODAY AND TOMORROW. New
York: Frederick A. Praeger, 1963. 232 p.

> For the nonspecialist. A summary and discussion within
> a socioeconomic framework of Europe's role in the At-
> lantic Community. Assumes the desirability of an At-
> lantic Community, and describes the main political and
> economic developments from the Marshall Plan to the
> EEC.

1112  McCloy, John J. THE ATLANTIC ALLIANCE: ITS ORIGINS
AND ITS FUTURE. New York: Columbia University Press, 1969.
83 p.

> Selections from the 1968 Benjamin F. Fairless Memorial
> Lecture Series concerning the current state of the At-
> lantic alliance, its importance, challenges, and future
> direction.

1113  Mally, Gerhard. INTERDEPENDENCE. Lexington, Mass.: D.C.
Heath and Co., 1976. 229 p.

> "A scholarly and pragmatic study of the 'phenomenon
> of interdependence' in the domains of security, eco-
> nomics, politics, and the environment. Particular em-
> phasis is placed upon the management of economic in-
> terdependence in the Atlantic area and upon the in-
> herent conflicts between the designs for intra-European
> and trans-Atlantic integration."

## EUROPEAN COMMUNITY

1114      . "United Europe and the Atlantic Community: A Study
of Contemporary Trends Toward Political Integration in Western
Europe and their Significance for Future Trans-Atlantic Relations."
Ph.D. dissertation, University of Pennsylvania, 1964.

1115      , ed. THE NEW EUROPE AND THE UNITED STATES:
PARTNERS OR RIVALS. Lexington, Mass., Toronto, and London:
published for the Atlantic Council of the United States by Lexington Books, 1974. 463 p.

> A collection of addresses, articles, and essays by both
> Europeans and Americans on the diplomatic, economic,
> and security issues of the Atlantic partnership.

1116  Mandel, Ernest. EUROPE VS. AMERICA: CONTRADICTIONS
OF IMPERIALISM. New York: Monthly Review Press, 1970. 160 p.

> A focus on the economic confrontation between Euro-

pean and American capitalism. Includes the British effort to enter the EC, the French revolt against Washington, the international monetary structure, and the
role of labor.

1117    Mayne, Richard, ed. THE NEW ATLANTIC CHALLENGE. New
York: John Wiley and Sons, 1975. 376 p.

The results of a symposium held in 1973 in Amsterdam.
Includes contributions by George Ball, Walter Hallstein, Raymond Aron, Zbigniew Brzezinski, and Nelson Rockefeller, among others, discussing topics under
these headings: "Economic Issues in an Interdependent
World," "Processes of Change in the Field of Security,"
and "New Perspectives in Foreign Policy." A study
useful for both professionals and graduate students.

1118    Mendershausen, Horst. A VIEW OF U.S.-RELATIONS IN 1964.
Santa Monica, Calif.: RAND Corp., 1964. 43 p.

1119    Middleton, Drew. THE ATLANTIC COMMUNITY: A STUDY IN
UNITY AND DISUNITY. New York: David McKay Co., 1965. 303 p.

A study of the Atlantic Community's continuing crisis
including a review of the state of the various Atlantic organizations like NATO. Also reviews the various national outlooks of France, Britain, Germany,
and Italy on the Atlantic Community.

1120    _____. CRISIS IN THE WEST. London: Martin Secker and
Warburg, 1965. 286 p.

Notes with dismay the decline of cooperation in the
Atlantic alliance and the strength of opposition to
European unity, including the revival of nationalism.
Also discusses the political situation in the major West
European states, the progress of unity, and the Soviet
challenge.

1121    Munk, Frank. ATLANTIC DILEMMA: PARTNERSHIP OR COM-
MUNITY? Dobbs Ferry, N.Y.: Oceana Publications, 1964.
177 p.

A functional analysis of the Atlantic alliance and alternatives to the present alliance in the "free world
community."

1122    Nunnerley, David. PRESIDENT KENNEDY AND BRITAIN. New
York: St. Martin's Press, 1972. 242 p.

A focus upon the leadership and policies of John Ken-

nedy and Macmillan which encouraged the "special
relationship" and caused Britain so much trouble with
de Gaulle and Europe.

1123   Perry, Bruce.   "Senator J. William Fulbright on European and Atlantic Unity."   Ph.D. dissertation, University of Pennsylvania, 1968.

1124   Pfaltzgraff, Robert L[ouis]., Jr.   THE ATLANTIC COMMUNITY.
New York: Van Nostrand Reinhold Co., 1969.   216 p.

Traces U.S.-European relations since the founding of
NATO.   Assesses the principal sources of tension
among Atlantic countries pointing particularly to imbalances in military affairs, technology, politics and
economics, and proceeds to show how they have led
to a disintegration of the Atlantic Community.

1125   Philip, Andre.   COUNSEL FROM AN ALLY:   REFLECTIONS ON
CHANGES WITHIN THE ATLANTIC COMMUNITY.   Columbia: University of Missouri Press, 1966.   xi, 79 p.

Three lectures by Philip, on France, the EC, and
the necessity of coordinating these two in the Atlantic alliance.

1126   Raestad, Arnold Christopher.   EUROPE AND THE ATLANTIC
WORLD.   Oslo: I Kommisjon hos Aschehoug, 1958.   114 p.

A philosophical essay on the necessity of forming an
Atlantic community including the United States and
the smaller powers like Norway which offer peculiar
merits to such a community.

1127   Rosenthal, Benjamin S., and Fraser, Donald M.   A GROWING
BOND: THE EUROPEAN PARLIAMENT AND THE CONGRESS.
REPORT ON THE FIRST OFFICIAL VISIT TO CONGRESS BY A
DELEGATION OF THE EUROPEAN PARLIAMENT, MAY 1972.
Washington, D.C.: Government Printing Office, 1972.   20 p.

1128   Russett, Bruce M.   COMMUNITY AND CONTENTION:   BRITAIN
AND AMERICA IN THE TWENTIETH CENTURY.   Cambridge, Mass.:
M.I.T. Press, 1963.   252 p.

A case study of Karl Deutsch's concept of a "security
community" as applied to the Atlantic Community.   Also discusses the way in which members act to accommo-
date one another's interests.   Included is a wealth of
material on Anglo-American relations and indexes challenging the closeness of the Anglo-American nexus.
Communications analysis used for the study.

1129　Schaetzel, J. Robert. THE UNHINGED ALLIANCE: AMERICA
AND THE EUROPEAN COMMUNITY. New York: published for
the Council on Foreign Relations by Harper and Row, 1975. 179 p.

A critique of American foreign policy towards the EC
and an assessment of the prospects for the future in
economic, political, and defense relations.

1130　Silberschmidt, Max. THE UNITED STATES AND EUROPE: RIVALS
AND PARTNERS. Translated by J.M. Brownjohn. London: Thames
and Hudson, 1972; New York: Harcourt Brace Jovanovich, 1972.
216 p.

A study of the United States and Europe. Treats their
likenesses and differences in a global context in order
to test the thesis of Atlantic cooperation.

1131　Steel, Ronald. THE END OF ALLIANCE: AMERICA AND THE
FUTURE OF EUROPE. New York: Viking Press, 1964. 148 p.

An assessment of Europe's resistance to America, and
the collapsing of the old alliance which began in 1945.

1132　Strausz-Hupe, Robert, et al. BUILDING THE ATLANTIC WORLD.
New York: Harper and Row, 1963. 400 p.

A study of American foreign policy which focuses upon
the military, politico-diplomatic, and economic aspects
of that policy towards Western Europe during the early
1960s.

1133　Streit, Clarence. FREEDOM'S FRONTIER: ATLANTIC UNION
NOW. New York: Harper and Row, 1961. 318 p.

A federalist's view of integration. Argues that Europe
is inexperienced in "democracy" and therefore should
unite into an Atlantic federation where democracy is
more deeply embedded.

1134　Szent-Miklosky, Istvan. "The Development of American Thinking on an Atlantic Community, 1945-62." Ph.D. dissertation,
Columbia University, 1962.

1135　Taber, George M. JOHN F. KENNEDY AND A UNITING EU-
ROPE: THE POLITICS OF PARTNERSHIP. Studies in Contemporary
European Issues. Brussels: College of Europe, 1969. 183 p.

An examination of President Kennedy's policy toward European-American integration including U.S. policy towards the British application for membership in the EC.

1136   Trezise, Phillip H.   THE ATLANTIC CONNECTION:   PROSPECTS,
       PROBLEMS, AND POLICIES.   Washington, D.C.:   Brookings Insti-
       tution, 1975.   100 p.

>      "An examination of the many problems and crises fac-
>      ing the transatlantic system, including unresolved trade
>      and investment issues, recurring European suspicions of
>      a U.S.-Soviet condominium, what kind of international
>      monetary regime should replace the Bretton Woods sys-
>      tem, and the formulation of an energy policy for the
>      Atlantic nations."
>
>                                                    Publisher

1137   Turner, Arthur Campbell.   THE UNIQUE PARTNERSHIP:   BRITAIN
       AND THE U.S.   New York: Pegasus, 1971.   166 p.

>      A history of the U.S.-U.K. relations.   Of special in-
>      terest is the post-World War II situation, and the de-
>      velopment of a unique partnership in light of conti-
>      nental Europe's efforts to unify.

1138   Turner, Arthur Campbell, et al.   PROBLEMS OF EUROPEAN IN-
       TEGRATION.   Proceedings of the Institute of World Affairs, 43d
       session, 1966.   Vol. 42.   Los Angeles:   University of Southern
       California Press, 1967.   139 p.

>      A collection of papers by Henry Kissinger and others
>      focusing upon practical issues for U.S. foreign policy
>      resulting from European integration, trading blocs,
>      Eastern Europe, and American narcissism.

1139   Tuthill, John W.   THE DECISIVE YEARS AHEAD.   Atlantic Pa-
       pers 4, 1972.   Westmead, Engl.: Saxon House, 1972.   77 p.

>      A balance sheet of European-American relations and a
>      program of suggestions for political action between the
>      two.

1140   Wilcox, Francis O., and Haviland, H. Field, Jr., eds.   THE
       ATLANTIC COMMUNITY:   PROGRESS AND PROSPECTS.   New
       York:   Frederick A. Praeger, 1963.   294 p.

>      A compendium by leading European and American spe-
>      cialists questioning whether cooperative relations among
>      Atlantic nations should be developed further, and by
>      what means.

## 2. United States and Atlantic Community (nonsecurity): Economic

1141   Bradley, Gene E., ed.   BUILDING THE AMERICAN-EUROPEAN

MARKET: PLANNING FOR THE 1970'S. Homewood, Ill.: published for the Atlantic Council of the United States by Dow-Jones and Richard Irwin, 1967. 272 p.

Directed to the private businessman. Fourteen essays by corporation executives, diplomats, and scholars. Reviews the economic, political, and cultural conditions in the Euro-market.

1142 Casadio, Gian Paolo. TRANSATLANTIC TRADE: USA-EEC CONFRONTATION IN THE GATT NEGOTIATIONS. Lexington, Mass.: D.C. Heath and Co., 1973. xii, 260 p.

A study of world trade policy focusing upon the "Kennedy round" of trade negotiations, and presenting a "European" view of the negotiations and their effects.

1143 Committee for Economic Development. THE EUROPEAN COMMON MARKET AND ITS MEANING TO THE UNITED STATES. New York: McGraw-Hill Book Co., 1959. 152 p.

A critical analysis of the questions which creation of the EEC raises for the United States and the world.

1144 _____. TRADE NEGOTIATIONS FOR A BETTER FREE WORLD ECONOMY: A STATEMENT ON NATIONAL POLICY BY THE RESEARCH AND POLICY COMMITTEE. New York: 1964. 33 p.

A study of European-American trade reform in the OECD-GATT framework.

1145 _____. THE UNITED STATES AND THE EUROPEAN COMMUNITY. New York: 1971. 75 p.

A wide-ranging discussion of the relations and effects on the United States of U.S.-EC relations, on British entry, agriculture, industrial exports, and investments.

1146 CONFERENCE ON THE IMPACT OF THE EUROPEAN COMMON MARKET ON THE AMERICAN ECONOMY. Columbia: University of Missouri Press, 1962. 79 p.

1147 Cooper, Richard N. THE ECONOMICS OF INTERDEPENDENCE: ECONOMIC POLICY IN THE ATLANTIC COMMUNITY. New York: published for the Council on Foreign Relations by McGraw-Hill Book Co., 1968. 302 p.

A superb exposition of the political problems involved in carrying out international economic policy within

the Atlantic Community. Seeks to balance international economic needs of integration against national
independence in discussing business policy, taxation,
and balance of payments policies, among others.

1148 Coppock, John O. ATLANTIC AGRICULTURAL UNITY: IS IT
POSSIBLE? New York: published for the Council on Foreign
Relations and Food Research Institute, Stanford University, by
McGraw-Hill Book Co., 1966. 234 p.

An economic discussion about agriculture in the Atlantic Community, including de Gaulle's view, the role
of agricultural labor, and national policies towards agriculture in the community.

1149 Curtis, Thomas B., and Vastine, John Robert. THE KENNEDY
ROUND AND THE FUTURE OF AMERICAN TRADE. New York:
Praeger Publishers, 1971. 239 p.

An account for both layman and expert of the Trade
Expansion Act of 1962 by one of the delegates, Curtis,
to the negotiations. Details the confrontation between
the United States and the EEC, especially regarding agricultural and industrial relations.

1150 Dillard, Dudley D. ECONOMIC DEVELOPMENT OF THE NORTH
ATLANTIC COMMUNITY. Englewood Cliffs, N.J.: Prentice-
Hall, 1967. 747 p.

Chronologically analyzes the North Atlantic economy
from the Middle Ages to the present relating and com-
paring European and American development. Also examines the political and economic relations, industrialization, labor organizations, war, balance of payments,
and actions of countries on both sides of the Atlantic
regarding developing areas.

1151 Erdman, P.E., et al. COMMON MARKETS AND FREE TRADE
AREAS. Menlo Park, Calif.: Stanford University Press, 1960.
37 p.

An outline of worldwide trends toward regional economic groupings, the factors and causes, the nature
of proposed schemes, and potential problems and issues
the United States will face as a result. The issues
relate to the impact of the EEC and European organizations on the United States.

1152 Gotshal, Sylvan. THE EUROPEAN COMMON MARKET: PROBLEMS
AND OPPORTUNITIES IN THE NEW FRONTIER OF AMERICAN BUSI-
NESS. New York: 1961. 64 p.

1153    Hinshaw, Randall. THE EUROPEAN COMMUNITY AND AMERI-
        CAN TRADE: A STUDY IN ATLANTIC ECONOMICS AND POLI-
        CY. New York: published for the Council on Foreign Relations
        by Frederick A. Praeger, 1964. 188 p.

> A study of the impact of European integration on U.S.
> and Atlantic economic strength.

1154    Humphrey, Don D. THE UNITED STATES AND THE COMMON
        MARKET: A BACKGROUND STUDY. Rev. ed. New York:
        Frederick A. Praeger, 1964. 190 p.

> A background study on the political and economic is-
> sues of U.S. trade policy towards the Common Market
> put in the overall context of U.S. foreign policy.

1155    Institute for World Affairs Education. University of Wisconsin, Mil-
        waukee. THE COMMON MARKET AND U.S. TRADE POLICY.
        Milwaukee: 1962. 72 p.

> Five essays on U.S. trade and how it affects and is
> affected by the EEC. Also the U.S. national interest,
> its economic competitiveness, and labor's view of the
> U.S. position are among the topics covered.

1156    Kindleberger, Charles P., and Shonfield, Andrew, eds. NORTH
        AMERICAN AND WESTERN EUROPEAN ECONOMIC POLICIES.
        New York: Macmillan Co., 1971. 551 p.

> A series of twenty-one papers which were the proceed-
> ings of a conference held by the International Economic
> Association concerning conflicts of economic interest
> between the United States and Europe, and the impli-
> cations for regionalism, interdependence, and integra-
> tion.

1157    Krause, Lawrence B. EUROPEAN ECONOMIC INTEGRATION
        AND THE UNITED STATES. Washington, D.C.: Brookings In-
        stitution, 1968. 265 p.

> An appraisal of the consequences for the United States
> of the formation of the EEC and EFTA. Studies on agri-
> culture, foreign investment, foreign relations, and mone-
> tary policies included.

1158    Layton, Christopher. TRANS-ATLANTIC INVESTMENT. Paris:
        Atlantic Institute, 1966. 163 p.

> An attempt to grapple with American investment in Eu-
> rope, the political and economic advantages it brings

and the problems it poses for a united Europe as well
as the partnership it creates between the United States
and Europe.

1159 McCreary, Edward. THE AMERICANIZATION OF EUROPE: THE
IMPACT OF AMERICANS AND AMERICAN BUSINESS ON THE
UNCOMMON MARKET. Garden City, N.Y.: Doubleday and
Co., 1964. 295 p.

Commentary and reporting on three hundred interviews
with American and European business and governmental
representatives. Seeks to analyze the importance of the
international corporation as a new unifying force in the
international field.

1160 Markham, Jesse W., et al. THE COMMON MARKET: FRIEND
OR COMPETITOR? New York: New York University Press, 1964.
123 p.

From the Charles C. Moskowitz Lectures at N.Y.U.,
this study assesses the economic and political forces
which led to the creation of the EEC, and also the
effects of U.S. corporate influence in Europe.

1161 Marting, Elizabeth, ed. THE EUROPEAN COMMON MARKET:
NEW FRONTIER FOR AMERICAN BUSINESS. New York: American Management Association, 1958.

1162 Myrdal, Gunnar. CHALLENGE TO AFFLUENCE. London: Victor Gollancz, 1963. 172 p.

A discussion of American economic stagnation as a major world problem. Describes the dynamics of stagnation and its implications especially for the Soviet Union
and Western Europe.

1163 Peccei, Aurelio. THE CHASM AHEAD. New York: Macmillan
Co., 1969. xvi, 297 p.

By Peccei of Italy's Olivetti, speaking as a businessman. Argues that technology is outstripping control
and that the only hope for mankind lies in a cooperative effort by the Atlantic Community.

1164 Rahl, James A., ed. COMMON MARKET AND AMERICAN ANTI-
TRUST: OVERLAP AND CONFLICT. New York: McGraw-Hill
Book Co. for the Antitrust Project of the Special Committee on the
European Common Market, New York City Bar Association, 1970.
461 p.

Extensive analysis of the extraterritorial scope of U.S.

antitrust laws and their conflict with restrictive-practice laws in the European Community, legally, politically, and economically.

1165 Servan-Schreiber, Jean-Jacques. THE AMERICAN CHALLENGE. New York: Atheneum Publishers, 1968. 291 p.

Asserts that American industry, based in Europe, will fast become the third most powerful industrial force in the world. Discusses its development and the steps by which Europe could fight back.

1166 Uri, Pierre. PARTNERSHIP FOR PROGRESS: A PROGRAM FOR TRANSATLANTIC ACTION. New York: published for the Atlantic Institute by Harper and Row, 1963. 126 p.

Proposals for, and discussion of, trade reform between Europe and the United States in the OECD-GATT context. A discussion of agricultural, commercial, and development problems and policies also included.

1167 Vernon, Raymond. SOVEREIGNTY AT BAY: THE MULTINATIONAL SPREAD OF U.S. ENTERPRISES. New York: Basic Books, 1971. x, 326 p.

1168 Wasserman, Max J., et al. THE COMMON MARKET AND AMERICAN BUSINESS. New York: Simmonds-Boardman, 1964. 300 p.

A survey of business conditions, both economic and legal, within the countries of the EEC, including labor regulations, trade union organization, transport, energy, and financial policies. A useful reference for both legal and business concerns.

## Chapter 6
## EUROPEAN SECURITY

## A. GENERAL AND OTHER

1169    Aron, Raymond. WAR AND INDUSTRIAL SOCIETY. London:
Oxford University Press, 1958. 63 p.

> Tries to determine whether industrial civilizations are
> inherently peaceful by tracing the development of Eu-
> ropean politics from the time of Auguste Comte to the
> present. Concludes that twentieth-century politics de-
> velop in accordance with tradition.

1170    Ball, George W. THE DISCIPLINE OF POWER. Boston: Little, Brown
and Co., 1968. 363 p.

> Within a broader context of world peace, Ball analyzes
> Western Europe, its move toward unity, Britain's special
> role, de Gaulle's effect on the United States and Eu-
> rope, the sharing of nuclear power, and other topics
> relating to Europe's role in the world power balance.

1171    Bloomfield, Lincoln P. WESTERN EUROPE TO THE MID-SEVENTIES:
FIVE SCENARIOS. Cambridge, Mass.: Center for International Studies, M.I.T., 1968. 102 p.

1172    Brown, Neville. EUROPEAN SECURITY, 1972-80. London: Royal
United Services Institute for Defense Studies, 1972. 168 p.

1173    Buchan, Alastair. EUROPE'S FUTURES, EUROPE'S CHOICES:
MODELS OF WESTERN EUROPE IN THE 1970'S. London: published for the Institute of Strategic Studies by Chatto and Windus,
1969. 167 p.

> An examination of possible models of the future of
> Western Europe to try to determine the effects on the

Atlantic alliance and on East-West relations. Also
seeks to assess the possibilities each model offers in
the solution of Europe's own problems, and to isolate
the choices facing policy makers in the future.

1174  Buchan, Alastair, and Windsor, Philip. ARMS AND STABILITY
IN EUROPE: A BRITISH-FRENCH-GERMAN ENQUIRY. London:
published for the Institute of Strategic Studies by Chatto and
Windus, 1963. 236 p.

A study of the defensive confrontation between the two
world alliances and its effect on Europe.

1175  Burrows, Sir Bernard, and Irwin, Christopher. THE SECURITY OF
WESTERN EUROPE: TOWARDS A COMMON DEFENSE POLICY.
London: published for the Federal Trust for Education and Research
by C. Knight, 1972. vii, 189 p.

Analyzes Europe's preparedness for integration of security and defense resources, as has been done economically. Includes the conditions for an integrated defense mechanism, and the possible outline of such an
organization.

1176  Calmann, John. EUROPEAN COOPERATION IN DEFENSE TECH-
NOLOGY: THE POLITICAL ASPECT. London: Institute for Strategic Studies, 1967. 23 p.

1177  Campen, S.I.P. van. THE QUEST FOR SECURITY: SOME ASPECTS
OF NETHERLAND'S FOREIGN POLICY, 1945-50. The Hague: Martinus Nijthoff, 1958. 308 p.

1178  De Rusett, Alan. STRENGTHENING THE FRAMEWORK OF PEACE.
London: Royal Institute of International Affairs, 1950. 225 p.

A study of proposals for amending, developing, or replacing present international tribunals for the mainte-
nance of peace. Proposals include strengthening the
UN, creating a world federal government, and unifying Europe.

1179  Deutsch, Karl W. ARMS CONTROL AND THE ATLANTIC AL-
LIANCE: EUROPE FACES COMING POLICY DECISIONS. New
York: John Wiley and Sons, 1967. 167 p.

Deals primarily with arms control aspects of the Deutsch
(and others) survey research studies begun at Yale in 1963
on elite and popular public opinion attitudes. This study
on French and West German elites. Relates arms control
and defense views to cooperation, stability, and integration.

1180    Gray, Richard Butler, ed.  INTERNATIONAL SECURITY SYSTEMS.
        Itasca, Ill.:  F.E. Peacock, 1969.  227 p.

> See especially R.J. Barnet's "Regional Security Sys-
> tems," an assessment of the possibilities regional or-
> ganizations have for promoting security, including U.S.
> efforts to promote regionalism in Europe, the Middle
> East, and the Far East.

1181    Griffiths, William E.  THE UNITED STATES AND THE SOVIET
        UNION IN EUROPE:  THE IMPACT OF THE ARMS RACE, TECH-
        NOLOGY AND THE GERMAN QUESTION.  Cambridge, Mass.:
        M.I.T., 1967.

1182    Hassner, Pierre.  CHANGE AND SECURITY IN EUROPE:  PART I:
        THE BACKGROUND;  PART II:  IN SEARCH OF A SYSTEM.  Adel-
        phi Papers, nos. 45 and 49.  London:  Institute For Strategic Stud-
        ies, 1968.

> Two brief papers on the history and development of a
> European security system including the German prob-
> lem and European security in a global context.

1183    Holland, Vance M.  "Selected National Policies Regarding Euro-
        pean Military Integration, 1945-55."  Ph.D. dissertation, Uni-
        versity of Washington, 1965.

1184    Ionescu, Ghita, ed.  BETWEEN SOVEREIGNTY AND INTEGRA-
        TION.  London:  GOVERNMENT AND OPPOSITION published
        by Croom, Helm, 1974.  192 p.

> Papers from the ninth International Political Science
> Association Congress which examined the potential for
> peace through the new world federations, particularly
> the EEC.

1185    Kaufmann, William, ed.  MILITARY POLICY AND NATIONAL
        SECURITY.  Princeton, N.J.:  Princeton University Press, 1956.
        vii, 274 p.

> See especially Craig's article "NATO and the New
> German Army."

1186    Kertesz, Stephen Denis.  THE QUEST FOR PEACE THROUGH
        DIPLOMACY.  Englewood Cliffs, N.J.:  Prentice-Hall, 1967.
        182 p.

> An analysis of past and present successes and failures
> of diplomacy in dealing with major international crises.
> Focuses on the use of large multinational organizations

like the UN, NATO, EEC, OEEC-OECD, and ECSC.
Also discusses the nature of this diplomacy and its limitations.

1187    Knorr, Klaus E.   UNION OF WESTERN EUROPE: A THIRD CENTER OF POWER?   DRAFT MEMORANDUM.   New Haven, Conn.: Yale Institute of International Studies, 1948.   iii, 118 p.

1188    Korbel, Josef.   DETENTE IN EUROPE: REAL OR IMAGINARY? Princeton, N.J.: Princeton University Press, 1972.   302 p.

A consideration of various aspects of European detente, including German foreign policies toward East Europe, and U.S.-Soviet relations.   The economic, ideological, and political advantages of a European detente also discussed.

1189    Lerner, Daniel, and Gorden, Morton.   EUROPEAN LEADERS LOOK AT WORLD SECURITY.   Cambridge, Mass.: M.I.T. Center for International Studies, 1960.   150 p.

A study of the development of the French, British, and German positions on the unification of Europe.   It is based upon interviews taken in the respective countries in 1954, 1956, and 1959.

BIBLIOGRAPHIE ZUR EUROPAISCHEN INTEGRATION

1190    Merritt, Richard L., and Puchala, Donald J[ames].   WESTERN EUROPEAN ATTITUDES ON ARMS CONTROL, DEFENSE, AND EUROPEAN UNITY 1952-63.   New Haven, Conn.: Yale University, Political Research Library, 1966.   299 p.

A summary of the questions and results of the USIA survey research in Western Europe (France, Germany, Italy, and Britain) on popular perceptions of world politics, and attitudes toward other countries and toward European integration.

1191    Morton, Gordon.   "European Security: British and French Elite Perspectives."   Ph.D. dissertation, M.I.T., 1963.

1192    Phillips, Walter Alison.   THE CONFEDERATION OF EUROPE: A STUDY OF THE EUROPEAN ALLIANCE, 1813-23, AS AN EXPERIMENT IN THE INTERNATIONAL ORGANIZATION OF PEACE.   Six lectures delivered in the university schools at Oxford, at the invitation of the delegates of the Common University Fund, Trinity Term,

1913. London: Longmans, Green and Co., 1914. 315 p.

A history and analysis of the Confederation of Europe as a forerunner to an integrated Europe.

1193   Smyth, J.G., ed. THE WESTERN DEFENSES. London: Allan Wingate, n.d. 144 p.

Ten essays devoted to a postwar look at various aspects of the Western alliance system including questions about Europe's role and the advantages of an integrated defense system.

1194   Stillman, Edmund, et al. ALTERNATIVES FOR EUROPEAN DE-FENSES IN THE NEXT DECADE. Croton-on-Hudson, N.Y.: Hudson Institute, 1964.

1195   Whitaker, Arthur P. SPAIN AND DEFENSE OF THE WEST. New York: published for the Council on Foreign Relations by Harper and Brothers, 1961. 408 p.

A detailed analysis of Spanish relations with the United States and Western Europe, especially concerning defense matters.

1196   Williams, Geoffrey Lee, and Williams, Alan Lee. CRISIS IN EU-ROPEAN DEFENCE: THE NEXT TEN YEARS. London and Tonbridge: C. Knight and Co., 1974. 334 p.

A study of the major defense issues and developments which Western Europe faces over the next decade; the "Europeanist" versus the "Atlanticist" arguments for defense, the forces uniting Europe's defenses, and those dividing them.

1197   World Council of Peace. THE WORLD PEACE COUNCIL AND EUROPEAN SECURITY: DOCUMENTS, 1971-72. Helsinki: Information Centre of the World Peace Council, 1972. 24 p.

1198   Wright, Moorhead III. "Libra: A Study of the Origins of the Balance of Power Idea in European Interstate Relations." Ph.D. dissertation, Johns Hopkins University, 1971.

## B. BRITAIN

1199   Brown, Neville. ARMS WITHOUT EUROPE: BRITISH DEFENCE IN THE MODERN WORLD. Baltimore: Penguin Books, 1967. 159 p.

An assessment of Britain's defense role both for herself

and for Western Europe, and a discussion of Britain's effect upon NATO, WEU, and Europe defensively.

1200    Cordier, Sherwood S.  BRITAIN AND THE DEFENSE OF WESTERN
        EUROPE IN THE 1970'S:  AN ANALYSIS OF THE MILITARY PO-
        TENTIAL OF ENGLAND IN THE MODERN WORLD.  New York:
        Exposition Press, 1973.  101 p.

        A study from the military perspective of Britain's chang-
        ing world position, her European and NATO commit-
        ments, her entry into the Common Market, and her
        evolving role in the European balance of power.

1201    Richard, Ivor, et al.  EUROPE OR THE OPEN SEA?  THE POLIT-
        ICAL AND STRATEGIC IMPLICATIONS FOR BRITAIN IN THE
        COMMON MARKET.  London:  C. Knight and Co., 1971.  187 p.

        A study of the macro and long-range issues, especially
        concerning the defense and security of West Europe,
        facing Britain's entry into the EC.

1202    Tunstall, W.C.B.  ·THE COMMONWEALTH AND REGIONAL DE-
        FENSE.  London: Athlone Press, 1959.  68 p.

        A monograph on the organizations and defense systems
        of the Commonwealth from the 1930s through World
        War II, including NATO.  Useful for understanding
        previous military requirements and preconditions for
        a European defense community.

## C.  CSCE AND MBFR (Conference on Security and Cooperation in Europe and Mutual and Balanced Force Reductions)

1203    Huopaniemi, Jukka.  PARLIAMENTS AND EUROPEAN RAPPROACHE-
        MENT:  THE CONFERENCE OF THE INTER-PARLIAMENTARY UNION
        ON EUROPEAN COOPERATION AND SECURITY.  Leiden, Nether-
        lands: A.W. Sijthoff, 1973.  138 p.

        "A report on the Inter-Parliamentary Conference on
        European Cooperation and Security (IPCES), held in
        Helsinki, Jan. 26-31, 1973.  Parliamentary interac-
        tion is discussed as well as the premises for coopera-
        tion in matters of security, economics, culture, peo-
        ples, and institutional structures."

                                EUROPEAN COMMUNITY

1204    Klaiber, Wolfgang, et al.  ERA OF NEGOTIATIONS:  EURO-

PEAN SECURITY AND FORCE REDUCTIONS. Lexington, Mass.:
D.C. Heath and Co., 1973. xiv, 192 p.

> "The book includes an historical analysis of European
> security, a discussion of East-West dialogue on CSCE
> and MBFR, a study of the security perspectives of the
> North Atlantic Treaty Organization and the Warsaw
> Pact, a delineation of issues involved in CSCE and
> MBFR, as well as an overview of the risks and oppor-
> tunities of the post-conference environment."

EUROPEAN COMMUNITY

1205    Nessler, E. THE PROPOSED EUROPEAN SECURITY CONFER-
ENCE. Paris: Western European Union, General Affairs Committee, 1971. 99 p.

1206    Palmer, Michael. THE PROSPECTS FOR A EUROPEAN SECURITY
CONFERENCE. London: published for PEP by Chatham House,
1971. 107 p.

> An analysis of the problems and prospects of a Euro-
> pean Security Conference including a delineation of
> the concepts "European" and "security."

1207    Planck, Charles Robert. "Arms Control, Disarmament, and Security
in Europe: An Analysis of the Negotiations, 1955-65." Ph. D.
dissertation, Johns Hopkins University, 1968.

1208    Szaz, Z. Michael, ed. MBFR AT THE CROSSROADS. By El-
bridge Durbrow et al. Washington, D.C.: American Institute
on Problems of European Unity, 1974. 114 p.

## D. EDC (European Defense Community and Pleven Plan)

1209    Butler, Michael D. EUROPEAN DEFENSE PROBLEMS IN THE
1970'S: THE CASE FOR A NEW EUROPEAN DEFENSE COMMU-
NITY. Cambridge, Mass.: Center for International Affairs, Harvard University, February 1974. 74 p.

1210    Leites, Nathan, and de la Malene, Christian. PARIS FROM EDC
TO WEU. Santa Monica, Calif.: RAND Corp., 1956. 194 p.

1211    May, Joseph Turner. "John Foster Dulles and the European Defense Community." Ph.D. dissertation, Kent State University,
1969.

1212    Patrick, Charles William. THE AMERICAN PRESS AND THE EU-
        ROPEAN ARMY PLAN: A STUDY OF THE REACTION OF THE
        AMERICAN PRESS WITH RESPECT TO THE EUROPEAN DEFENSE
        COMMUNITY, 1950-54. Ambilly, France: Imprimerie: Les
        Presses de Savoie, 1966. 183 p.

1213    Thompson, Ralph John. "United States Policy and Pressure in West-
        ern Europe: The European Defense Community and the Multilateral
        Nuclear Force." Ph.D. dissertation, Fletcher School of Law and
        Diplomacy, 1968.

## E. FRANCE

1214    Furniss, Edgar S., Jr. FRANCE: KEYSTONE OF WESTERN DE-
        FENSE. Garden City, N.J.: Doubleday and Co., 1954. 77 p.

        A study of the Franco-American Friendship Treaty,
        French commitment to the West, her economy and de-
        fenses, her military and political institutions, and the
        role France plays vis-a-vis her other European partners.

1215    Kohl, Wilfrid. FRENCH NUCLEAR DIPLOMACY. Princeton,
        N.J.: Princeton University Press, 1972. 412 p.

        A well-balanced study of de Gaulle's nuclear policy,
        and the effects of his policy on NATO, on the other
        European states, and on European integration.

1216    Lerner, Daniel, and Aron, Raymond, eds. FRANCE DEFEATS
        THE EDC. New York: Frederick A. Praeger, 1957. 225 p.

        Nine independent views of France and the EDC by
        French participants and observers both for and against
        the French position.

## F. GERMANY

1217    Bathurst, Maurice Edward, and Simpson, J.L. GERMANY AND
        THE NORTH ATLANTIC COMMUNITY: A LEGAL SURVEY. New
        York: published for the London Institute of World Affairs by
        Frederick A. Praeger, 1956. 217 p.

        An examination from a legal viewpoint of the position
        of the Federal Republic of Germany in NATO and the
        events leading up to Germany's admission, 1944-55.

1218    Bluhm, Georg. DETENTE AND MILITARY RELAXATION IN EU-

ROPE: A GERMAN VIEW. Adelphi Paper no. 40. London: Institute for Strategic Studies, 1967. 15 p.

A monograph arguing for more integration within NATO, the EC, and WEU as a result of East-West detente.

1219 Craig, Gordon A. NATO AND THE NEW GERMAN ARMY. Memorandum no. 8. Princeton, N.J.: Princeton University, Center of International Studies, 1955. 30 p.

Part of a symposium series on military policy and national security. A monograph briefly discussing the kind of force a German army is likely to be, the way in which it will fit into the NATO structure, and the problems it will raise for Europe and the Atlantic alliance during its integration.

1220 Dobrich, John Richard J. "West German Rearmament and European Integration: The European Defense Community Treaty in France and Western Germany." Ph.D. dissertation, The New School for Social Research, 1958.

1221 Foerster, F.W. EUROPE AND THE GERMAN QUESTION. New York: AMS Press, 1975. xviii, 474 p.

1222 Hanrieder Wolfram F. THE STABLE CRISIS: TWO DECADES OF GERMAN FOREIGN POLICY. New York: Harper and Row, 1970. xvi, 221 p.

A discussion of West German foreign policy goals such as security, recovery, reunification, and relations between the national and international system including an analysis of German nuclear power, rearmament, and EURATOM.

1223 Hartmann, Frederick H. GERMANY BETWEEN EAST AND WEST: THE REUNIFICATION PROBLEM. Englewood Cliffs, N.J.: Prentice-Hall, 1965.

A discussion of the reunification problem and Germany's position between East and West as well as the difficulties this causes for NATO, for European defense, and for the European Economic Community.

1224 Lutz, Hermann. GERMAN-FRENCH UNITY: THE BASIS FOR EUROPEAN PEACE. Chicago: Henry Regnery, 1957. 257 p.

A history of German-French relations and an attempt to show why and how they are the key to peace and unity in Europe.

1225 McGeehan, Robert. THE GERMAN REARMAMENT QUESTION: AMERICAN DIPLOMACY AND EUROPEAN DEFENSE AFTER WW II. Urbana: University of Illinois Press, 1971. 280 p.

A study of the American demand for a German military contribution from a simple call for troops to elaborate integrating institutions in Europe like the EDC and NATO.

1226 Richardson, James L. GERMANY AND THE ATLANTIC ALLIANCE: THE INTERACTION OF STRATEGY AND POLITICS. Cambridge, Mass.: Harvard University Press, 1966. vii, 403 p.

A study of Germany's role in NATO and the Western defense system taking into consideration her own peculiar problems relating to World War II and reunification. A discussion of Germany's role in the defense of Western Europe and the implications for a unified Europe included.

1227 Russett, Bruce M. ARMS CONTROL IN EUROPE: PROPOSALS AND POLITICAL CONSTRAINTS. Denver: University of Denver, 1967. 85 p.

An assessment of various policies on German reunification and arms control in relation to respective European nations and their political parties, shifts over time, and patterns developing relative to national, regional, and international defense.

1228 Schmidt, Helmut. DEFENSE OR RETALIATION: A GERMAN VIEW. New York: Frederick A. Praeger, 1962. 264 p.

One of the most important continental contributions to the analytical literature on Western defense in the NATO era, whose author later was the German minister of defense and then chancellor. An argument for the effectiveness and strengthening of conventional forces.

1229 Schnitzer, Ewald W. PUBLIC DISCUSSION IN WESTERN GERMANY OF THE DEFENSE OF EUROPE, MARCH TO JUNE 1952. Santa Monica, Calif.: RAND Corp., 1952. 87 p.

1230 Speier, Hans. GERMAN REARMAMENT AND ATOMIC WAR: THE VIEWS OF GERMAN MILITARY AND POLITICAL LEADERS. Evanston III.: Row-Peterson, 1957. 272 p.

A discussion of the views of German military and political leaders between 1952 and 1957 on facets of German rearmament, its meaning to the Western security system, to NATO, to WEU, and to the EDC.

## G. NATO (North Atlantic Treaty Organization) AND UNITED STATES

1231   Alting von Geusau, Frans A.M., ed. NATO AND SECURITY IN
THE SEVENTIES. Boston: D.C. Heath and Co., 1971. 158 p.

A discussion of NATO and its capability to meet crises in the Mediterranean area and Eastern Europe. A
general discussion of NATO's political role between
East and West Europe as well as the security conference.

1232   Amme, Carl H. NATO WITHOUT FRANCE: A STRATEGIC AP-
PRAISAL. Stanford, Calif.: Hoover Institution, 1967. 195 p.

Analysis of the special military aspects of European integration and the practical matters concerning the use
of nuclear weapons for deterrence and defense of the
West.

1233   Atlantic Institute. THE ATLANTIC PAPERS: POLITICAL AND
STRATEGIC STUDIES. By Alastair Buchan et al. New York:
published for the Atlantic Institute by Dunellen, 1971. 356 p.

A collected series of Atlantic Institute monographs concerning the Atlantic nations' convergence and diver-
gence, Eastern Europe, and NATO security.

1234   Ball, Mary Margaret. NATO AND THE EUROPEAN UNION
MOVEMENT. New York: published for the London Institute of
World Affairs by Frederick A. Praeger, 1959. 486 p.

An organizational study of the origins, aims, structure,
principal activities and problems of the organizations
of the European and Atlantic areas including the relationship between European organizations and NATO.

1235   Barnet, Richard J., and Raskin, Marcus G. AFTER TWENTY
YEARS: THE DECLINE OF NATO AND THE SEARCH FOR A
NEW POLICY IN EUROPE. New York: Random House, 1965.
243 p.

Argues that the Atlantic alliance and the "Great Society" are in fundamental conflict and that disengagement from Europe is a more auspicious course for the
United States to take for the sake of both Europeans
and Americans.

1236   Baumann, Carol Edler. POLITICAL COOPERATION IN NATO. Madison, Wis.: National Security Studies Group at the University of Wisconsin, 1960. 108 p.

1237   Beaufre, General Andre.  NATO AND EUROPE.  Translated by
       Joseph Green.  New York:  Alfred A. Knopf, 1966.  170 p.

       An analysis of the development of NATO and the sta-
       tus of European unity.  Discusses the structure and strat-
       egy of NATO defenses and the recent changes in at-
       titudes and organization.

1238   Beckett, Sir W. Eric.  THE NORTH ATLANTIC TREATY, THE
       BRUSSELS TREATY AND THE CHARTER OF THE UNITED NATIONS.
       London:  Stevens and Sons, 1950.  75 p.

       An examination of NATO and the Western union in re-
       lation to the United Nations.

1239   Beer, Francis A.  INTEGRATION AND DISINTEGRATION IN
       NATO:  PROCESSES OF ALLIANCE COHESION AND PROSPECTS
       FOR ATLANTIC COMMUNITY.  Columbus:  Ohio State University
       Press, 1969.  330 p.

       Assesses the prospects for NATO in view of member-
       state goals and the crisis precipitated by the French
       withdrawal from military activities.  Further, analyzes
       the extent to which effective policy concensus and in-
       tegrated programs can be achieved under the present
       organizational structure.

1240   Bell, Coral.  NEGOTIATION FROM STRENGTH:  A STUDY IN
       THE POLITICS OF POWER.  London:  Chatto and Windus, 1962.
       224 p.

       Primarily a study in American foreign policy after 1950
       focusing on U.S. defense postures, e.g., "negotiations
       from strength," and the way in which this posture af-
       fected European defense politics, and, in turn, how
       this affects U.S. defense policy through NATO.

1241   Boyd, Andrew K.H., and Metson, William.  ATLANTIC PACT,
       COMMONWEALTH AND UNITED NATIONS.  New York: Hutch-
       inson  for the United Nations Association, 1949.  100 p.

1242   Branston, Ursala.  BRITAIN IN NATO:  A POLITICAL STUDY.
       London:  Conservative Political Centre, 1956.  63 p.

       A brief history of the first seven years of NATO's ex-
       istence and a look at extending NATO into broader,
       nonmilitary areas of cooperation.  Also a discussion
       of Atlantic federal union.

1243   Buchan, Alastair.  CRISIS MANAGEMENT:  THE NEW DIPLOMACY.

Boulogne-sur-Seine, France:  Atlantic Institute, 1966.  63 p.

A particularly sharp focus on the interrelationship between political consultation and crisis in NATO partly
as a result of French withdrawal from the military committee, and partly as a result of a changing European
sense of community.

1244    _____ .  NATO IN THE 1960'S:  THE IMPLICATIONS OF IN-
TERDEPENDENCE.  New York:  Frederick A. Praeger, 1960.  131 p.

An analysis of NATO and the implications of interdependence for its defensive and political capabilities.

1245    Cerny, Karl H., and Briefs, Henry W., eds.  NATO IN QUEST
OF COHESION.  New York:  Frederick A. Praeger, 1965.  476 p.

Twenty-five essays by Americans and Europeans on
NATO and its role in the Atlantic alliance, its relation to Europe, and its particular problems.

1246    Cleveland, Harlan.  NATO:  THE TRANSATLANTIC BARGAIN.
New York:  Harper and Row, 1970.  204 p.

A policy monolog by a former U.S. ambassador to
NATO describing the challenges of NATO, ABM,
SALT talks, French withdrawal from NATO's military
committee, and Europe's role in the alliance.

1247    Cleveland, Harold Van Buren.  THE ATLANTIC IDEA AND ITS
EUROPEAN RIVALS.  New York:  published for the Council on
Foreign Relations by McGraw-Hill Book Co., 1966.  186 p.

An analysis of the dichotomy between European unity
and the Atlantic alliance especially in the areas of
economics and defense.  Concludes that common security interests are still the most dominant links within
the Atlantic alliance and outweigh the conflicts arising from the needs for European unity.

1248    Cromwell, William C.  THE EURO-GROUP AND NATO.  Research Monograph Series no. 18.  Philadelphia:  Foreign Policy
Research Institute, 1974.  55 p.

1249    Daniels, Walter Machray, comp.  DEFENSE OF WESTERN EUROPE.
New York:  H.W. Wilson and Co., 1950.  242 p.

A collection of article reprints on a variety of topics
concerning the defense of Western Europe including
NATO, its organization and effectiveness, economic
factors in defense, and proposals for political union.

1250    Duchene, Francois. BEYOND ALLIANCE. The Atlantic Papers,
        NATO Series no. 1. Boulogne-sur-Seine, France: Atlantic In-
        stitute, 1965. 63 p.

        A discussion of the changing role of NATO brought
        on by the changed nature of the East-West threat and
        a changed relationship among the NATO partners, spe-
        cifically between the United States and an integrated
        Europe.

1251    Fedder, Edwin H. NATO: THE DYNAMICS OF ALLIANCE IN
        THE POSTWAR WORLD. New York: Dodd-Mead and Co., 1973.
        155 p.

        A study of the nature and function of alliances in
        general and NATO in particular as well as Europe's
        role in the alliance vis-a-vis the United States. Ar-
        gues for greater responsibility-sharing by the United
        States.

1252    Foster, Richard B., et al., eds. STRATEGY FOR THE WEST:
        AMERICAN-ALLIED RELATIONS IN TRANSITION. New York:
        Crane Russak and Co., 1974. 258 p.

        "Papers and synthesis of a conference on Western stra-
        tegic problems held to stimulate greater West European
        defense cooperation and calling on the United States
        to help Europe help itself."

                        ATLANTIC COMMUNITY QUARTERLY

1253    Fox, William T.R., and Fox, Annette B. NATO AND THE RANGE
        OF AMERICAN CHOICE. New York: Columbia University Press,
        1967. 352 p.

        A very readable description of the alliance's origins
        and evolution, its structures, policies, and methods
        with emphasis on the U.S. role. Useful comparisons
        of NATO with other alliances and international or-
        ganizations which lead the authors to conclusions
        about "organized security alliances" generally.

1254    Fox, William T.R., and Schilling, Warner R., eds. EUROPEAN
        SECURITY AND THE ATLANTIC SYSTEM. New York: Columbia
        University Press, 1973. 276 p.

        Seven essays concerning European security arrangements
        including the role of NATO, the influence of the Eu-
        ropean Community, and the roles of Britain, France,
        and West Germany.

1255   Furniss, Edgar S., Jr. THE WESTERN ALLIANCE: ITS STATUS
AND PROSPECTS. Columbus: Ohio State University Press, 1965.
182 p.

> Nine articles dealing with the theme of the United
> States and Europe cooperating in NATO, and the ef-
> fects that cooperation has on Europe and European in-
> tegration.

1256   Geiger, Theodore. THE FORTUNES OF THE WEST: THE FUTURE
OF THE ATLANTIC NATIONS. Bloomington: Indiana University
Press, 1972. 352 p.

> A study of the foreign policies of the United States
> and the Soviet Union including a discussion of the
> impact of European unity on world policy.

1257   Geiger, Theodore, and Cleveland, Harold Van Buren. MAKING
WESTERN EUROPE DEFENSIBLE: AN APPRAISAL OF THE EF-
FECTIVENESS OF THE UNITED STATES POLICY IN WESTERN
EUROPE. Monograph no. 74. Washington, D.C.: National
Planning Association, 1951. 85 p.

> A study of the defenses of Western Europe from eco-
> nomic, political, and military perspectives, the role
> of the United States in defense and the role of Europe.
> Includes proposals like the Pleven Plan to integrate
> Europe.

1258   Howard, Michael Eliot. DISENGAGEMENT IN EUROPE. Baltimore: Penguin Books, 1958. 92 p.

1259   Hunt, Brigadier K. NATO WITHOUT FRANCE: THE MILITARY
IMPLICATIONS. London: Institute for Strategic Studies, 1966.
26 p.

1260   Hunter, Robert Edwards. SECURITY IN EUROPE. Bloomington:
Indiana University Press, 1972. 281 p.

> An analysis of the political context of European secu-
> rity and defense, including NATO and the Warsaw Pact
> from the cold war to detente.

1261   Ismay, Lord. NATO: THE FIRST FIVE YEARS, 1949-54. Paris:
International Secretariat, NATO, 1954. 280 p.

> A concise analysis of NATO, the reason the treaty
> was signed, its meaning, the workings of NATO--both
> civil and military--and its accomplishments.

1262     Jordan, Robert S., ed. EUROPE AND THE SUPERPOWERS: PER-
CEPTIONS OF EUROPEAN INTERNATIONAL POLITICS. Boston:
Allyn and Bacon, 1971. 301 p.

> A post cold-war analysis written for Americans by Eu-
> ropeans expressing their impressions and reactions to
> the superpowers, and the global conflict in which Eu-
> rope is an actor.

1263     Joshua, Wynfred, and Hahn, Walter F. NUCLEAR POLITICS:
AMERICA, FRANCE, AND BRITAIN. The Washington Papers,
vol. 1. Washington, D.C.: Center for Strategic and International Studies, Georgetown University, 1973. 84 p.

> An examination of the French and British nuclear ca-
> pability in light of Europe's own defense needs and
> the possibility of nuclear cooperation with the United
> States. The chapter entitled "The Political Factors
> Bearing Upon Nuclear Cooperation: Incentives and
> Constraints," of special interest.

1264     Kaplan, Morton A. THE RATIONALE FOR NATO: EUROPEAN
COLLECTIVE SECURITY; PAST AND FUTURE. Washington, D.C.:
American Enterprise Institute for Public Policy Research, 1973.
94 p.

> Written for a specialized audience. A descriptive
> analysis of post-World War II events in Europe which
> concludes that conditions are not radically altered
> militarily between the East bloc and the West, and that
> the NATO rationale remains intact. Also develops
> a strategy of deterrence and tries to show how it might
> be implemented.

1265     Kissinger, Henry A. THE NECESSITY FOR CHOICE: PROSPECTS
FOR AMERICAN FOREIGN POLICY. New York: Harper and
Brothers, 1961. 370 p.

> An analysis of some of the major issues facing U.S.
> foreign policy including U.S. policy towards Europe,
> specifically in the military and defense context of
> NATO.

1266     _____. THE TROUBLED PARTNERSHIP: A REAPPRAISAL OF
THE ATLANTIC ALLIANCE. New York: published for the Council on Foreign Relations by McGraw-Hill Book Co., 1965. 266 p.

> An inquiry into the future of the Atlantic Community
> in political as well as economic and military terms.
> Urges an allied nuclear force composed of the United
> State, France, and Britain to be under the control of

the NATO Council rather than the proposed concept of a multilateral force.

1267    Knorr, Klaus E.  THE ATLANTIC ALLIANCE:  A REAPPRAISAL. New York:  Foreign Policy Association, 1974.  63 p.

1268    _____, ed.  NATO AND AMERICAN SECURITY.  Princeton, N.J.: Princeton University Press, 1959.  342 p.

Twelve articles on NATO and its strategy dealing directly with European and national perspectives on NATO.

1269    McLachlan, Donald L.  [Lord Brand].  ATLANTIC ALLIANCE: NATO'S ROLE IN THE FREE WORLD.  London:  Royal Institute of International Affairs, 1952.  172 p.

A report by the Chatham House study group chaired by Lord Brand.

1270    Macridis, Roy C., ed.  MODERN EUROPEAN GOVERNMENTS: CASES IN COMPARATIVE POLICYMAKING.  Englewood Cliffs, N.J.:  Prentice-Hall, 1968.  244 p.

See especially Andrews's article "De Gaulle and NATO," a case analysis of de Gaulle's decision to withdraw from NATO.  Other articles on European integration included.

1271    Mendershausen, Horst.  TERRITORIAL DEFENSE IN NATO AND NON-NATO EUROPE.  Santa Monica, Calif.:  RAND Corp., 1973.  xiv, 100 p.

1272    Mensonides, Louis J., and Kuhlman, James A., eds.  AMERICA AND EUROPEAN SECURITY.  East-West Perspectives, vol. 2. Studies under the auspices of the East-West Foundation, an international research organization.  Leiden, Netherlands:  A.W. Sijthoff, 1975.  200 p.

A series of studies on European security and the Atlantic Community including East-West detente, fundamentals of U.S. foreign policy towards Europe, and the role of the multinational corporations.  Articles by Berkhouwer, R. Wood, W. Feld, A. Gyorgy, et al.

1273    Middleton, Drew.  THE DEFENSE OF WESTERN EUROPE.  New York:  Alfred A. Knopf, 1952.  313 p.

A history and analysis of the political and military

situation in Europe during the early 1950s. Includes
a call for the revival of NATO, asking for a more
unified and concerted effort by Europe and America
towards NATO.

1274  Moore, Ben T.  NATO AND THE FUTURE OF EUROPE.  New
York:  Harper and Row, 1958.  263 p.

A study of NATO and the impact of military technology and nuclear strategy on Europe as well as the
prospects for integration.  Also analyzes NATO in the
context of other European organizations like the EEC.

1275  Mulley, F.W.  THE POLITICS OF WESTERN DEFENSE.  New
York:  Frederick A. Praeger, 1962.  282 p.

An analysis of the political implications of military
defenses and the integration of military forces.  Looks
at the problems of nuclear sharing as well.  The emphasis is on NATO.

1276  Neuchterlein, Donald E.  ICELAND: RELUCTANT ALLY.  Ithaca,
N.Y.:  Cornell University Press, 1961.  213 p.

A study of Icelandic foreign policy from 1939 to 1960
during which Iceland, an isolated Nordic country, entered NATO.  Included are the concerns of the United
States and Western Europe for Iceland as a strategic
territory.

1277  Neustadt, Richard E.  ALLIANCE POLITICS.  New York: Columbia University Press, 1970.  xii, 167 p.

A study of the U.S.-British relations on two issues,
Suez and Skybolt, and an attempt to assess the meaning of these two events on the Atlantic alliance.

1278  Newhouse, John, et al.  U.S. TROOPS IN EUROPE: ISSUES,
COSTS, AND CHOICES.  Washington, D.C.:  Brookings Institution, 1971.  163 p.

Analyzes U.S. and European attitudes, policies, and
options towards both NATO and an integrated defense
community.  Major focus on United States.

1279  Osgood, Robert E.  NATO: THE ENTANGLING ALLIANCE.
Chicago:  University of Chicago Press, 1962.  416 p.

A review of American foreign policy and its influence
in NATO, the place of NATO within the overall po-

litical and military purposes of the Western alliance,
and the functions NATO could perform for the European Community and for a more closely integrated Atlantic Community.

1280    Owen, David. THE POLITICS OF DEFENSE. New York: Taplinger Publishing Co., 1972. 249 p.

Written for a general audience. Focuses on decision
making in security matters and assesses NATO, the
national deterrents in Europe, and an integrated European defense. Finally, considers future decision
making in Europe, the need for autonomy from the
United States, and the need for a U.S. commitment
to Europe.

1281    Roach, James R., ed. THE UNITED STATES AND THE ATLAN-
TIC COMMUNITY: ISSUES AND PROSPECTS. Austin: University of Texas Press, 1967. 87 p.

An examination of the present place of NATO as a
peace-keeping force. Advocates a revision of the policies and functions of NATO to meet changes in the
world situation, partially caused by NATO. Considers
the implications of the economic recovery of Europe,
the end of colonialism, the lessening of the Soviet
threat, advances in technology, and the unification of
Europe.

1282    Royal Institute of International Affairs. ATLANTIC ALLIANCE:
NATO'S ROLE IN THE FREE WORLD. New York: 1952. 172 p.

Conclusions of a Chatham House study group assessing
the NATO alliance, examining the possibilities of a
European Defense Community, and urging the establishment of a more inclusive Atlantic Community.

1283    Ruehl, Lothar. THE NINE AND NATO: THE ALLIANCE AND
THE COMMUNITY; AN UNCERTAIN RELATIONSHIP. Atlantic
Papers, no. 2. Paris: Atlantic Institute for International Affairs,
1974. 43 p.

1284    Salvadori, Massimo. NATO: A TWENTIETH CENTURY COM-
MUNITY OF NATIONS. New York: D. Van Nostrand Co.,
1957. 189 p.

A short history of NATO and its achievements. Also
included are readings and excerpts from the "Charter
of Liberty" of the North Atlantic Community, as well
as excerpted documents from NATO itself.

1285 Schilling, Warner R., et al. AMERICAN ARMS AND A CHANG-
ING EUROPE: DILEMMAS OF DETERRENCE AND DISARMAMENT.
New York: Columbia University Press, 1973. 217 p.

A revised version of a report submitted to the U.S.
Arms Control and Disarmament Agency concerning U.S.
choices towards European security. Describes various
models of possible security arrangements for Western
Europe and discusses the effects of integration, or lack
of it, on security, as well as the effects of various
security arrangements on Europe and further integration.

1286 Schuetze, Walter. EUROPEAN DEFENSE COOPERATION AND
NATO. Paris: Atlantic Institute, 1969. 59 p.

A monograph on the feasibility and desirability of European cooperation or integration on defense matters.

1287 Snyder, Glenn H. DETERRENCE AND DEFENSE: TOWARD A
THEORY OF NATIONAL SECURITY. Princeton, N.J.: Princeton University Press, 1961. 294 p.

A partial theory of defense and deterrence including
an analysis of NATO from its American and European
perspectives.

1288 Stanley, Timothy W. NATO IN TRANSITION: THE FUTURE OF
THE ATLANTIC ALLIANCE. New York: published for the Council on Foreign Relations by Frederick A. Praeger, 1965. 414 p.

A denial that the original purpose of NATO has been
outlived. An analysis of the origins and present political and strategic implications of NATO for the Atlantic alliance.

1289 Stanley, Timothy W., and Whitt, D.M. DETENTE DIPLOMACY:
UNITED STATES AND EUROPEAN SECURITY IN THE 1970'S.
New York: Dunellen Publishing Co., 1970. 170 p.

Reviews the U.S. long-term interest in Europe and
the military balance. Analyzes the problems of Germany and Berlin, U.S. troop reduction, the NATO
alliance, and the Warsaw Pact.

1290 Stillman, Edmund, and Wiener, Anthony J. EUROPEAN DE-
FENSE, AMERICAN INTEREST, AND THE PROSPECT FOR NATO.
With contributions from Frank E. Armbruster and David A. Robison.
Harmon-on-Hudson, N.Y.: Hudson Institute, 1964. 184 p.

1291    Strausz-Hupe, Robert. THE BALANCE OF TOMORROW: POWER
        AND FOREIGN POLICY IN THE UNITED STATES. New York:
        G.P. Putnam's Sons, 1945. 302 p.

        An accounting of the future possibilities of war and
        peace with a statement of the author's opinion of the
        best long-range foreign policy for the United States,
        including a discussion of the reasons the United States
        should encourage a West European federation.


1292    Truitt, Wesley Byron. "The Troops to Europe Decision: The Pro-
        cess, Politics, and Diplomacy of a Strategic Commitment." Ph.D.
        dissertation, Columbia University, 1968.


1293    United Nations Association of the United States. TOWARD THE
        RECONCILIATION OF EUROPE: NEW APPROACHES FOR THE
        UNITED STATES, THE UNITED NATIONS, AND NATO: A RE-
        PORT. New York: 1969. 36 p.


1294    U.S. Senate. Foreign Relations Committee. PROBLEMS AND
        TRENDS IN ATLANTIC PARTNERSHIP: SOME COMMENTS ON
        THE EUROPEAN ECONOMIC COMMUNITY AND NATO. Wash-
        ington, D.C.: Government Printing Office, 1962. viii, 48 p.

        A study of the development of functional European in-
        tegration including the negotiations between Britain
        and the six founding members on the EC, and the ef-
        fects of integration on the Atlantic partnership.


1295    Vandevanter, E., Jr. STUDIES ON NATO: AN ANALYSIS OF
        INTEGRATION. Santa Monica, Calif.: RAND Corp., 1966.
        xi, 102 p.


1296    Warne, J.D. NATO AND ITS PROSPECTS. New York: Freder-
        ick A. Praeger, 1954. vii, 110 p.


1297    Waterman, Harvey. "Europe and Strategic Weapons: Implications
        for American Foreign Policy." Ph.D. dissertation, University of
        Chicago, 1963.


1298    Wolfers, Arnold, ed. ALLIANCE POLICY AND THE COLD
        WAR. Baltimore: Johns Hopkins University Press, 1959. xi,
        314 p.

        Included are ten articles on alliances and alliance
        strategy. Roger Hilsman's article "On NATO Strat-
        egy." especially useful for considering the relevance
        of NATO to European defense and integration. The

article by Hans Morgenthau, "Alliances in Theory and Practice," also a useful conceptual study of alliance and integration.

1299 _____. EUROPEAN-AMERICAN COLLOQUIUM: CHANGING EAST-WEST RELATIONS AND THE UNITY OF THE WEST. Papers presented 1 and 2 May 1964 at the Washington Center of Foreign Policy Research, School of Advanced International Studies, Johns Hopkins University. Washington, D.C.: 1964.

Nine essays dealing with detente and security problems between the East bloc and the West, including European views on the United States, and the U.S. view of Europe and its security.

1300 Zu Lowenstein, Hubertus, and Von Zuhlsdorff, Volkmar. NATO AND THE DEFENSE OF THE WEST. New York: Frederick A. Praeger, 1962. 383 p.

## H. SOVIET UNION AND EAST BLOC

1301 Beglov, Spartak Ivanovich. EUROPEAN SECURITY: PROBLEM NUMBER ONE. Moscow: Novosti Press Agency Publishing House, 1971. 54 p.

1302 Efremov, Alexandr. A BASIS FOR LASTING PEACE IN EUROPEAN SECURITY AND COOPERATION. Moscow: Novosti Press Agency Publishing House, 1973. 103 p.

1303 King, Robert R., and Dean, Robert W., eds. EAST EUROPEAN PERSPECTIVES ON EUROPEAN SECURITY AND COOPERATION. New York: Praeger Publishers, 1974. xxi, 254 p.

1304 Levine, Viktor. COLLECTIVE SECURITY IN EUROPE. Moscow: Novosti Press Agency Publishing House, [1960?]. 55 p.

A review of Soviet peace initiatives towards Europe beginning in 1954, including the usual support for de Gaulle, and objections to German "revanchism." More of a policy statement by the Soviet Union on European defense and security than an analysis of the interplay between Europe and Moscow.

1305 Lomko, Y.A., ed. EUROPEAN SECURITY: A SPECTRUM OF OPINIONS; PEOPLE FROM TWENTY-ONE COUNTRIES SPEAK ON PROBLEMS OF SECURITY AND COOPERATION IN EUROPE. Moscow: Moscow News Agency, 1972. 99 p.

1306    Mensonides, Louis J., and Kuhlman, James A., eds. CHANGES
        IN EUROPEAN RELATIONS. East-West Perspectives, vol. 1.
        Studies under the auspices of the East-West Foundation, an inter-
        national research organization. Leiden, Netherlands: A.W.
        Sijthoff, 1975. 200 p.

            Nine analyses dealing primarily with Europe's role
            in security matters between East and West and includ-
            ing such topics as Europe's effect on detente, Yugo-
            slavia's approach to European security, the view of
            the Soviet Union towards European security, and that
            of the United States. Essays by Z. Brzezinski, R.
            Donaldson, A. Ghibutiu, G. Mally, and others.

## 1. WEU (Western European Union)

1307    Borcier, Paul. THE CONTRIBUTION OF THE ASSEMBLY OF
        WEU TO SOCIAL AND CULTURAL COOPERATION IN EUROPE.
        Monograph, Nov. 1959. Paris: Western European Union, As-
        sembly, 1959. 46 p.

            A review of the general characteristics of social and
            cultural cooperation among WEU members, and a pre-
            sentation of the results.

1308    _____. THE POLITICAL ROLE OF THE ASSEMBLY OF WEU.
        Strasbourg, France: [WEU], 1963. 50 p.

            A short overview of the activities of the assembly of
            the Western European Union and in particular its politi-
            cal initiatives in spite of its legal impotence.

                                BIBLIOGRAPHIE ZUR EURO-
                                PAISCHEN INTEGRATION

1309    Foster, J.G. BRITAIN IN WESTERN EUROPE: WEU AND THE
        ATLANTIC ALLIANCE. London: Oxford University Press, 1956.
        120 p.

            An analysis of the significance of the Western Euro-
            pean Union, a military alliance including England,
            France, West Germany, and Italy designed to bring
            about German rearmament. Also examines the history
            of West European integration movements since 1946.

1310    Hawtrey, Ralph George. WESTERN EUROPEAN UNION: IMPLI-
        CATIONS FOR THE UNITED KINGDOM. London: Royal Institute
        of International Affairs, 1949. 126 p.

            An examination of the extent to which a closer union

of Western Europe would affect the position and policies, economic, political, and strategic, of Britain.
Included is an analysis of the cost and contribution
Britain would make, and the effects on the Commonwealth.

1311    Kressler, Diane Arlene.   "Western European Union:  A Study of
        WEU and its Role in European Integration, 1954-66."   Ph.D. dis-
        sertation, University of Pennsylvania, 1967.

1312    Royal Institute of International Affairs.   BRITAIN IN WESTERN
        EUROPE:  WEU AND THE ATLANTIC ALLIANCE.   London: Chat-
        ham House study group, 1956.   xii, 121 p.

        A post-World War II history of the developments lead-
        ing up to the WEU, and an assessment of its signifi-
        cance to Europe and to the Atlantic alliance.

1313    Western European Union.   Assembly.   TEN YEARS OF SEVEN-
        POWER EUROPE.   Paris:  1964.   149 p.

1314    Western European Union.   General Affairs Committee.   A RETRO-
        SPECTIVE VIEW OF THE POLITICAL YEAR IN EUROPE, 1970.
        Paris:  1971.   226 p.

## Chapter 7

## REFERENCE SOURCES

## A. BIBLIOGRAPHIES

1315    ABC POLITICAL SCIENCE. ADVANCE BIBLIOGRAPHY OF CON-
        TENTS: POLITICAL SCIENCE AND GOVERNMENT. Santa Barbara,
        Calif.: ABC-Clio Press, 1969-- .

        A listing of the tables of contents of over 300 periodi-
        cals both in English and other languages. Authors and
        subjects indexed in each of the eight annual issues.
        Also indexed annually.

1316    Atlantic Institute. ATLANTIC STUDIES. Boulogne-sur-Seine,
        France: 1964-- .

        An annual publication listing and describing current
        and prospective studies on the Atlantic relationship.

1317    Aufricht, Hans, comp. GENERAL BIBLIOGRAPHY ON INTER-
        NATIONAL ORGANIZATION AND POST-WAR RECONSTRUC-
        TION. New York: n.p., 1942. 28 p.

1318    Beljaars, G.A.C., comp. BIBLIOGRAPHIE HISTORIQUE ET CUL-
        TURELLE DE L'INTEGRATION EUROPEENNE [Historical and cul-
        tural bibliography of European integration]. Brussels: Commission
        Belge de Bibliographie, 1957. 143 p.

        An annotated bibliography primarily in French and
        German covering the history of the European idea
        since 1918, attempts at unification between 1918 and
        1939, presents attempts and activities, and the European
        organizations.

1319    Bildungswerk Europaische Politik. BIBLIOGRAPHIE ZUR EURO-
        PAISCHEN INTEGRATION [Bibliography of European integration].
        Dusseldorf, Germany: 1962. 178 p.

        An annotated bibliography with sections including the

theory and ideas of integration, organizations and institutions, internal and external relations of the EC,
economic problems, and bibliographic and other works.
Annotations in German, but sources identified by their
original language, English, French, German, and Italian.

1320    Blaber, D., et al., comps.  THE ATLANTIC COMMUNITY:  AN
INTRODUCTORY BIBLIOGRAPHY.  2d ed.  2 vols.  Leiden,
Netherlands:  published for the Conference on Atlantic Community
by A.W. Sijthoff, 1962.  700 p.

An annotated bibliography covering some 600 books
and articles published on the Atlantic Community in
English, French, German, and Italian between 1945
and 1961.

1321    Boettcher, Winfried, comp.  GREAT BRITAIN AND EUROPE,
1940-72.  Vol. 2, PERIODICALS.  Dusseldorf, Germany:  Droste
Verlag, 1973.  591 p.

One of the most comprehensive listings of articles concerning Britain and Europe.  Volume compiled exclusively from some twenty-six British general and specialist periodicals, and weekly publications like the
ECONOMIST.  Organized by year of publication.
Bibliography not annotated but contains both an author and subject index.

1322    Boettcher, Winfried, et al., comps.  GREAT BRITAIN AND EU-
ROPE, 1940-70.  Vol. 1, BOOKS AND BROCHURES.  Dusseldorf, Germany:  Droste Verlag, 1971.  164 p.

A comprehensive bibliography of publications between
1940 and 1970 concerning Britain and Europe in various aspects including European integration.

1323    Carson, Sally, comp.  EUROPEAN INTEGRATION AND U.S.-
EUROPEAN RELATIONS:  AN INTRODUCTORY ANNOTATED
BIBLIOGRAPHY OF GENERAL PERIODICAL ARTICLES AND PAM-
PHLET MATERIAL.  New York:  Council for Intercultural Studies
and Programs, 1974.  11 p.

A brief annotated bibliography of some of the more
recent general articles and pamphlet materials as well
as several books which would be of interest to under-
graduate students and teachers.

1324    Cosgrove, Carol Ann, comp.  A READER'S GUIDE TO BRiTAIN
AND THE EUROPEAN COMMUNITIES.  London:  Political and
Economic Planning, 1970.  106 p.

1325    Crocker, Isabelle C., and Karp, Basil, comps. WESTERN EURO-
        PEAN UNIFICATION: A SELECTED BIBLIOGRAPHY. New York:
        American Committee on United Europe, 1959.

1326    Dexter, B.D., et al., comps. THE FOREIGN AFFAIRS 50-YEAR
        BIBLIOGRAPHY: NEW EVALUATIONS OF SIGNIFICANT BOOKS
        ON INTERNATIONAL RELATIONS 1920-70. New York: published
        for the Council on Foreign Relations by R.R. Bowker Co., 1972.
        936 p.

            An extensive resource on European integration as well
            as on individual European countries.

1327    Drummond, Olive Frances, comp. THE COMMON MARKET,
        SOURCES OF INFORMATION: SELECT LIST--EEC ADDRESSES,
        DIRECTORIES, STATISTICS. Edinburgh: Edinburgh College of
        Commerce Library, 1972. 46 p.

1328    European-Atlantic Movement. THE EUROPEAN AND ATLANTIC
        COMMUNITIES: A GUIDE TO SOURCE MATERIALS AND TEACH-
        ING AIDS. 2d ed. Exeter, Engl.: 1966. 48 p.

1329    European Communities, Commission. CATALOGUE DES PUBLICA-
        TIONS, 1952-71. Vol. 1. Brussels: 1972. 306 p.

1330    European Community Information Service. EUROPEAN COMMU-
        NITY. Washington, D.C.: 1954-- .

            A monthly publication including, besides articles and
            reports on European integration, an annotated listing
            of recent books dealing with the EC and Atlantic top-
            ics. Official publications of the EC also listed and
            annotated.

1331    _____. A GUIDE TO THE STUDY OF THE EUROPEAN COM-
        MUNITY. Rev. ed. London: 1967. 20 p.

            A bibliography of the European Community and its
            British-related activities, both official publications
            and other sources. Films and visual aids also included.

1332    _____. PUBLICATIONS OF THE EUROPEAN COMMUNITIES.
        Washington, D.C.: July 1962. 60 p.

            A catalog of the titles of official publications by the
            various institutions and common services of the EC.

1333    _____. A SELECT GUIDE TO THE EUROPEAN COMMUNITIES.

Washington, D.C.: 1973. 16 p.

> A selected bibliography of basic and recent texts in
> English on European integration and related topics.
> Also lists and describes official publications.

1334   European Community Institute for European Studies. UNIVERSITY
STUDIES ON EUROPEAN INTEGRATION. Brussels: 1963-- .

> An annual handbook and bibliography listing the var-
> ious institutions and centers for European studies. Sum-
> marizes current research and future projects, also.

1335   European Free Trade Association. SELECTED PUBLICATIONS ON
THE EUROPEAN FREE TRADE ASSOCIATION AND EUROPEAN
INTEGRATION. Rev. ed. Washington, D.C.: EFTA Informa-
tion Office, 1963. 52 p.

1336       . SELECTED PUBLICATIONS ON THE EUROPEAN FREE
TRADE ASSOCIATION AND EUROPEAN INTEGRATION: SUP-
PLEMENT. Washington, D.C.: EFTA Information Office, 1964.
18 p.

1337   European Parliament. General Directorate of Parliamentary Documentation and Information. MONTHLY BULLETIN OF EUROPEAN
DOCUMENTATION: SPECIAL ISSUE: GUIDE TO DOCUMENTA-
TION ON THE EUROPEAN PARLIAMENT. [Luxembourg]: 1965.
151 p.

1338   Fondation Nationale des Sciences Politiques. INDEX TO POST-
1944 PERIODICAL ARTICLES ON POLITICAL, ECONOMIC AND
SOCIAL PROBLEMS. Boston: G.K. Hall.

> From the Center for Contemporary Documentation of
> the F.N.S.P. Paris. Covers 1500 periodicals of which
> about one-third are French. The remainder from other
> sources.

1339   FOREIGN AFFAIRS BIBLIOGRAPHY. New York: Harper and
Row, 1919-52; R.R. Bowker, 1952-62.

> A selected and annotated list of books. Arranged
> analytically, chronologically, and regionally.

1340   Haas, Ernst B., comp. "Regional Integration: Selected Bibliography." INTERNATIONAL ORGANIZATION 24 (1970): 1003-20.

> A three-part bibliography devoted to integration. Or-
> ganized as follows: "Theory and Method," "Organi-
> zations, General," "Organizations, Specific Regions

and Activities." Part 3 includes West Europe, East
Europe, Atlantic affairs, the Middle East, and West
Africa.

1341   Harmon, Robert B., comp. POLITICAL SCIENCE: A BIBLIO-
GRAPHICAL GUIDE TO THE LITERATURE. 2d Supplement.
Metuchen, N.J.: Scarecrow Press, 1972. vii, 594 p.

A general bibliographical guide for political science
containing numerous sources on European integration,
federation, and community.

1342   _____. POLITICAL SCIENCE BIBLIOGRAPHIES. Vol. 1. Metuchen, N.J.: Scarecrow Press, 1973. 181 p.

1343   Hennessy, James, comp. BRITAIN AND EUROPE SINCE 1945:
A BIBLIOGRAPHICAL GUIDE. AN AUTHOR, TITLE AND CHRO-
NOLOGICAL INDEX TO BRITISH PRIMARY SOURCE MATERIAL ON
EUROPEAN INTEGRATION ISSUED SINCE 1945. Brighton, Engl.:
Harvester Press, 1973. 98 p.

The first Harvester Primary Social Sources (PSS) bibliography. A unique collection for primary sources from
single interest pressure groups, and political and social
movements on European integration. Indexes all news-
papers, journals, pamphlets, leaflets, open letters,
and so forth released by nearly one hundred pressure
groups concerned with Britain and integration.

1344   Holler, Frederick, comp. THE INFORMATION SOURCES OF
POLITICAL SCIENCE. Santa Barbara, Calif.: ABC-Clio Press,
1971. 264 p.

A general reference for materials on political science:
bibliographies, directories, dictionaries, and hand-
books. Includes a section on Western Europe.

1345   INTERNATIONAL BIBLIOGRAPHY OF POLITICAL SCIENCE.
Chicago: Aldine Publishing Co.; London: Stevens and Sons,
1953.

1346   INTERNATIONAL ENCYCLOPEDIA OF THE SOCIAL SCIENCES.
New York: Macmillan Co., 1968.

Includes the principal concepts, theories, historical
development, and empirical findings in the social
sciences. Contains also an encyclopedic overview
of integration.

1347    INTERNATIONALE BIBLIOGRAPHIE DER ZEITSCHRIFTEN-LITERA-
        TURE. Osnabruck, Germany: Dietrich, 1965.

        The largest subject index to periodical articles in all
        fields of human knowledge. English and foreign-
        language articles listed under German headings, though
        the English translations are included.

1348    INTERNATIONAL INDEX TO PERIODICALS: A QUARTERLY
        GUIDE TO PERIODICAL LITERATURE IN THE SOCIAL SCIENCES
        AND HUMANITIES. New York: H.W. Wilson, 1916-65.

1349    AN INTRODUCTORY BIBLIOGRAPHY OF THE ATLANTIC COM-
        MUNITY. 2 vols. Leiden, Netherlands: A.W. Sijthoff, 1961.
        600 p.

1350    Johnson, Harold S., with Singh, B., comps. INTERNATIONAL
        ORGANIZATION: A CLASSIFIED BIBLIOGRAPHY. East Lansing:
        Asian Studies Center, Michigan State University, 1969. 261 p.

1351    Kitter, Audrey, comp. THE U.S. AND THE EEC: AMERICAN
        REACTION TO AN INVOLVEMENT IN THE "COMMON MAR-
        KET." Los Angeles: Center for the Study of Armament and Dis-
        armament, California State University, Los Angeles, 1973. ix,
        62 p.

1352    Liboiran, Albert A., comp. FEDERALISM AND INTERGOVERN-
        MENTAL RELATIONS IN AUSTRALIA, CANADA, THE UNITED
        STATES AND OTHER COUNTRIES: A BIBLIOGRAPHY. Kingston,
        Ontario: Institute of Intergovernmental Relations, Queen's Uni-
        versity, 1967. vi, 231 p.

        An unannotated list of works relating to federalism and
        integrated relations in the last one hundred years.
        Contains about thirty-five hundred sources.

1353    Macaulay, Alexander John, comp. THE COMMON MARKET,
        PRINCIPLES AND POLICIES: SELECT LIST; PERIODICAL ARTI-
        CLES. Edinburgh: Edinburgh College of Commerce Library,
        1972. 29 p.

1354    Macdonald, Hugh Ian, comp. THE EUROPEAN ECONOMIC COM-
        MUNITY: BACKGROUND AND BIBLIOGRAPHY. Toronto: Cana-
        dian Institute of International Affairs, 1962. 16 p.

1355    Mason, John Brown, comp. RESEARCH RESOURCES: ANNOTATED
        GUIDE TO THE SOCIAL SCIENCES. Vol. 1, INTERNATIONAL RE-

LATIONS AND RECENT HISTORY. 2d ed. Santa Barbara, Calif.: ABC-Clio Press, 1971.

A guide to indexes, abstracts, periodicals, books, and government publications on international relations.

1356    Medsker, Karen, comp. EUROPEAN INTERNATIONAL ORGANI-ZATIONS AND INTEGRATION MOVEMENTS: REPORTS AND ANALYSES. A SELECTED BIBLIOGRAPHY OF NON-BOOK MA-TERIALS APPEARING BETWEEN 1965 AND EARLY 1970. Bloom-ington: Bureau of Public Discussion, Indiana University, 1970. 7 p.

1357    National Book League with the European-Atlantic Movement. EU-ROPEAN AND ATLANTIC AFFAIRS. London: 1971. 29 p.

A selected list of the major publications on European integration and Atlantic Relations.

1358    NORTH ATLANTIC TREATY ORGANIZATION BIBLIOGRAPHY. Paris: NATO-OTAN, 1964. 205 p.

A listing of the official NATO publications, books, articles about NATO, and reviews which regularly print articles about NATO. Covers political, mili-tary, economic, legal, and cultural aspects of NATO as well.

1359    Organization for European Economic Cooperation. GENERAL CATALOGUE OF BOOKS PUBLISHED FROM 1948-58. Paris: n.d. 109 p.

1360    Paklons, L.L., comp. EUROPEAN BIBLIOGRAPHY/BIBLIOGRAPHIE EUROPEENNE. Bruges, Belgium: De Temple, 1964. 217 p.

1361    Partington, Lena, comp. THE EUROPEAN COMMUNITIES: A GUIDE TO THE LITERATURE AND AN INDICATION OF SOURCES OF INFORMATION. London: Department of the Environment, Library, 1974. iv, 101 p.

More of a handbook of sources than a conventional bibliography. Useful especially for British-related as-pects of the European Community. Contains basic in-formation and resources about the EC, the addresses of the various organs, their membership and publica-tions, organizations in the U.K. concerned with the EC, places where research on European Studies is be-ing conducted in Britain, and a listing of EC-member embassies in the U.K.

1362    Pehrson, Hjalmar, and Wolf, Hanna, comps. Leiden, Nether-
        lands: published for the European Cultural Center, Geneva, by
        A.W. Sijthoff, 1965. 472 p.

>       A selective and annotated bibliography concerning Eu-
>       rope as a cultural entity and as a unit, rather than
>       as individual countries. Nine sections; covers history,
>       politics and law, federalism and economics as well as
>       general topics and reference sources.

1363    Perumbulavil, Vilasini, comp. THE EUROPEAN ECONOMIC COM-
        MUNITY AND NEW ZEALAND: A CHECKLIST. Wellington, New
        Zealand: Library School, National Library Service, 1965. 44 p.

1364    Pogany, Andras H., and Pogany, Hortenzia L., comps. POLITI-
        CAL SCIENCE AND INTERNATIONAL RELATIONS: BOOKS REC-
        OMMENDED FOR THE USE OF AMERICAN CATHOLIC COLLEGE
        AND UNIVERSITY LIBRARIES. Metuchen, N.J.: Scarecrow Press,
        1967. xvii, 387 p.

>       A selection tool for small or medium-sized college
>       libraries, as well as students and faculty looking for
>       representative books on a particular subject. Lists
>       about six thousand works.

1365    Pryce, Roy, comp. "Political Science and Integration in Europe."
        GOVERNMENT AND OPPOSITION 2, no. 3 (1967): 457-61.

1366    PUBLIC AFFAIRS INFORMATION SERVICE BULLETIN (PAIS). New
        York: PAIS, 1915-- .

>       A subject index to current books, pamphlets, period-
>       ical articles, and government documents in political
>       science, economics, law, and public affairs. Covers
>       about one thousand periodicals.

1367    READERS' GUIDE TO PERIODICAL LITERATURE. New York:
        H.W. Wilson, 1900-- .

>       An index of U.S. periodicals of broad, general char-
>       acter.

1368    Robinson, Jacob, comp. INTERNATIONAL LAW AND ORGANI-
        ZATION: GENERAL SOURCES OF INFORMATION. Leiden,
        Netherlands: A.W. Sijthoff, 1967. 560 p.

>       An extensive and annotated bibliography.

1369    Speeckaert, Georges Patrick, comp. INTERNATIONAL INSTI-

TUTIONS AND INTERNATIONAL ORGANIZATION: A SELECT
BIBLIOGRAPHY. Brussels: published with assistance from UNESCO
and in collaboration with the International Federation for Documentation, 1956. 116 p.

1370 _____. SELECT BIBLIOGRAPHY ON INTERNATIONAL ORGANI-
ZATION, 1885-1964. Brussels: Union of International Associations, 1965. 150 p.

> About 350 titles. Listings by author, on general top-
> ics of international organization. About 750 additional
> titles listed according to specific organizations, includ-
> ing numerous European ones. Not annotated.

1371 Stewart, Charles F., and Simmonds, George B., comps. A BIBLI-
OGRAPHY OF INTERNATIONAL BUSINESS. New York: Columbia University Press, 1964. 603 p.

> An unannotated bibliography of 8,000 entries covering
> books and articles published in English after 1950.
> Lists materials on comparative business systems, gov-
> ernmental and international organizations, including
> individual national and regional studies.

1372 SUBJECT GUIDE TO BOOKS IN PRINT: AN INDEX TO THE
PUBLISHERS' TRADE LIST ANNUAL. New York: R.R. Bowker,
1957-- .

1373 SUBJECT GUIDE TO FORTHCOMING BOOKS. New York:
R.R. Bowker, 1966-- .

> An annually updated edition of SUBJECT GUIDE TO
> BOOKS IN PRINT which lists already-published works
> and those to be published within six months. Often
> the first listing of new sources.

1374 Szabo, A., and Posner, W.H., comps. BIBLIOGRAPHY ON EU-
ROPEAN INTEGRATION: LIST OF THE BOOKS, DOCUMENTS,
AND PERIODICALS ON EUROPEAN INTEGRATION IN SAN
DIEGO STATE COLLEGE LIBRARY. San Diego, Calif.: San
Diego State College Library, 1967. 62 p.

1375 Tamuno, Olufunmilayo G., comp. THE EEC AND DEVELOPING
NATIONS, 1958-66. A BIBLIOGRAPHY. Vol. 1. Ibadan,
Nigeria: Nigerian Institute of Social and Economic Research,
1967. 51 p.

1376 U.S. Department of Agriculture. AGRICULTURE IN THE EURO-

PEAN ECONOMIC COMMUNITY: AN ANNOTATED BIBLIOG-
RAPHY, 1958-66. ERS, foreign no. 213. Washington, D.C.:
1968. 77 p.

1377    U.S. Department of State. Division of Library and Reference
Services. INTEGRATION OF WESTERN EUROPE: MILITARY,
ECONOMIC, POLITICAL; AN ANNOTATED BIBLIOGRAPHY.
Washington, D.C.: 1952.

1378    U.S. Department of the Army. NUCLEAR WEAPONS AND NATO.
Washington, D.C.: 1970. viii, 450 p.

   A bibliography with abstracts of books, articles, and
   documents issued between 1965 and 1969 concerning
   the Atlantic alliance, West European security, the
   East-West strategic balance, and arms control.

1379    U.S. Library of Congress. THE UNITED STATES AND EUROPE:
A BIBLIOGRAPHICAL EXAMINATION OF THOUGHT EXPRESSED
IN AMERICAN PUBLICATIONS. Washington, D.C.: 1948-50.

   An annotated listing of books and articles on the European situation generally and on each country. Though
   discontinued in 1950, covers a critical and formative
   period of American postwar policy towards Europe.

1380    U.S. Library of Congress. European Affairs Division. INTRO-
DUCTION TO EUROPE: A SELECTIVE GUIDE TO BACKGROUND
READING. Washington, D.C.: 1950. SUPPLEMENT, 1950-55.
Compiled by Helen F. Conover.

   An annotated and very useful guide to European studies.

1381    U.S. Mission to the European Communities. SPECIAL BOOK COL-
LECTION ON EUROPEAN INTEGRATION: CATALOG. 2d ed.
Brussels: 1961. 55 p.

1382    Universal Reference System. BIBLIOGRAPHY OF BIBLIOGRAPHIES
IN POLITICAL SCIENCE, GOVERNMENT AND PUBLIC POLICY.
Princeton, N.J.: Princeton Research Publishing Co., 1968.

   A very detailed compilation which uses the Grazian
   indexing system.

1383    University Microfilms. DISSERTATION ABSTRACTS: INTERNA-
TIONAL ABSTRACTS OF DISSERTATIONS AVAILABLE ON MICRO-
FILM, OR AS XEROGRAPHIC REPRODUCTIONS. Ann Arbor,
Mich.: 1938-- .

A monthly and annual compilation of abstracts of doc-
toral dissertations submitted by more than 250 institutions in the United States and abroad. Contains a
keyword and author index.

1384　Waer, David Kent, comp. COMMON MARKET ANTITRUST: A
GUIDE TO THE LAW, PROCEDURE AND LITERATURE. The Hague:
Martinus Nijhoff, 1964. 67 p.

1385　Warr, Louise, comp. BRITAIN AND EUROPE DURING 1973: A
BIBLIOGRAPHICAL GUIDE. AN AUTHOR, TITLE AND CHRONO-
LOGICAL INDEX TO BRITISH PRIMARY SOURCE MATERIAL ON
EUROPEAN INTEGRATION ISSUED DURING 1973. Sussex, Engl.:
Harvester Press, 1974. 45 p.

A companion to Harvester's PSS microfiche collection
of material produced during 1973 on Britain and Europe.

1386　Wild, J.E., comp. THE EUROPEAN COMMON MARKET AND
THE EUROPEAN FREE TRADE ASSOCIATION. 3d rev. ed. London: Library Association, 1962. 64 p.

1387　Zelletin, Gerda, comp. BIBLIOGRAPHIE ZUR EUROPAISCHEN
INTEGRATION. 2d rev. and exp. ed. Cologne, Germany:
Bildungswerk Europaische Politik, 1965. 209 p.

An updated and considerably expanded version of the
earlier work. Annotations in German though the citations given in the original language (French, English,
German, and Italian). Divided as in first edition.

## B. YEARBOOKS

1388　American Committee on United Europe. EUROPEAN UNION: A
SURVEY OF PROGRESS. New York: 1951-- .

An annual survey of the activities and organizations
concerned with European union.

1389　ANNUAIRE EUROPEEN/EUROPEAN YEARBOOK. The Hague:
Martinus Nijhoff, 1955-- .

A comprehensive coverage of European organizations
and their work, including a chronology of events, decisions, publications of the various organizations, and
a bibliography.

1390    EUROPA YEARBOOK. London: Europa Publications, 1959-- .

Devoted to international organizations, their aims and
activities as well as information on individual countries, parties, judicial systems, and the economy of
each country of the world.

1391    Hansell, S., ed. YEARBOOK OF NORDIC STATISTICS. Vol. 9.
1970. THE NORDIC COUNTRIES' TRADE WITH THE EEC. New
York: Transatlantic Arts, 1971. 228 p.

A compilation of statistical data on Scandinavia focusing on information for regional topics: the population, industrial production, and international trade.

1392    STATESMAN'S YEARBOOK. New York: St. Martin's Press,
1864-- .

An annual history describing the structure, purpose,
and activities of international organizations, including
the regional European ones.

1393    YEARBOOK OF AGRICULTURAL COOPERATION, 1967. Edited
by the Plunkett Foundation for Cooperative Studies. London:
Basil Blackwell, 1967. ix, 315 p.

An annual study devoting particular attention to cooperative agricultural development in twelve European
countries, to the new problems and opportunities brought
about by the European Common Market, and to verti-
cal integration.

1394    YEARBOOK OF THE EUROPEAN CONVENTION ON HUMAN
RIGHTS. The Hague: Martinus Nijhoff, 1958-- .

An annual review of the activities of the Commission
and cases concerning the convention. Of interest not
only to lawyers, but also to those concerned with human rights, and with their region-wide acceptance and
applicability.

1395    YEARBOOK OF THE EUROPEAN CONVENTION ON HUMAN
RIGHTS, THE EUROPEAN COMMISSION AND EUROPEAN COURT
OF HUMAN RIGHTS. The Hague: Martinus Nijhoff, 1955-57.

Included are the basic texts, selected decisions, and
general information on activities and development in
the field of human rights.

1396    THE YEARBOOK OF WORLD AFFAIRS. London: Stevens and
        Sons for the Institute of World Affairs, 1946-- .

        A collection of articles published annually on inter-
        national affairs, frequently including chapters on as-
        pects of European integration. A cumulative index
        to volumes 1-25 located in the 1971 volume of the
        yearbook.

## C. HANDBOOKS

1397    BACKGROUND DATA ON THE COMMON MARKET. No. 1.
        London: European Data Publishing Co., January 1972.

        A series explaining what the Common Market is, how
        it began, how it works, and containing an analysis
        of the Treaty of Rome and progress reports on its ap-
        plication.

1398    Calmann, John. WESTERN EUROPE: A HANDBOOK. New
        York: Frederick A. Praeger, 1967. xxii, 697 p.

        A handbook providing basic and essential information
        on all Western European countries--statistical, de-
        scriptive, economic, political, and other data, in-
        cluding that on the European Community.

1399    Council of Europe. THE CONSULTATIVE ASSEMBLY: PROCE-
        DURE AND PRACTICE. 4th ed. Strasbourg, France: 1961.
        382 p.

        "The fourth edition of the Consultative Assembly's PRO-
        CEDURE AND PRACTICE. Intended primarily for Euro-
        pean parliamentarians. A rich resource for the struc-
        ture and procedure. Annexes contain a chronological
        overview of the activities of the Assembly from 1949
        to 1960."

                                BIBLIOGRAPHIE ZUR EURO-
                                PAISCHEN INTEGRATION

1400    Council of Europe. Directorate of Information. CONCISE HAND-
        BOOK OF THE COUNCIL OF EUROPE. Strasbourg, France:
        1954. 85 p.

1401    Council of Europe. Secretariat-General. HANDBOOK OF EURO-
        PEAN ORGANIZATIONS. Strasbourg, France: 1956. 172 p.

        Detailed information on WEU, the OEEC, EPU, Coun-
        cil of Europe, and the ECSC.

1402   European Communities. Statistical Office. BASIC STATISTICS
       OF THE COMMUNITY: 1970. Luxembourg: 1970. 224 p.

       A 1969 comparison of seventeen European countries and
       the United States, Canada, Japan, and the Soviet Union
       on a variety of topics, including agriculture, popula-
       tion, labor force, energy, trade, and standard of liv-
       ing.

1403   _____. THE COMMON MARKET TEN YEARS ON:  TABLES
       1958-67. Brussels and Luxembourg: 1968. 109 p.

1404   Henig, Stanley, and Pinder, John, eds. EUROPEAN POLITICAL
       PARTIES: A HANDBOOK. London:  George Allen and Unwin
       for Political and Economic Planning, 1969. 565 p.

       A structural-functional and comparative analysis of each
       major party in the Western democratic countries. Seeks
       to assess the role of party in the development of inte-
       gration and linkages in cross-national integration.

1405   INTERNATIONAL ORGANIZATIONS AND INTEGRATION. Lei-
       den, Netherlands: A.W. Sijthoff, 1968. 1,141 p.

       A collection of documents relating to the United Na-
       tions and to the regional agencies, including the Eu-
       ropean regional organizations.

1406   Keesing's Publications. TREATIES AND ALLIANCES OF THE
       WORLD: AN INTERNATIONAL SURVEY COVERING TREATIES
       IN FORCE AND COMMUNITIES OF STATES. New York: Charles
       Scribner's Sons, 1968. 214 p.

       A one-volume guide to the major multinational alliances.
       Contains basic data on each agreement including the
       time and place of signature, participating nations,
       and their representatives as well as a summary of the
       purposes and conditions of the treaties. Includes the
       major European regional alliances.

1407   1976 EUROPEAN COMMUNITY DIRECTORY AND DIARY. Dublin:
       Institute of Public Administration, 1975. 237 p.

       "A directory, a desk diary, a digest of statistical and
       other information, and a handy reference book to the
       European Community."

                           EUROPEAN COMMUNITY

1408   Palmer, Michael, and Lambert, John. A HANDBOOK OF EU-

ROPEAN ORGANIZATION. New York: Frederick A. Praeger, 1968. 520 p.

Concise summaries of the structure and activities of the major European organizations like the Council of Europe, NATO, the EEC, and others, and the way in which these organizations have transformed relations among the countries of Western Europe in political, economic, and defense affairs.

1409 Panhuys, H.F., Brinkhorst, L.J., et al., eds. INTERNATIONAL ORGANIZATION AND INTEGRATION: A COLLECTION OF THE TEXTS OF DOCUMENTS RELATING TO THE UNITED NATIONS, ITS RELATED AGENCIES AND REGIONAL INTERNATIONAL ORGANIZATIONS. Leiden, Netherlands: A.W. Sijthoff, 1968. 1,141 p.

A treaty and documentary reference including over 250 of the 1,100 pages on the European Communities. Annotated.

1410 Peaslee, Amos Jenkins, ed. INTERNATIONAL GOVERNMENTAL ORGANIZATIONS: CONSTITUTIONAL DOCUMENTS. Rev. 3d ed. The Hague: Martinus Nijhoff, 1974.

A collection of the basic documents of various international organizations, including the European regional organizations. Contains an appended bibliography.

1411 Simmonds, K.R., et al., eds. EUROPEAN COMMUNITY TREATIES. With editorial assistance by Sweet and Maxwell's legal editorial staff. London: Sweet and Maxwell, 1972. 334 p.

The treaty texts for the ECSC, EEC, and EURATOM, the 1965 Executive Merger Treaty, the 1970 Budgetary Treaty, and the 1972 Treaty of Accession for Britain, Ireland, and Denmark are set forth.

1412 UNITED NATIONS DIRECTORY OF NATIONAL BODIES CONCERNED WITH URBAN AND REGIONAL RESEARCH. New York: United Nations, 1968. 134 p.

A directory of principal, national research bodies in almost all ECE countries concerned with urban and regional research.

1413 Weil, Gordon L., ed. A HANDBOOK ON THE EUROPEAN ECONOMIC COMMUNITY. New York: published for the European Community Information Service by Frederick A. Praeger, 1965. 479 p.

A concise compilation of the basic EEC documents and excerpts covering every major aspect of the EEC through the SEVENTH GENERAL REPORT of the EEC. The institutions, origins of the EC, external relations, association policies, economic and financial affairs, internal market, social affairs, agriculture, energy, administration, and judicial decisions included. An extensive bibliography appended.

1414 WESTERN COOPERATION: A REFERENCE HANDBOOK. Central Office of Information Reference Pamphlet, no. 11. London: Her Majesty's Stationery Office, 1956. viii, 127 p.

An overview of European cooperation including historical coverage as well as consideration of the various organizations: economic (ERP, OEEC, ECSC), defense (NATO, WEU), and cultural and social cooperation (Council of Europe).

# Chapter 8
# GUIDE TO OFFICIAL PUBLICATIONS

The following information has been excerpted from the European Community Information Service's SELECTIVE GUIDE.

> "There are three main types of publications, documents, statistical information, and Information Service publications. Most of the documents are published by the Publications Office of the EC in Luxembourg but may be obtained from the European Community Information Service in Washington, D.C. at 2100 M Street, NW. Standing orders can be placed for all periodicals and annual reports, or the materials may be consulted in the library of the Washington Office or at the European Community Information Service, 277 Park Ave. N.Y., N.Y. 10017."

1415    TREATIES INSTITUTING THE EUROPEAN COMMUNITIES.

> "1973 edition. Texts of the ECSC, EEC and Euratom Treaties with revisions on the merger of the executive institutions, financing arrangements, and documents concerning the accession of Great Britain, Ireland, and Denmark."

1416    BULLETIN OF THE EUROPEAN COMMUNITIES. 1968-- . Monthly.

> "Detailed Monthly account of the Communities' activities plus supplements containing major Commission proposals and memoranda. Reduced rates for students, professors, and university libraries."

1417    DEBATES OF THE EUROPEAN PARLIAMENT. 1973-- . In English.

> "Transcript of the European Parliament's proceedings."

1418    EUROSPECTRA. 1969-74. Quarterly.

> "Quarterly survey of scientific and technological activity in the Community."

1419   GENERAL REPORT ON THE ACTIVITIES OF THE EUROPEAN COM-
       MUNITIES. 1967-- . Annual.

           "Annual progress report on the Communities submitted
           by the Commission to the European Parliament."

1420   OFFICIAL JOURNAL OF THE EUROPEAN COMMUNITIES. 1958-- .
       Daily.

           "Proposals, regulations, directives, decisions, and
           other acts of the Commission and the Council; sum-
           mary of decisions of the Court of Justice, minutes
           and written questions of the European Parliament."

1421   REPORTS OF THE COURT OF JUSTICE. 1952-- . Irregular.

           "Proceedings and decisions of the Court."

1422   WORKING DOCUMENTS. English ed. 1973-- . Approximately
       600/year.

           "Reports by the Parliament's standing committees on
           subjects to be debated by the Parliament."

1423   MISCELLANEOUS REPORTS. 1952-- . Irregular.

           "The Commission publishes many reports on its work in-
           cluding an annual survey of investment in the coal and
           steel industries, an annual survey of the social situation
           in the Community, an annual report on competition policy,
           quarterly economic surveys and monthly reports and graphs
           on the economic situation, technical abstracts on scien-
           tific research, and occasional studies done for or by the
           Commission."

1424   EUROPEAN COMMUNITY. 1954-- . Monthly.

           "A monthly magazine devoted to news and feature ar-
           ticles on the Communities. Reviews new books on
           European integration and advertises new official Com-
           munity publications."

1425   EUROPEAN COMMUNITY NEWS. 1972-75. Fortnightly.

           "A fortnightly newsletter containing news, short fea-
           tures and policy statements by Community officials."
           Ceased publication in 1975, September.

1426   BACKGROUND NOTES. English ed. 1972-- . Irregular.

           "Occasional expository articles on current issues, ac-
           tions, and policies of the Communities."

# Chapter 9

# RELEVANT PERIODICALS

The following periodicals have devoted numerous articles, over time, to European integration or related subjects.

AGENOR: EUROPEAN REVIEW. Brussels, Belgium: Societe Cooperative Agenor, 1967-- . Quarterly.

AGRA EUROPE. Tumbridge Wells, Engl.: Agra Europe Ltd., 1963-- . Weekly.

ATLANTIC COMMUNITY NEWS. Washington, D.C.: Atlantic Council of the United States, 1974-- . Monthly.

ATLANTIC COMMUNITY QUARTERLY. Washington, D.C.: Atlantic Council of the United States, 1963-- .

BACKGROUND OF THE COMMON MARKET. London: European Data Publishing Co., 1972-- . Irregular.

COMMON MARKET LAW REPORTS. London: 1962-73. Bimonthly.

COMMON MARKET LAW REVIEW. Leiden, Netherlands: A.W. Sijthoff for the British Institute of International and Comparative Law, 1963-- . Quarterly.

COMMON MARKET NEWS: THE THREE-WEEKLY JOURNAL REPORTING ON THE AFFAIRS OF THE EUROPEAN COMMUNITY. London: European Economic Data Publishing Co., 1970-- .

COMPARATIVE POLITICAL STUDIES. Beverly Hills, Calif.: Sage Publications, 1968-- . Quarterly.

COMPARATIVE POLITICS. New York: City University of New York, 1968-- . Quarterly.

CONTEMPORARY AFFAIRS. Rawalpindi, Pakistan: Bureau of National Research and Reference, 1969-- . Quarterly.

ECONOMIC BULLETIN FOR EUROPE. New York: United Nations Publications, 1949-- . Semiannual.

ECONOMIST. London: Economist Newspaper Ltd., 1843-- . Weekly.

EFTA BULLETIN. Geneva: European Free Trade Association, 1960-- . Monthly.

EFTA REPORTER. Geneva: European Free Trade Association, 1962-- . Monthly.

EUROPEAN BULLETIN AND PRESS. Sarbiton, Engl.: Central European Federalists, 1971-- . Semiannual.

EUROPEAN BUSINESS REVIEW. Paris: 1964-- . Quarterly.

EUROPEAN COMMUNITY. Washington, D.C.: European Community Information Services, 1954-- . Monthly.

EUROPEAN ECONOMIC REVIEW. Amsterdam, Netherlands: North Holland Publishing Co. for the Association Scientifique Europeenne d'Economie Appliquee, 1969-- . Quarterly.

EUROPEAN INTELLIGENCE: A REVIEW OF THE EUROPEAN BUSINESS ECONOMY. Fortnightly Report on Company Initiatives, EEC (Mergers, Affiliations) Plus Community News and Articles. Turnbridge, Engl.: 1964-- . Bimonthly.

EUROPEAN JOURNAL OF POLITICAL RESEARCH. Amsterdam, Netherlands: Elsevier Scientific Publishing Co. for the European Consortium for Political Research, 1973-- . Quarterly.

EUROPEAN MARKET REPORT. Richmond, Engl.: Samson Publications, 1972-- . Weekly.

EUROPEAN REVIEW. London: Birkett Press, 1950-- . Quarterly.

EUROPEAN STUDIES (Teacher's Series). London: European Studies Committee. Quarterly.

EUROPEAN STUDIES NEWSLETTER. Pittsburgh: Council for European Studies, University of Pittsburgh, 1972-- . Bimonthly.

EUROPEAN STUDIES REVIEW. Beverly Hills, Calif.: Sage Publications, 1971-- . Quarterly.

EUROPEAN TEACHER. Wicklow, Ireland: Wicklow Press for the European Association of Teachers, Irish Section, 1962-- . 3/year.

EUROPEAN TRENDS. London: Economist Intelligence Unit, 1964-- . Quarterly.

EUROPE LEFT. London: Labour Committee for Europe, 1970-- . Monthly.

FOREIGN AFFAIRS: AN AMERICAN QUARTERLY REVIEW. New York: Council on Foreign Relations, 1922-- .

FOREIGN POLICY. New York: National Affairs, 1970-- . Quarterly.

FORWARD IN EUROPE. Strasbourg, France: Council of Europe, 1959-- . 4/year.

GERMAN TRIBUNE: A WEEKLY REVIEW OF THE GERMAN PRESS. Hamburg: Friedrich Reinecke Verlag, Gmbh, 1962-- .

GOVERNMENT AND OPPOSITION. London: Government and Opposition Ltd. for the London School of Economics and Political Science, 1965-- . Quarterly.

INTERNATIONAL AFFAIRS. London: Royal Institute of International Affairs, Chatham House, 1922-- . Quarterly.

INTERNATIONAL ORGANIZATION. Madison: University of Wisconsin Press, 1947-- . Quarterly.

INTERNATIONAL PERSPECTIVES. Amsterdam, Netherlands: World Association of World Federalists, 1974-- . Bimonthly.

INTERNATIONAL STUDIES QUARTERLY. Beverly Hills, Calif.: Sage Publications for the International Studies Association, 1957-- .

JOURNAL OF COMMON MARKET STUDIES. Oxford, Engl.: Basil Blackwell-Mott, 1962-- . Quarterly.

JOURNAL OF COMMONWEALTH AND COMPARATIVE POLITICS. London: Frank Cass and Co., Ltd., for the Institute of Commonwealth Studies, 1961-- . 3/year.

# Relevant Periodicals

JOURNAL OF INTERNATIONAL AFFAIRS. New York: Columbia University, School of International Affairs, 1947-- . Semiannual.

NATO REVIEW. Brussels, Belgium: North Atlantic Treaty Organization, 1953-- . Bimonthly.

NEW EUROPE. London: European Movement, 1972-- . Monthly.

NEWSLETTER ON LEGISLATIVE ACTIVITIES. Strasbourg, France: Council of Europe, Directorate of Legal Affairs, 1972-- . 6/year.

OECD OBSERVER. Paris: Organization for Economic Cooperation and Development, 1962-- . Bimonthly.

PARLIAMENTARY AFFAIRS. London: Hansard Society for Parliamentary Government, 1947-- . Quarterly.

POLITICAL QUARTERLY. London: Political Quarterly Publishing Co., 1930-- .

POLITICAL STUDIES. London: Oxford University Press for the Political Studies Association of the United Kingdom, 1953-- . 4/year.

WORLD POLITICS: A QUARTERLY JOURNAL OF INTERNATIONAL RELATIONS. Princeton, N.J.: Princeton University Press for the Center of International Studies, 1948-- .

WORLD TODAY. London: Oxford University Press for the Royal Institute of International Affairs, 1945-- . Monthly.

# Chapter 10

# RECOMMENDED HOLDINGS

# FOR SMALL OR PRIVATE LIBRARIES

## THEORETICAL AND CONCEPTUAL STUDIES OF INTEGRATION AND COOPERATION

Balassa, Bela. THE THEORY OF ECONOMIC INTEGRATION. London: George Allen and Unwin, 1962. 304 p. (12)*

Haas, Ernst B. BEYOND THE NATION-STATE: FUNCTIONALISM AND INTERNATIONAL ORGANIZATION. Stanford, Calif.: Stanford University Press, 1964. x, 595 p. (39)

_____. THE UNITING OF EUROPE: POLITICAL, SOCIAL, AND ECO-NOMIC FORCES, 1950-57. Stanford, Calif.: Stanford University Press, 1958. 552 p. (40)

Mitrany, David A. A WORKING PEACE SYSTEM. London: Royal Institute of International Affairs, 1943; Chicago: Quadrangle Books, 1966. 221 p. (42)

Riker, William H. FEDERALISM: ORIGIN, OPERATION, SIGNIFICANCE. Boston: Little, Brown and Co., 1964. 169 p. (34)

Taylor, Paul. INTERNATIONAL COOPERATION TODAY: THE EUROPEAN AND UNIVERSAL PATTERN. London: Elek Books, 1971. 165 p. (48)

---

* This number and those in parentheses that follow are the citation numbers for these works in this bibliography.

## GENERAL, HISTORICAL, AND INSTITUTIONAL STUDIES OF INTEGRATION (Excluding the European Economic and Atomic Energy Communities)

Aron, Raymond. THE CENTURY OF TOTAL WAR. Garden City, N.Y.: Doubleday and Co., 1954. 379 p. (194)

Denton, Geoffrey R., ed. ECONOMIC INTEGRATION IN EUROPE. Reading University Studies on Contemporary Europe, no. 3. 2d ed. London: George Weidenfeld and Nicolson, 1972. 365 p. (144)

Diebold, William. THE SCHUMAN PLAN: A STUDY IN ECONOMIC CO-OPERATION, 1950-59. New York: Frederick A. Praeger for the Council on Foreign Relations, 1959. 750 p. (98)

Fawcett, J.E.S. THE APPLICATION OF THE EUROPEAN CONVENTION ON HUMAN RIGHTS. Oxford: Clarendon Press, 1969. 368 p. (69)

Henderson, W.O. THE ZOLLVEREIN. 2d ed. Chicago: Quadrangle Books, 1959. 375 p. (134)

Mayne, Richard, ed. EUROPE TOMORROW: SIXTEEN EUROPEANS LOOK AHEAD. London: published for Chatham House and Political and Economic Planning by Fontana, 1972. 352 p. (247)

Palmer, Michael, et al. A HANDBOOK OF EUROPEAN ORGANIZATIONS. New York: Frederick A. Praeger, 1968. 519 p. (253)

Robertson, A.H. THE COUNCIL OF EUROPE: ITS STRUCTURE, FUNCTIONS AND ACHIEVEMENTS. 2d ed. London: published for the London Institute of World Affairs by Stevens and Sons, 1961. 288 p. (85)

_____. EUROPEAN INSTITUTIONS: CO-OPERATION, INTEGRATION, UNIFICATION. 3d ed. London: published for the London Institute of World Affairs by Stevens and Sons, 1973. 427 p. (259)

Rougemont, Denis de. THE IDEA OF EUROPE. Translated by N. Guterman. New York: Macmillan Co., 1966. 434 p. (95)

## THE EUROPEAN COMMUNITIES: BACKGROUND, POLICIES, AND INSTITUTIONS (Excluding the ECSC Studies Contained in the Above Section)

Andrews, Stanley. AGRICULTURE AND THE COMMON MARKET. Ames: Iowa State University Press, 1973. 183 p. (420)

Bouvard, Marguerite [Galembert]. LABOR MOVEMENTS IN THE COMMON MARKET COUNTRIES: THE GROWTH OF A EUROPEAN PRESSURE GROUP. New York: Praeger Publishers, 1972. xxx, 272 p. (657)

Camps, Miriam. EUROPEAN UNIFICATION IN THE SIXTIES: FROM THE VETO TO THE CRISIS. New York: published for the Council on Foreign Relations by McGraw-Hill Book Co., 1966. 267 p. (351)

Coombes, David. POLITICS AND BUREAUCRACY IN THE EUROPEAN COMMUNITY: A PORTRAIT OF THE COMMISSION OF THE EEC. London: published for PEP by George Allen and Unwin, 1970. 343 p. (463)

Deniau, J.F. THE COMMON MARKET: ITS STRUCTURE AND PURPOSE. 2d ed. London: Barrie and Rockliff, 1961. 170 p. (358)

Feld, Werner J. THE COURT OF THE EUROPEAN COMMUNITIES: NEW DIMENSIONS IN INTERNATIONAL ADJUDICATION. The Hague: Martinus Nijhoff, 1964. 127 p. (588)

Friedrich, Carl J. EUROPE: AN EMERGENT NATION? New York: Harper and Row, 1969. 269 p. (525)

Kitzinger, Uwe W. THE CHALLENGE OF THE COMMON MARKET. Oxford: Basil Blackwell, 1961. 168 p. (383)

Lindberg, Leon N[ord]. THE POLITICAL DYNAMICS OF EUROPEAN ECONOMIC INTEGRATION. Stanford, Calif.: Stanford University Press, 1963. 367 p. (473)

Lindsay, Kenneth. EUROPEAN ASSEMBLIES: THE EXPERIMENTAL PERIOD 1949-59. New York: Frederick A. Praeger, 1960. 267 p. (636)

Mayne, Richard. THE RECOVERY OF EUROPE: FROM DEVASTATION TO UNITY, 1945-73. Rev. ed. Garden City, N.Y.: Anchor Books, 1973. 458 p. (394)

Pryce, Roy. THE POLITICS OF THE EUROPEAN COMMUNITY. Totowa, N.J.: Rowman and Littlefield, 1973. 187 p. (404)

Spinelli, Altiero. THE EUROCRATS: CONFLICT AND CRISIS IN THE EUROPEAN COMMUNITY. Baltimore: Johns Hopkins University Press, 1966. 229 p. (481)

Swann, Dennis. THE ECONOMICS OF THE COMMON MARKET. 3d ed. Harmondsworth, Engl.: Penguin Books, 1975. 267 p. (512)

## EUROPEAN COMMUNITIES AND MEMBER-STATE RELATIONS

Beloff, Nora. THE GENERAL SAYS NO: BRITAIN'S EXCLUSION FROM EUROPE. Baltimore: Penguin Books, 1963. 181 p. (715)

Camps, Miriam. BRITAIN AND THE EUROPEAN COMMUNITY, 1955–63. Princeton, N.J.: Princeton University Press, 1964. 547 p. (723)

Jebb, Gladwyn [Lord Gladwyn]. THE EUROPEAN IDEA. New York: Frederick A. Praeger, 1966. 159 p. (812)

Kitzinger, Uwe W. DIPLOMACY AND PERSUASION: HOW BRITAIN JOINED THE COMMON MARKET. London: Thames and Hudson, 1973. 433 p. (754)

Pinder, John. BRITAIN AND THE COMMON MARKET. London: Cresset Press, 1961. 134 p. (773)

_____. EUROPE AGAINST DE GAULLE. London: published for the Federal Trust by Pall Mall Press, 1963. 160 p. (890)

Shanks, Michael, and Lambert, John. THE COMMON MARKET TODAY AND TOMORROW. New York: Frederick A. Praeger, 1962. 253 p. (787)

Willis, F. Roy. FRANCE, GERMANY AND THE NEW EUROPE, 1945–67. New York: Oxford University Press, 1968. 431 p. (904)

_____. ITALY CHOOSES EUROPE. New York: Oxford University Press, 1971. 373 p. (933)

## EUROPEAN COMMUNITIES AND EXTERNAL RELATIONS

Benoit, Emile. EUROPE AT SIXES AND SEVENS: THE FREE TRADE ASSO-
CIATION AND THE UNITED STATES. New York: Columbia University Press,
1961. 275 p. (991)

Coppock, John O. ATLANTIC AGRICULTURAL UNITY: IS IT POSSIBLE?
New York: published for the Council on Foreign Relations and Food Research
Institute, Stanford University by McGraw-Hill Book Co., 1966. 234 p. (1148)

Feld, Werner J. THE EUROPEAN COMMON MARKET AND THE WORLD.
Englewood Cliffs, N.J.: Prentice-Hall, 1967. 184 p. (940)

Hanrieder, Wolfram F., ed. THE UNITED STATES AND WESTERN EUROPE:
POLITICAL, ECONOMIC AND STRATEGIC PERSPECTIVES. Cambridge, Mass.:
Winthrop Publishing Co., 1974. xiii, 311 p. (1096)

Henig, Stanley. EXTERNAL RELATIONS OF THE EUROPEAN COMMUNITY:
ASSOCIATIONS AND TRADE AGREEMENTS. London: Political and Economic
Planning, 1971. 145 p. (944)

Hoffmann, Stanley. GULLIVER'S TROUBLES OR THE SETTING OF AMERICAN
FOREIGN POLICY. New York: McGraw-Hill Book Co., 1967. 556 p.
(1102)

John, Ieuan, ed. EEC POLICY TOWARDS EASTERN EUROPE. Hants, Engl.:
Saxon House; and Lexington, Mass.: D.C. Heath and Co., 1975. 149 p.
(1051)

Okigbo, P.N.C. AFRICA AND THE COMMON MARKET. Evanston, Ill.:
Northwestern University Press, 1967. 183 p. (976)

Orvik, Nils, ed. FEARS AND EXPECTATIONS: NORWEGIAN ATTITUDES
TOWARD EUROPEAN INTEGRATION. Oslo: Universitets Forleget, 1972.
371 p. (1019)

Schaetzel, J. Robert. THE UNHINGED ALLIANCE: AMERICA AND THE
EUROPEAN COMMUNITY. New York: published for the Council on Foreign
Relations by Harper and Row, 1975. 179 p. (1129)

Streeten, Paul, and Corbet, Hugh, eds. COMMONWEALTH POLICY IN A
GLOBAL CONTEXT. Toronto: University of Toronto Press, 1971. 232 p.
(1028)

## EUROPEAN SECURITY

Buchan, Alastair. EUROPE'S FUTURES, EUROPE'S CHOICES: MODELS OF WESTERN EUROPE IN THE 1970S. London: Chatto and Windus for the Institute of Strategic Studies, 1969. 167 p. (1173)

Cleveland, Harold Van Buren. THE ATLANTIC IDEA AND ITS EUROPEAN RIVALS. New York: published for the Council on Foreign Relations by McGraw-Hill Book Co., 1966. 186 p. (1247)

Fox, William T.R., and Schilling, Warner R., eds. EUROPEAN SECURITY AND THE ATLANTIC SYSTEM. New York: Columbia University Press, 1973. 276 p. (1254)

Lerner, Daniel, and Aron, Raymond, eds. FRANCE DEFEATS THE EDC. New York: Frederick A. Praeger, 1957. 225 p. (1216)

Newhouse, John, et al. U.S. TROOPS IN EUROPE: ISSUES, COSTS, AND CHOICES. Washington, D.C.: Brookings Institution, 1971. 163 p. (1277)

Osgood, Robert E. NATO: THE ENTANGLING ALLIANCE. Chicago: University of Chicago Press, 1962. 416 p. (1279)

Palmer, Michael. THE PROSPECTS FOR A EUROPEAN SECURITY CONFERENCE. London: Chatham House and Political and Economic Planning, 1971. 107 p. (1206)

Richardson, James L. GERMANY AND THE ATLANTIC ALLIANCE: THE INTERACTION OF STRATEGY AND POLITICS. Cambridge, Mass.: Harvard University Press, 1966. 403 p. (1226)

# AUTHOR INDEX

This index includes all authors, editors, and compilers cited in the text. Numbers refer to entry numbers. The index is alphabetized letter by letter.

# Author Index

# Author Index

# Author Index

Giunta, Agatino John 99
Glaser, Kurt 1041, 1042, 1043
Godson, Joseph 1093
Goerner, E.A. 223
Goldman, Alan Richard 304
Goldschmidt, Bertrand 539
Goodman, Eliot R. 1094
Goodwin, Geoffrey L. 28
Goodwin, M. 224
Goormaghtigh, John 100, 225
Gorden, Morton 388, 1189
Gordon, Kermit 1095
Gorell Barnes, Sir William 942
Gorgey, Laszlo 1049
Gormley, W. Paul 564
Gorz, Andre 663
Gotshal, Sylvan 1152
Government and Opposition [London]
    4, 366
Government Stationery Office
    [Dublin] 845
Government Stationery Office
    [London] 1009, 1414
Gowda, K. Venkatagiri 985
Granick, David 471
Graubard, Stephen R. 367
Graupner, R. 600
Gray, Richard Butler 1180
Green, Andrew Wilson 608, 609
Green, R.H. 970
Grieves, Forest L. 610
Griffiths, William E. 1181
Groom, A.J.R. 38
Gross, Feliks 226
Grosser, Alfred 871
Grosshans, H. 178
Guerard, Albert 227
Gunther, John 228
Gurland, Robert 368
Gustavson, Carl G. 151

# H

Haagerup, Niels J. 849
Haas, Ernst B. 39, 40, 55, 81,
    1340
Hager, Wolfgang 946
Hague, D.C. 806
Hahn, Walter 1263
Haigh, Anthony 526

Haines, C. Grove 229, 230
Hajda, Joseph 231
Hallberg, H. Peter 232
Hallett, Graham 427, 428
Hallstein, Walter 369, 370, 371
Hamlin, D.L.B. 372
Han, S.S. 491, 743
Hanrieder, Wolfram F. 1096, 1222
Hansell, S. 1391
Hardy, Stephen 570
Haritos, Jeremy G. 872
Harlow, J.S. 873
Harmon, Robert B. 1341, 1342
Harris, Seymour 305
Harrison, Reginald J. 56
Hartley, Livingston 1097
Hartmann, Frederick H. 1223
Hassner, Pierre 943, 1098, 1182
Hasson, J.A. 540
Hauser, Gustave M. 601
Hauser, Rita E. 601
Haviland, H. Field, Jr. 306, 1140
Hawtrey, Ralph George 1310
Hay, Denys 88
Hay, Peter 325, 574, 611
Hazard, Paul 89
Headley, Anne Renouf 744
Healey, Derek T. 429
Heath, Edward 811
Heathcote, Nina 430
Hedges, Barry 832
Heilbroner, Robert L. 373
Heiser, H.J. 833
Heisler, Martin O. 233
Helms, Andrea Rose Carroll 694
Henderson, W.O. 134, 374
Hene, Derek H. 745, 746
Henig, Stanley 944, 1404
Hennessy, James 1343
Herriot, Edouard 179
Herter, Christian A. 1100
Hertig, Serge 498
Hess, John L. 874
Hickmann, Warren Leroy 307
Hinshaw, Randall 1153
Hitchens, Harold Lee 308
Hitiris, Theodore 1053
Hodges, Michael 375
Hodson, H.V. 1101
Hoepli, Nancy L. 376
Hoffman, George W. 398

# Author Index

# Author Index

Schwarz, John Erwin 642
Scitovsky, Tibor 20
Scott, J.H.M. 265
Scott, John 1023
Scottish Conservative Central Office 785
Seidman, A. 970
Self, Peter 454
Selly, Clifford 455
Sennholz, Hans F. 266, 267
Serfaty, Simon Henry 896, 897
Servan-Schreiber, Jean-Jacques 898, 1165
Sexter, Dorothy Achenbaum 704
Shackleton, M.R. 268
Shanks, Michael 786, 787
Shears, Ursala H. 920
Shepherd, Robert J. 410
Sherer, Walter 111
Shimm, Melvin G. 411
Shockley, Barbara Jean Larson 87
Shonfield, Andrew 412, 1156
Sidjanski, Dusan 249, 638
Silberschmidt, Max 1130
Silj, Alessandro 899
Silver, Jacob 900
Simmonds, George B. 1371
Simmonds, K.R. 572, 1411
Simpson, J.L. 1217
Sinanian, Sylva 1058
Sinclair, Sol 1024
Singh, B. 1350
Sisson, C.H. 788
Sjostedt, Gunnar 61
Slaughter, Richard Arthur 62
Slotta, Peter Luis 901
Smith, A.M. 527
Smith, Gordon 269
Smith, Howard K. 270
Smith, Keith Allen 705
Smith, Munroe 573
Smyth, J.G. 1193
Snyder, Glenn H. 1287
Society for International Development 963
Sohler, Katherine B. 789
Solomon, Rhona Rachel 527, 1059
Soper, Tom 1025, 1026, 1027
Sorensen, Max 849
Sovani, N.V. 989
Spaak, Paul-Henri 125

Spanier, David 790
Speeckaert, Georges Patrick 1369, 1370
Speerenberg, D.P. 112
Speier, Hans 1230
Spiegel, Steven 321
Spinelli, Altiero 413, 481
Stadler, K.R. 528
Stanley, Timothy W. 1288, 1289
Stead, W.T. 190
Stearns, Peter N. 674
Steel, Ronald 1131
Stein, Eric 574, 602, 603
Stewart, Charles F. 1371
Stewart, Margaret 675
Stikker, Dirk U. 126
Stillman, Edmund 1194, 1290
Stingelin, Peter 950
Stohler, Jacques 19
Stolper, Wolfgang 921
Storing, Herbert J. 454
Strange, Susan 791
Strauss, Erich 839, 840
Strauss, Franz-Josef 295, 922
Strausz-Hupe, Robert 1132, 1291
Streeten, Paul 21, 1028
Streit, Clarence 296, 1133
Study Group on Economic and Monetary Union 511
Sullivan, Nicholas J. 792
Summers, Robert E. 318
Swann, Dennis 503, 512, 513, 604
Swift, William J. 793
Szabo, A. 1374
Szaz, Z. Michael 1208
Szent-Miklosky, Istvan 1134

# T

Taber, George M. 1135
Tamuno, Olufunmilayo G. 1375
Taussig, Andrew John 923
Taylor, Paul 38, 48
Tharp, Paul A., Jr. 331
Thomas, Hugh 794
Thompson, Dennis 514, 577
Thompson, Ralph John 1213
Thumm, Garold W. 271
Times Publishing Company [London] 795, 796
Tinbergen, Jan 22, 414, 415

# Author Index

# SUBJECT INDEX

This subject index should be used in conjunction with the table of contents. For example, all entries concerned primarily with European Free Trade Area (EFTA) are listed under section 5:C in the table of contents. Those entries have not been repeated in the subject index. Rather, entries in other sections of the bibliography concerned only partially with EFTA and which could not be found otherwise in the table of contents are listed in the subject index. This index is alphabetized letter by letter. Numbers refer to entry numbers.

# Subject Index

256